Karma Yoga: Yoga of Action

Karma Yoga: Yoga of Action

Based on the Teachings of Sri Swami Satchidananda

O. R. Krishnaswami

Dev Publishers & Distributors
New Delhi

Published by:
Dev Publishers & Distributors
2nd Floor, Prakash Deep,
22, Delhi Medical Association Road,
Darya Ganj,
New Delhi-110002
Phone : 011-4357 2647
e-mail: devbooks@hotmail.com
website: www.devbooks.co.in

NOTE

In this Text the words 'man,' 'he' and 'him' are used in a generic sense and refer to both men and women.

ISBN 978–93–81406–54-0
First published 2016

Printed in India by Sarat Impressions Pvt. Ltd., Kolkata

Contents

Preface

This Text on **Karma Yoga (Yoga of Action**) was assembled from the transcribed talks of Sri Gurudev (Spiritual Master) Sri Swami Satchidananda and from the works of Swami Vivekananda, Swami Abedananda (Brother-monk of Swami Vivekananda), Swami Sivananda and other Saints and writers, which are listed under references and cited in the footnotes. I acknowledge my grateful indebtedness to all of them. If there are any errors and faults, I am personally responsible.

This Text is much more comprehensive than any other text on Karma Yoga. It covers all aspects of Karma Yoga with guidelines for practicing it. There are four major paths for attaining the life's goal of Self-realization or God-realization, namely, Bhakti Yoga, Raja Yoga, Jnana Yoga and Karma Yoga. Karma Yoga is the approach to God through selfless service. It spiritualizes our day-to-day activities and service to others and by its magic touch, work becomes worship and Yoga.

The compilation of this work was entirely due to the inspiration and Grace of my beloved Sri Gurudev and the Supreme Lord. Indeed Sri Gurudev (visible manifestation of God) and the Lord worked through this humble soul. With deep devotion I dedicate this Text to the Lotus Feet of Sri Gurudev and the Lord for having used this soul as an instrument in their Hands.

May this Text inspire and guide the students of Yoga in their sincere practices for achieving the ultimate purpose of life, Self-realization.

O. R. KRISHNASWAMI

Satchidananda Ashram-Yogaville

Acknowledgement

I am deeply grateful to Sri Swami Satchidananda Maharaj, my Spiritual Master, who inspired me to compile this Text as an instrument in his hands.

I am indebted to the authors of books listed under references and cited in footnotes, from whose thoughts I derived enlightenment.

I am indebted to Swami Murugananda who archived all of Sri Swami Satchidanada's Satsangs on his computerized database of the SASTRI PROJECT, from which references to Sri Gurudev's teachings were taken.

I am grateful to the Administrative Body of Satchidananda Ashram-Yogaville, Buckingham, Virginia for having provided me with all the facilities for working on this project.

I am also thankful to my third son Karthi Krishnaswami who presented me with a laptop computer and also procured several books for my study and reference.

I am also thankful to my family which gave me love, encouragement and support for doing this work.

O. R. KRISHNASWAMI

1

The Goal of Life and Yoga

Worldly life

We live in this world as human beings. We are mostly busy with earning our livelihood. We also aspire for social status and try to amass as much wealth as possible hoping to live comfortably. Some go further and become millionaires floating in affluence. We seek sensual pleasures prompted by desires for objects of senses. Our desires are endless. Innumerable objects are produced to satisfy our desires. What for do we live? What is the purpose behind all this?

Happiness

Happiness seems to be the main purpose behind all our desires, aspirations and efforts. We all seem to be thinking that happiness is something to come from outside, from worldly objects and sensual pleasures, something to be grabbed from somewhere. Is the happiness that comes from outside is real and lasting? No. It is just momentary, and it is mixed with manifold miseries. Every external object that gives us some fleeting happiness is subject to change. Position and power will disappear at any time. One wrinkle or one pimple will do to destroy our beauty. One simple misunderstanding is enough to mar our relationship. Today's millionaire may become a homeless beggar tomorrow. The worldly life is like that. So no permanent happiness can come from outside. Is then there is no permanent happiness? Yes, it is. But it does not come from external objects. Our very nature itself is peace and joy. Unfortunately we are not aware of that and go on searching for it from outside objects and experiences and get entangled in a continuous stream of desires and face the consequent stress, distress and disturbances. We cling desperately to the thirst for life.

Until we give up that thirst, the strong attachment to this transient, conditioned existence, we have no hope of catching even a glimpse of our real divine nature – eternal freedom, bliss and peace. The realization of this Divinity or the Self within us is the goal of life. There is only one way to attain to that goal, and that is to give up our attachment to the little life of lower self, i.e., our attachment to the worldly objects and sensual pleasures. It is indeed a most difficult thing to give up our clinging to this worldly life. Nevertheless it is achieved through the practice of Yoga.

Yoga

The Sanskrit word *Yoga* was derived from its root *yuj*, which means 'to join' or 'to unite.' What are the two things, which join together? Although the human soul or the *jivatman* is a facet of the Supreme Spirit or *Paramatman,* the Divine Reality, and in essence both are the same, the *jivatman* has subjectively separated from *Paramatman* or God. However, after going through an evolutionary cycle in the manifested universe, it becomes reunited with *Paramatman.* The union of *jivatman* with *Paramatman,* and the method through which this union is attained, both are called Yoga. However, there is no absolute union of *Atman* (Self) with God (*Brahman*); the practice of Yoga enables the embodied soul to realize its true nature, namely, *Atman* which is same as *Brahman*. The false identification of the soul with the body, mind, senses and intellect is loosely described as the feeling of separation from God and also the bondage of *jivatman.* As a culmination of Yogic practice, the *jivatman* sheds its false feeling of separation and bondage and becomes one with God or *Paramatman.* So in its technical sense, 'Yoga' refers to that enormous body of spiritual virtues, attitudes, precepts and techniques (that have been developed in India over several millennia), which purify the mind and heart of a human being and enable him to realize his true nature, the Divinity within.

The Paths of Yoga

There are many paths to the realization of the Self, just as there are many paths to the summit of a mountain. They primarily consist of *Karma Yoga* (the Path of Selfless Action), *Bhakti Yoga* (the Path of Devotion), *Jnana Yoga* (the Path of knowledge) and *Raja Yoga* (the Path of Meditation). The word "Yoga" in a generic sense refers to all the different paths. The paths vary so as to suit the varying temperaments and capacities of human beings, but all the paths lead to the same goal of Self-realization. The different paths of Yoga are not mutually exclusive. They simply represent a difference of emphasis.

Karma Yoga

The Sanskrit word *Karma* means action. So 'Karma Yoga' means Yoga of Action. The tendency to perform action is innate in all beings, and none can remain inactive. Of those who are particularly of an active temperament, what is required is not cessation from action but the proper control and direction of their activity. Work with attachment to its fruits binds the soul, but selfless work performed in a spirit of worship becomes a means for attaining freedom. Selfless action does not bind the doer, as he has no sense of doership or attachment to the fruits of his action. Sri Krishna says in the *Bhagavad Gita*[1] :

> One who does actions, offering them to the Divine, and forsaking attachment is not tainted by evil, just as a lotus leaf is not tainted by water. (5.10)
> Though ever engaged in actions, one, having taken refuge in Me (the Lord),
> Attains to the eternal and immutable state of being by My grace. (18.56)

The work that is offered to God becomes worship and Yoga. Karma Yoga helps a person to live successfully and usefully in the world while remaining above it, unaffected by its fetters, just as lotus leaves on the water.

Bhakti Yoga

This is a Yoga of Devotion, a path of love and devotion to God. It is an intense longing and love for God. It enables the aspirant to constantly remember God. It purifies his emotions and elevates his mind to the consciousness of the Reality. He surrenders all his thoughts, words and deeds to the Lord and adores Him with an unflinching devotion. By the constant remembrance of the Lord, the devotee imbibes into his own being the Divine attributes. He yearns from the depth of his heart for the union with his beloved Lord. Worldly love does not satisfy this deep passion of the soul. The devotee's entire mind flows, as it were, in a continuous stream towards the Lord. The Lord is not a being dwelling somewhere in a far off heaven, but is seated in his own heart. In order to see Him and to feel His Divine presence he has only to look within. "The Lord," says Sri Krishna, "dwells in the hearts of all beings . . . . Take refuge in Him with all thy being; by His Grace you shall attain supreme peace and the eternal abode." (*Bhagavad Gita*, 18. 61, 62). By total devotion and self-surrender to God, one can attain to God or the ultimate Reality. Bhakti Yoga is simple and suitable for all those of an emotional nature.

Jnana Yoga

The word *Jnana* means knowledge. So Jnana Yoga is a Yoga of Knowledge. This path involves intense discrimination (*Viveka*). One with a contemplative mind tries to seek answer to the basic question: "Who am I? Am I a body or mind? If not, what else?" He discriminates between the real and the unreal, between the transient and the eternal. Such persistent discrimination and self-inquiry ultimately lead to Enlightenment or the Knowledge of Self. Ramana Maharishi, the great Indian sage of the twentieth century, was a great Jnana Yogi.

The seeker, who is having a philosophic turn of mind, is not satisfied with the little pleasures of the worldly life. He is eager to know his true nature and the reality behind the phenomenal world. He does not feel any great attraction for the personal aspects of the Divinity. He yearns to attain to the Infinite, his true Self. Speaking of the followers of the Path of Knowledge, Sri Krishna observes in the *Bhagavad Gita*:

> Those who have their intellect absorbed in That, whose Self is That, established in That, with That as their supreme goal, (they) attain to the highest salvation, their impurities being cleaned by Knowledge. (5.17) relative existence, even here in this world, has been conquered by those, whose minds rest in evenness. As the infinite Self is even and without imperfection, they are established in It. (5.19).

Raja Yoga

This 'Royal Path' (*Raja*) is highly scientific. It is as old as human civilization. It is a Yoga of Meditation. It was codified by the ancient saint (of India) Patanjali in his *Yoga Sutras*. Raja Yoga encompasses the teachings of all the different paths; it concerns itself with three realms—the physical, the mental and the spiritual. By practicing Raja Yoga regularly, one learns to control his desires, emotions and thoughts and thus to purify his mind, and finally to attain *Samadhi*, the state of Super-consciousness.

The man of a contemplative bent of mind, endowed with tremendous will power, wants to control the whole of Nature, external and internal. But spasmodic attempts at concentration will only lead to failure and mental depression. The restless mind is to be brought under control slowly and steadily through practice and renunciation. Speaking of the Yoga of Meditation, Sri Krishna says, "With intellect steadfast, with the mind fixed on the Self, let the yogi attain quietude little by little, without thinking of anything else. By whatever cause the restless, unsteady mind wanders away, let him, restraining it from wandering, bring it back under the control of the Self alone. Verily, supreme bliss comes to the Yogi, whose mind is perfectly tranquil, whose passions are quieted, who is free from impurities, and who has become one with the all-pervading Being." (*Bhagavad Gita*, 6.25-27).

Complementarity of Paths

The different Paths of Yoga are not mutually exclusive. They are complementary to one another. An aspirant cannot really follow any one of these four paths to the exclusion of the rest; he may only lay greater emphasis upon one or the other. For instance, Meditation is to be practiced as a discipline, no matter which path the aspirant may follow. Besides, the aspirant must cultivate discrimination and gain spiritual knowledge to practice even Bhakti Yoga and Karma Yoga. And even the aspirant who practices Bhakti Yoga or Jnana Yoga or Raja Yoga has to be active and perform actions without expecting their fruits or dedicate them to the Lord. Above all every aspirant, irrespective of the path chosen by him, must have devotion to God or love for the Chosen Ideal. Thus in reality, there is a combination of Yogas in every aspirant's life, because perfection is attained only by developing all aspects of one's own personality – physical, mental, moral and emotional – i. e., by attaining an all-round or over-all spiritual growth. In fact, one-sided development is fraught with dangers. Work sometimes becomes aimless and leads to mere restlessness. Yoga of Meditation at times degenerates into physical mortification and pursuit of psychic powers. Devotion often deteriorates into meaningless sentimentalism. Knowledge may also lapse into dry intellectualism and morbid inactivity. Hence there is a great necessity for combining the different paths in order to safeguard against the dangers of following one path to the exclusion of others. Let work be combined with Meditation, and knowledge be tempered with devotion. Let us try to be equally established in all the Yogas and bring about a harmonious development of all our latent spiritual powers. This all-sided personality is the healthiest ideal for any spiritual aspirant to pursue. This is why, in the teachings of *Bhagavad Gita* and of Sri Ramakrishna, emphasis has been laid upon synthesizing all the Yogas in one's life. In the Integral Yoga Institutes established by Sri Swami Satchidananda, the apostle of peace, in the United States of America and other countries, this total approach is rightly called 'Integral Yoga.' 'Integral' means a synthesis or harmonious blending. Integral Yoga is a combination of Hatha Yoga, Pranayama, Bhakti Yoga, Karma Yoga, Jnana Yoga and Raja Yoga. It gives Yoga an affirmative and dynamic form. Its goal is complete self-integration. Action, devotion, wisdom and peace are equally important elements in such integration. Over-emphasis upon any one of these elements leads to lop-sided development and disturbs the balance of life.

All the above elements are inter-dependent and inter-related. Devotion in its full flowering is inseparable from wisdom and selfless action. Devotion, in its spiritual essence, is an attribute of wisdom. It flows from the vision of the interdependence of all life and the oneness of all existence. It is the joyful expression of the soul freed from the bonds of selfishness.

Similarly, knowledge, in its full flowering, is inseparable from devotion and action. Knowledge is not an ivory-tower contemplation, but a comprehensive awareness of the nature of existence. It is the vision of oneness of all things and beings. It awakens the jnani to the timeless dimension of being.

In the same way, action is not a mere means to self-purification resulting in salvation. The liberated individual participates in the creative adventure of life. His action is a total and joyful self-giving at the altar of welfare of all beings. Liberated person's action rises above the limits imposed by scriptural injunctions and fixed cultural patterns.

Yoga is thus the means to achieve the life's goal of Self-realization, our real nature. Only human beings can attain the Knowledge of Self. Human birth is rare indeed. Sankaracharya[2] in his *Vivekachudamani* says,

> "There are three things that are rare indeed and are due to the grace of God, viz., a human birth, the longing for liberation and the protecting care of a perfected sage. (3)
>
> "One who, having obtained the human birth, is foolish enough not to exert himself for self-liberation, verily commits suicide, for he kills himself by clinging to things unreal. (4)
>
> "What greater fool is there than a person who having obtained the rare human birth, neglects to achieve the real end of this life (Liberation)." (5)

The *Chandogya Upanishad*, one of the oldest Upanishads[3] declares,

> "He, who has found out and knows the Self, has attained all the worlds, and all desires." (8.7. 1)

Yoga enables us to purify our minds and hearts and reach the goal of Self-realization, which is a state of eternal freedom, peace and bliss. The *Mundaka Upanishad* declares,

> "As the flowing rivers, having relinquished their names and forms, merge into the ocean, so the knower, being free from name and form, attains to the Supreme Divine Being." (3. 2. 8)
> "Verily, he, who knows the supreme Brahman becomes Brahman himself. He crosses over sorrow and all sins. Liberated from the knots of the heart, he becomes immortal." (3. 2. 9)

One who reaches the goal of Self-realization becomes united with supreme Divine being, and thus attains Liberation from suffering and the cycle of births and deaths. (For details, *see* Chapter 39. Freedom from Karma and Rebirth, and Chapter 40. Liberation, *below*).

References

1 *Bhagavad Gita* is an ancient Indian scripture dealing with Yoga. It gives a philosophy of life relevant to all times.
2 Sankaracharya (AD 788-820) was one of the greatest saints and philosophers of India. He was the foremost exponent of *Advaita Vedanta* (the Doctrine of Non-dualism).
3 The *Upanishads* are ancient scriptures of India. They are rich in profound philosophical thoughts. They contain the eternal divine knowledge of *Brahman* (God) and show the pathway to Self-realization.

2

What is Karma?

Meaning

The Sanskrit word *karma* is derived from the verbal root *kri*, 'to act' or 'to do,' and the word is now almost naturalized into English. It has several meanings:

- It means not only "action," but also the "effect" or the "result" or "reaction" of an action. The result or effect of an action is part of the action and cannot be separated from it.
- Karma is the sum total of acts performed by a person both in the present life and in the preceding births.
- It also means "duty" to be performed according to one's station of life.
- It signifies the destiny or storehouse of one's tendencies that give rise to his future birth.
- It is sometimes understood as fate referring to the consequences of actions performed in previous birth or births.
- As action is both a cause and an effect at the same time, so the word *karma* includes both the cause and the effect.
- Any thought, any word or any deed that produces an effect is a Karma. Thus breathing, thinking, talking, seeing, hearing, eating, walking, willing, desiring, nay, all the actions of body, mind and senses are all Karmas.

Our nature consists of knowing, feeling and willing. These three fashion our Karmas. A desire for an object arises in our mind. Then we think how to get it. And we exert to get it. Thus desire, thought and action always go together. They are the three threads, as it were, that are twisted into the cord of Karma. Being governed by the irresistible Law of Causation, they produce reactions. The reactions or consequences of Karmas are experienced as pleasure or pain depending on their nature. (For details *see* Chapter 9. Universal Laws, *below*).

No escape

Every action will leave its result; every cause will yield its effect, and these do not go away, but are stored in their subtle forms as impressions (*samskaras*) in the subconscious mind (*see* Chapter 4. What causes Karmas?, *below*). The stored impressions wait for an opportunity to come to the surface and bring their reactions. You do not always get the reactions in the same order in which you perform the actions; it depends on the nature of the actions performed. If you eat some undesirable food and soon thereafter put your finger into a candle flame, your first Karma is eating the food and your second is putting your finger into the flame. But the second Karma brings a result immediately. The first Karma may not germinate for one or two days; then you will get a stomach-ache. Whatever you have done, you will surely have to get the reaction. There is no getting away from Karma. It is like a boomerang that comes back to one who throws it.

Heredity

Karma has nothing to do with heredity. A deformed child may be born to a perfect healthy couple. The child has not inherited its deformity from the family, but acquired it as the effect of its own past actions performed in its previous birth. Is a person blind because in some past life the person has blinded another entity? The answer is that not the act itself, but the inner consent given to it is the determining factor. A hangman in life need not necessarily end up by himself being hanged in another life, if, in the course of his duties, he merely carried out his duty (*dharma*), as it were, without having any attachment to the task.

Nothing Accidental

There is no room left for a chance or accident. What we call accident is, in reality, the effect of some definite cause that we may not know or cannot trace due to our limited knowledge. In ancient times, tribal people used to attribute the accident events or events produced by unknown causes, to some supernatural or providential powers. Even today there are many who believe in accidents. But in reality, all accidents have natural causes whether we know them or not. All chance-events such as diseases, earthquakes, cyclones, thunderstorms, hurricanes and volcanoes are the results of some causes.

Knowing about Karma can be helpful. If by chance you are insulted or struck by someone for what seems to be no apparent reason, you can think, "Probably, it is my Karma. I must have hurt somebody earlier and escaped from being hurt in return. Now it comes back to me and I accept." There is no effect without a cause; no one will hurt you if you are really innocent. You may be innocent today, but days before, years before, even the life before, you probably were not innocent. So you can say to your oppressor, "Okay, you helped me purge my Karma. Thank you so much." You sow better Karma when you do not return hatred with hatred. Pouring love on hate is like pouring water on fire. It needs strong will to do that. Accepting injury without returning it is the highest spiritual practice.

The only way to purge your Karma is by sowing seeds of selfless actions. No teacher, no Guru, no scripture, no temple, no church can purge you of your Karma. Even God will not take away your Karma. It is only when you discover how to perform perfect actions that you transform Karma into Karma Yoga, and through Karma Yoga, your heart, mind and body are soon cleaned. (For details, *see* Chapter 14. Karma Yoga, *below*).

Mixed Effects

There is no action that does not bear good and bad effects at the same time. We cannot breathe or live without injuring other beings;

our very lives are crowding out other lives – human beings, animals, plants or other living beings.

Ordinarily, in judging the result of an action when we find the preponderance of good over evil, we call it good. When evil predominates, that action is evil or bad.

Group Karmas

Karma operates not only among individuals but also among groups such as families, tribes and whole peoples. But this fate is self-created. The fortunes or misfortunes of a nation are not wholly due to the capacity or foolishness of those who govern it. They are partly the reflection of the capacity and foolishness of the people themselves. Either in the past or in the present, both the people and the rulers of the country would have helped to create the causes and conditions that reach their climax with open sufferings. Until a transformation in their way of thinking occurs and the doctrine of Karma is faithfully observed, they will have to face intermittent recurrence of conflicts with consequent sufferings. Of course, it is the imperative duty of administrators and religious leaders to lead and guide peoples rightly.

3

The Categories of Karma or Kinds of Karma

Karmas are broadly classified into three main categories: *Sanchita* (Dormant or accumulated), *Prarabdha* (Active) and *Agami* or *Kriyamana* (Potential) Karmas. *Sanchita* Karma means 'stored' Karma. It is the sum total of all the accumulated Karmas of the past. It remains dormant in the subconscious mind. It may become active at the appropriate time. *Prarabdha* Karma is Karma that has already started bearing fruit. It is the *Prarabdha* Karma that is responsible for the present incarnation or birth. *Agami* or *Kriyamana* Karma is that now being performed or yet to be performed in the present life.

In Yoga texts there is a beautiful analogy. *Sanchita* Karmas are like the bundle of arrows stored in the quiver of a bow man on his back; the *Prarabdha* Karma is like the arrow that he has shot and already in flight. *Kriyamana* Karmas are the arrows that are being made or yet to be made. One has control over the *Sanchita* and the *Kriyamana*, but he must surely work out his *Prarabdha.*

Sanchita Karma

This includes both good and bad actions performed by us in our previous births. They lie dormant in subtle forms in the subconscious mind. They will become active when conditions become favorable. It is our passion and attachment that give energy to dormant Karmas. Yogis neutralize them with the power of non-attachment. Passion and attachment are like the nutrients a seed needs in order to sprout. Once you no longer provide these nutrients, the seed of Dormant Karmas will loose their capacity to grow into Active Karmas. But the practice of non-attachment alone may not be able to neutralize the effect of powerful Dormant Karmas. In addition to non-attachment, intense spiritual practice with firm will and determination is necessary to achieve it. (*See* Chapter 18. Practice of Karma Yoga, *below*).

Sanchita Karmas are destroyed by Self-knowledge or God-realization. When a spiritual seeker gets illumination through direct intuitive knowledge that he is not body-mind complex, but the eternal *Atman* (Self), then the subtle impressions of the accumulated actions lying in the mental space are burnt by the fire of Self-knowledge, and so they can no longer bind the liberated Yogi. (*See* Chapter 39. Freedom from Karma and Rebirth, and 40. Liberation, *below*).

Prarabdha Karma

This is a set of one's own previous actions that gave rise to the present birth. It is like the arrow that has already left the bow and cannot return. What is enjoyed, suffered and experienced in this life is the effect of one's own *Prarabdha* Karma. It is, therefore, unavoidable and must be accepted with a poised mind. Any effort to avoid will bring about additional Karmas.

But how can we say that a particular Karma belongs to the category of *Prarabdha* Karma? Certain events happen unexpectedly to us in spite of all our efforts to avoid them. This unavoidability, this unexpectedness and our helplessness in spite of the apparent capability to remedy it are the symptoms of the Fructifying Actions.

With their developed psychic power, enlightened souls may know in advance of these unavoidable events, but they make no attempt to avoid them. There are many readings given by Edgar Cayce,[1] that end abruptly ,saying, "We are through for the present," with a subsequent untimely death of the entity. (Langley, *Edgar Cayce on Reincarnation,* pp. 111-13). Death is virtually fixed and its time, place and manner depend upon the Active Karmas.

Prarabdha Karma can only be exhausted by experiencing its

fruits in the present life. A child is born blind, deaf or dumb. This is due to its *Prarabdha* Karma. The life-span or longevity, happiness and suffering are all due to *Prarabdha* Karma. A virtuous person suffers. A scoundrel is prosperous. An aged mother loses her only son who was her sole support. A young girl loses her husband soon after her marriage. Such instances are countless. In all such cases *Prarabdha* Karmas operate precisely. *Prarabdha* Karmas constitute our destiny or fate.

It is difficult to change the *Prarabdha* Karmas. They run at the speed of time and so it is almost impossible to change their direction. The laws governing *Prarabdha* Karma are similar to Newton's First and Second Laws of Motion. Newton's First Law states that an object moving in a straight line will continue in a straight line unless acted upon by an outside force. An object in motion will stay in motion, unless an outside force acts on it. This is known as the Principle of Inertia, for a force to change an object's motion, it must first to overcome the inertia of the object. The same is true of *Prarabdha* Karmas. They will continue to move in a particular direction at a set rate of speed unless acted upon by an outside force.

In Yogic texts we find tales and parables about Karmic predicaments. In some cases even great sages and Divine incarnations could not overcome the inertia of Active Karmas. Here is a story to illustrate the dynamics of *Prarabdha* Karma.

Once there was a beggar who was not successful in begging. Even after begging all day long, he hardly ever get enough to eat, so he was always half-starved. One day Parvati, the concert of Lord Shiva, noticed the beggar's misery and deeply moved. She asked Shiva to help him.

> "O Parvati," Shiva replied, "poverty and prosperity, misery and happiness and other such conditions in life are the result of one's own past Karma. It cannot be changed. This poor man is purging his past Karma through his suffering."

But Parvati argued, "O Lord, You are omniscient and capable of doing anything you wish. When a person is not in a position to help himself, others have to help him. Please help him."

The compassion of Parvati made Shiva relent. "Tell me, in what manner do you want me to help him?"

" Lord, put a heap of gold coins on the road that he walks every day."

"So be it," said Shiva.

Immediately a heap of gold appeared on the road just ahead of the beggar.

At the same moment, the beggar thought, "I wonder how blind people walk? How do they manage? Let me try it and find out." So he closed his eyes and passed by the gold without seeing it.

"See, Parvati," said Shiva, "His destiny is so strong that neither you nor I can stop it." By its very nature destiny is entrenched and almost insurmountable.

Prarabdha is of three kinds: (1) *Iccha Prarabdha* (acts of own will), (2) *Aniccha Prarabdha* (acts of God), and (3) *Pareccha Prarabdha* (acts compelled by others).

Iccha Prarabdha. These are events that happen according to your own will. You do things according to your desire, but later you regret. You know the evil consequences of your actions, yet you are impelled to do them by your cravings. You know, for example, that smoking is bad for your health, yet you smoke if you have addicted to smoking.

Learn to handle your desires intelligently and do not allow them to grow into uncontrolled cravings. Cravings can never be satisfied. You may crave for wealth, pleasures of senses, name, fame and glory. No matter how much you attain you are never satisfied.

Aniccha Prarabdha. These are acts of Nature, over which you have no control. Hurricanes, floods, earthquakes, dreadful epidemics and accidents are examples of *Aniccha Prarabdha.*

Instead of developing a sense of fear and insecurity about such unexpected events, take whatever precautions that are possible, but deep down remain relaxed.

You have faced many natural calamities in the countless past embodiments. You are not the body. You are immortal Atman. Why should you tremble? One day death will come to your present body, and should always be prepared for it. Entrust yourself in Divine hands, and feel free. God knows what is best for you.

Pareccha Prarabdha are acts that you perform under other's compulsion. When others hurt you or throw you into a worse situation, do not curse them and try to take revenge upon them, tit for tat. Such revenge would only add to your evil Karma. Instead, understand the Divine message behind such suffering. Your evil Karma of the past is working itself out through those people. Instead of nurturing hatred and ill will toward them, feel thankful to them for having helped you to purge your past Karma. As saint Kabir of Northern India sang, "Sow flowers for them who sow thorns for you." Your good act will purify you. Others who hurt you will receive their due punishment, though you feel no ill will toward them.

Agami Karmas

These are the current actions that will fructify in future. They are like the arrows that are getting ready for use. *Agami* are actions only to those who are egoistic and selfish and have the sense of doership. *Agami* are not actions to a realized sage, as he has no desires, no selfishness and no sense of doership.

Just as a potter, having set the wheel in motion, removes his hand allowing the wheel to revolve till the momentum previously imparted to it is exhausted, so also the sage even after attaining liberation through the Knowledge of Self continues to enjoy the fruit of his *Prarabdha* Karma up to the end of the present body. *Prarabdha* are exhausted by no other means than by enjoying their fruits. But they cannot produce the seed of *Sanchita* Karma on account of his desirelessness and non-attachment. The enjoyment of the fruits of *Prarabdha* falls to his lot by the force of *Prarabdha*. He has no desire for them. So their enjoyment does not in any way affect him. The experience of happiness and misery, like parched seed, is impotent to produce any *Sanchita* Karma. Thus the liberated sage gets disentangled from the fetters of all actions.

Prarabdha and Self-effort

Prarabdha is self-effort of a previous birth. You can neutralize the effects of *Prarabdha* through rightly directed self-effort. Markandeya, who was destined to live for sixteen years only, through self-effort of intense austerity and worship fought against the King of Death and attained the state of immortality. (For details, *see* Chapter 34. Destiny and Self-effort, *below*).

Often Indians are called fatalists, as they accept Karmic effects as fate or destiny. But Karma is not a fatalistic doctrine. (*See* Chapter 33. Fatalism vs. Free will, *below*). It is a logical theory that explains differences in our births and temperaments and guides us in molding our future.

Prarabdha concerns the present only. The future is in your hands. You can change your destiny. You have free will to act. You have the faculty of reason to determine what is right and what is wrong. You can cultivate right thinking and do right actions. Your free will gives an opportunity to change your destiny and character. Rightly directed self-effort can enable even a scoundrel to become a saint. This is a challenge. It can be met by proper guidance and from firm determination.

A knowledge of the threefold Karmas and their interrelationships is essential for shaping our future destiny. But this is not enough to enable us to formulate an approach for attaining mastery over Karmas. To do that we need to know what causes Karmas and where the Karmic drama is enacted.

References

1. Edgar Cayce (1877-1945) was a famous clairvoyant. He had given some 2,500 life-readings based on clairvoyance. He gave his readings when he was under trance like sleep. (For further details, *see* "Remembrances of Past lives" in Chapter 29. The Doctrine of Reincarnation, *below*).

4

What Causes Karmas?

Prakriti

According to Samkhya philosophy and Yoga science, everything in the universe – mind, senses, intellect, elements (air, water, fire, etc.) – has evolved from *Prakriti* (Primordial Nature). *Prakriti* is eternal; it is the prime cause of the entire universe and all that exists in it. *Prakriti* is composed of three intrinsic forces (*gunas*): *sattva* (purity), *rajas* (restlessness) and *tamas* (inertia). When these forces remain in perfect balance, *Prakriti* remains in its unmanifested form. When this balance is disturbed, *Prakriti* becomes manifest.

Everything in the manifested world consists of *sattva*, *rajas* and *tamas* in varying degrees. *Sattva* is characterized by light, illumination, clarity, purity and goodness. *Rajas* is the force of activity, movement, restlessness, agitation and ambition. *Tamas* is the force of darkness, heaviness, inertia, dullness, delusion and sloth. (For details, *see* Chapter 5. Three Gunas, *below*).

When the equilibrium of these forces is disturbed, evolution begins. The first thing derived from *Prakriti* is the mind, both the cosmic mind and the individual mind. The mind like all other evolved things consists of three *gunas* of *sattva*, *rajas* and *tamas*. At any time any one of them will be predominant, while the other two forces remain subordinate. The interplay of these three forces causes the mind continually shift from one state to another. This is the reason for the constant change and restlessness of the mind. By turns and by varying degrees it is distracted, stupefied, disturbed and controlled. When *sattva* is dominant, the mind remains calm and controlled.

When *rajas* is dominant, the mind becomes restless and disturbed. When *tamas* is predominant, the mind becomes dull and stupefied.

These varying mental states influence the endless thoughts and desires that flow as a running stream in the mind. What we think that we become. It is the thoughts and desires that give rise to actions.

Thus we find that it is our endless thought-waves and desires that cause Karmas. It is our ego or sense of "I and mine" that is responsible for our desires and consequent actions. In order to understand this process of creation of Karma we must know how our minds work.

Mind

Mind ordinarily operates at two levels: conscious and unconscious or subconscious. Conscious mind works during our waking state. It functions in response to sense stimuli. Using the senses as its instruments, the conscious mind gathers data related to external objects and perceives them. With the functioning of the intellect, the objects are identified as good or bad and the mind decides to respond to them positively or negatively. The conscious mind stores information at each step, some in the conscious memory and others in the subconscious.

We are normally unaware of what is going on in the subconscious mind. It is where all our memories, past experiences, emotional urges, desires, etc. are stored in the form of subtle impressions (*samskaras*). We do not have conscious access to this level of mind.

Today information revolution is taking place in the world. Our minds are overloaded with information flowing from all directions. At the same time due to the use of calculators and computers and exposure to fast moving images, our attention span is shrinking rapidly. We are using the conscious mind less and dumping more information into already congested subconscious. As a result most of our activities are governed by the subconscious mind, on which we have no control. Thus we have become slaves of our subconscious mind. For instance, we know that advertisements rarely present the complete truth, yet most of us are heavily influenced by them. For example, messages from cigarette and liquor advertisements have deeply implanted in our subconscious mind. As a result the conscious mind's awareness of their damaging effects on our health is not always able to stop many of us from using those substances.

Right from the birth we are trained only to use the conscious mind and we do not know how to bring the contents of the subconscious mind to the conscious level and deal with them. The subconscious mind remains locked and we do not know what is hidden there. Our tendencies, dispositions and subtle desires (*vasanas*) are deeply influenced by the impressions buried in the subconscious mind. It is these impressions that motivate the conscious mind to employ the body and sensory organs to perform actions. Here is a story from *Bhagavatam*[1] to illustrate this point.

Once upon a time there was a sage named Saubhari who lived in solitude. For many years he dedicated himself totally to the practice of austerities and meditation, and by the time he reached a ripe old age everyone in the kingdom knew him. General public, traders, philosophers and even the royal family respected him.

One day Saubhari went to bathe in a nearby lake, and remained in the water to do his special twilight meditation. As he opened his eyes to take water in his palms, he noticed a group of small fishes frolicking with their mother. They seemed to be having such fun that the sage used his extraordinary intuitive power to understand why they were so happy—and he was surprised to realize the profound joy the mother fish felt at being the parent of so many young ones. "The fishes in the lake are so joyful," the sage thought, "I have spent my whole life doing spiritual practices, and I have not experienced this. I too should have children, I must get married." With this thought he came out of the lake and began formulating a plan.

After making inquiries, the sage learned that the king had several daughters; all of them were of marriageable age, so he decided to visit the king. When the king heard that Saubhari had come to see him, he greeted him with great respect and asked how he could serve him. The holy man replied frankly that he wanted to get married and had heard that the king's daughters were of marriageable age.

Although the king had great reverence for the sage, he did not like to give any of his daughters in marriage to such an old man. But at the same time, he could not refuse him bluntly. So, humbly he said that since his daughters were grown up, it would be better if their feelings were respected. If any of them agreed to marry the sage, the king would give his consent. The sage understood what the king meant, so using his wisdom and yogic power, he rejuvenated himself and reversed his age, transforming himself into a handsome young man.

When he met the princesses, one after the other, all agreed to marry him, so he wed all of them and brought them to his ashram. There he lived the life of a householder and he had several children, two with each wife.

This simple story tells us about the effects of the subconscious on the conscious decision-making. Watching the group of fishes happily around their mother was not the main motivating force behind the sage's decision to get married. That incident simply revived memories—the subtle impressions of being married and having children—that were buried in his subconscious. The sight was like a pebble thrown into a lake; the ripples kept spreading outward until they reached the shore of the sage's conscious mind. In the same way, stimulated by external events, our *samskaras* are awakened and influence our conscious decision to act.

There are innumerable dormant Karmas stored in the subconscious. Some are powerful, others relatively weak; some are primary, others secondary. Generally, the main Karmas are accompanied by a number of secondary Karmas. Only one Karma or a group of Karmas fructifies at a time as our *Prarabdha* Karma and acts upon us and dictate our behavior. The main active Karma is like a blue print for a house. The secondary Karmas are like the finishing materials and decorative details that complete the house. The architect has nothing to say about what color of the carpets we use, what color we paint our shutters or how we arrange our furniture. These are secondary details. Just as the house owner has choice over these details, we mostly have choice in manipulating our secondary Karmas.

According to the scriptures such as Patanjali's *Yoga Sutras* it is possible to create powerful Karmas that override other Karmas, by performing our present actions skillfully without attachment to their fruits. Similarly we create a powerful negative Karma by hurting someone who is helpless, one who trusts us or one who is totally dedicated to spiritual life. Such a negative Karma also overrides other Karmas.

Samskaras (Impressions)

All our perceptions, thoughts, words and all mental and physical actions produce *samskaras* or subtle impressions in our subconscious mind. The impressions of our past thoughts, desires and actions become our inherent tendencies and influence our current behavior. Let us see how powerful inborn tendencies are. A prince had, in a previous birth, been the son of a washer man. While playing with his friends in his incarnation as the prince, he said to them, "Hay, stop those games, I shall show you a new one. I shall lie on my belly, and you will beat the clothes on my back as the washer man does, making swishing sound."

A Conflicting Situation. In a conflicting situation caused by a clash of various problems, the mind gets agitated and confused. For example, in one afternoon, a technical consultant gets a call from a customer to come immediately to solve an urgent problem. In the next moment there is a call from the school to say a thunderstorm is expected and he should pick up his children. Intent on visiting the customer's factory, he calls his wife at work to ask her to pick up the children but to his dismay she tells him she is having some problem with her car and needs a ride home herself. When there is such a clash of problems our mind is likely to become agitated and confused. How we might deal with such a situation depends upon which *guna* is dominant. People dominated by *sattvic guna* are composed, those dominated by *rajasic* are agitated, and those dominated by *tamasic guna* are depressed. So if we increase the level of *sattva* we can make the mind to function in a balanced way. When the *sattvic guna* becomes predominant we can think clearly and make right decisions, and thus create positive or good Karmas. How can we increase the level of *sattva*?

Cultivation of *Sattva guna*

To increase the level of *sattva* we have to be vigilant in all areas of our life style: diet, sleep, reading, recreation and exercise. We must take *sattvic* food, and avoid rajasic and tamasic food.

Foods that give energy and calmness of mind are *sattvic* foods. They are the most desirable foods for human beings for maintaining sound physical and mental health. The most ideal foods in this category are fruits, nuts and seeds that are eaten in the natural state. They are, however, difficult to digest, and should not be taken in too large a quantity. Other *sattvic* foods are vegetables, soybean roots, pure milk and grains. To know what a well-known Doctor recommends on the basis of extensive research findings, refer *Dr. Dean Ornish's Program for Reversing Heart Disease,* New York: Ballantine Books, 1995, Chapter 10.

Foods that stimulate the system and create mental and physical unrest are *rajasic.* They include coffee, tea, canned foods, those grown with chemicals, meat, spices, onion, garlic, hot pepper, alcohol, tobacco, and intoxicating drugs. They cause over-stimulation, discomfort, and lead to various serious diseases. These rajasic foods should be avoided.

Foods that lead to lethargy are *tamasic,* and they also should be avoided. They include meat, stale and rotten foods and highly refined foods as white sugar, white flour, polished rice, pickled foods, leftovers and preservative-added foods.

Moderation in diet, work, rest and sleep is essential for yogic life. Buddha after passing through severe austerities, adopted and taught a moderate path. Lord Krishna says in *Bhagavad Gita*:

Yoga is not for one who eats too much, nor for one who does not eat at all, nor for one who sleeps too much, nor for one who does not sleep at all. (6. 16)

Yoga becomes destroyer of pain for one who is moderate in eating and recreation, who is moderate in sleep and wakefulness. (6.17)

Reading should be selective. We should read ennobling and elevating texts such as spiritual and moral scriptures and books written by realized persons. We should avoid reading vulgar and horror stories and books which stimulate base emotions and materialistic outlook.

Although our efforts to increase the level of *sattvic* force do not destroy our dormant and active Karmas, they will neutralize the *tamasic* and *rajasic* effects of these Karmas.

But in creating potential Karmas we have greater freedom of choice. If we practice with determination to make right decisions and act on them, we create positive potential Karmas. These Karmas will be deposited in the subconscious mind and later will influence our present and future actions and tendencies.

Mind's Intrinsic Powers

According to the sage Vyasa,[2] the mind is endowed with seven intrinsic powers. They are:

- *Sankalpa Shakti* – the power to be and the power to become.
- *Cheshta* – purposeful movement.
- *Jivana* – the capacity to contain the life-force and to keep an organism alive.
- *Parinama* – the capacity to keep changing from one mood to another. This is the mind's capacity to control itself..
- *Samskara* – the capacity to store the subtle impressions of an action or any information the mind gathers from any source.
- *Dharma* – the power that naturally inclines the mind toward freedom and inner fulfillment.

Due to lack of spiritual training we usually experience only the functioning of *samskara*, through which the mind continuously stores the subtle impressions of our thoughts and actions. The subconscious mind is expanded in this process. *Jivana* gives life to all the stored contents. It keeps the past impressions alive, *cheshta* stirs these subtle impressions, giving them momentum to manifest. Thus it is the mind's own power that awakens the stored Karmas to become active Karmas.

Besides, our decision-making faculty is heavily influenced by the powerful impressions stored in the subconscious mind. That is why even though we know what is wrong at a conscious level, we continue to do it. Our personality traits and character evolve along the pattern established by the contents of our subconscious mind. (*See* Chapter 8. Karma and Character, *below*).

References

1. *Bhagavatam* is one of the ancient scriptures of Hinduism. It deals with the life and teachings of Lord Krishna.
2. Vyasa was an ancient sage of India and the compiler of the *Vedas*, the foundational scripture of Hindus and the reputed author of the epic *Mahabharatam* and *Brahma Sutras*.

5

Three *Gunas* (Modes of Nature)

Introduction

As actions are influenced by *gunas*, a clear understanding of the three *gunas* and their operations is essential for a Karma Yogi.

The whole structure of the manifested universe is considered to rest on the three *gunas: sattva, rajas* and *tamas* (*Yoga Sutras*, 2.18). All human beings and other creatures are subject to the interplay of the three *gunas*. All the objects of the universe possess these *gunas*. The *Bhagavad Gita* says,

> "There is no creature on earth or in heaven among the gods which is free from the three *gunas* of *Maya*." (18.40)

Everything in the world is pervaded by the *gunas* and can be classified according to the predominating *guna*.

Nature of *Gunas*

Sattva, rajas and *tamas* are distinct. Yet they function in coordination with one another. The nature of *sattva guna* is purity, peace and serenity; that of *rajas* is activity, restlessness, sensuality, desire, attachment and enjoyment; and that of *tamas* is slothfulness, inertia, confusion, delusion and ignorance. When one of the gunas is dominant, the other two remain subdued. A Yogic aspirant should always be vigilant and see that *tamas* and *rajas* remain tamed with the help of *sattva* so that he can continue to march on the path of Yoga undisturbed and undistracted. In order to accomplish this, earnest effort should be made, and he should meditate and pray regularly.

The state of society and international relations simply reflects the inner condition of human beings. Wars and strife are the externalization of inner conflicts. The welfare of society and the harmonious and friendly relations between nations depend more upon people establishing inner harmony in their own minds by the cultivation of *sattva.*

Sattva

Sattva is purity, harmony and goodness. It is stainless and luminous. It produces knowledge and happiness. It enlightens the intellect. It is helpful for maintaining mental and emotional equilibrium. When *sattva* is predominant, one remains serene and happy. A *sattvic* person cultivates fearlessness. He is endowed with discrimination between real (*sat*) and unreal (*asat*). He is free from egoism. He enjoys peace of mind, inner harmony and tranquility. He controls senses; he performs selfless service; he has no attraction for the objects of senses. He is humble, pious, generous, merciful, forbearing, loving, caring and sharing. He practices ethical discipline. He remains in a state of peace and joy. He sees unity in diversity. He knows what causes bondage and what dispels it.

Rajas

Rajas is passion or activity and ambition. It pleases the mind keeps alive the passions. It creates attachment or aversion towards the objects of the world. A *rajasic* person is full of cravings and desires. He is forced to act for their fulfillment. He becomes attached to those who help him to fulfill his desires and hates those that stand in his way. He runs after sensual pleasures and his desires become insatiable as a flame fed by oil. He is egoistic. He possesses the sense of "I and mine." He is ever greedy and restless. The more he acquires, the more passionate and greedy he becomes. Desires multiply. Nothing gives him satisfaction. He loses his power of discrimination. He runs after name, fame and comforts and involves himself in endless activities. He has no peace of mind. He is attached to action and its fruits. He uses others as tools for his own self-aggrandizement. He is motivated by selfishness and binds himself by Karmas or effects of his selfish actions.

Rajasic mind likes certain persons, objects and places now, and after some time it becomes disgusted with them, and wants new persons for company. It finds pleasure in sightseeing, and visiting new places. It always wants new sensations and variety. It is proud, egoistic, greedy and jealous. It makes a person constantly active and restless. It has a tendency to look into the defects of others. It also remembers the bad deeds or wrongs done by others and forgets easily their good acts. These tendencies intensify hatred and cause frequent disturbances in mind, and they may lead to hypertension and many other diseases. *Rajasic* mind has no compassion for others' sufferings.

It is *rajasic* mind that splits, separates and divides. It is under the sway of unconscious habits of wrong doings. Criminals when interrogated confess that they knew that they should not have acted in the way they did, but that they committed their offences out of habit. It is *rajas* that led them to commit serious crimes.

Tamas

Tamas means sloth, and inertia; it produces ignorance and destroys the sense of discrimination. It creates delusion, and so one cannot decide things on time. Thus it leads one to inaction. A *tamasic* person is thoughtless and ignorant. He is negligent and indolent. He forgets everything. He completely identifies himself with the body and begins to fight with people if they speak ill of him. He has no sense of proportion and no sense of balance or poise. A *tamasic* person remains in a state of sleepiness and lethargy, and in such a state of mind he goes through negative withdrawal. For him life is full of gloom; he does not experience joy or delight. Such a person becomes fat and flabby and is prone to disease. *Tamas* leads one to many illnesses; *tamasic* person becomes passive and suffers from all the diseases related to passivity. He does not want to move; he remains in a semi-conscious state. He is controlled by negative emotions. He is depressed, dependent and helpless. Life becomes burdensome for him.

Gunas and Actions (*Karmas*)

There is an intimate connection between the *gunas* and Karmas. It is the *gunas* that goad one to act. Self is non-doer, a silent witness. It is the body and mind that act. *Sattvic* person performs virtuous deeds without attachment to their fruits. He dedicates them to God or His manifestations. *Sattva* facilitates Yoga practice and helps one to become liberated from the bondage of Karma. *Sattvic* person performs actions with tranquil mind, and without egoism.

Rajasic person performs actions with selfish motives and the reactions of his actions cause pain and suffering. He is haunted by the fear of death. He seeks wealth by all means. He works for his own glory, fame and self-aggrandizement. The *tamasic* person remains in the darkness of ignorance. He is lazy and vicious. He acts without thought of what damage or injury his action might cause.

Gunas and Rebirth

If a person dies when the *sattva guna* remains predominant, he takes birth in the homes of wise parents. But one who casts off his body in *rajas* is reborn in a family of pleasure-seekers. If *tamas* is predominant when one drops off the body, he is reborn in a dull, lazy and desolate family.

Gunas and Spirituality

The modes of *sattva, rajas* and *tamas* constantly intervene in human life. When *sattva guna* leads one to the light of knowledge, one becomes a sage. When *rajas* predominates, the desire for enjoyment victimizes the human mind. One then loses all sense of discrimination and indulges in sensual enjoyment. When *tamas* predominates, one becomes dull and lazy and does nothing creative and useful.

From *sattva* arises knowledge, from *rajas* desire is born, and from *tamas* arises ignorance. A *sattvic* person marches upward towards liberation; a *rajasic* person remains in the middle; and a *tamasic* one moves downward under the influence of base qualities.

In the first step on the spiritual journey, a Yogi aspirant should not allow the *tamasic* quality to rise its head. He should prevent his mind from going to the grooves of negativity and passivity. Failure and lack of confidence in life lead one to such a negative state.

In the next step he should learn not to look for objects of pleasure. Sensual enjoyment robs his inner vitality that is the very basis of human unfoldment. Taming and keeping *tamas* and *rajas* under control, he should cultivate *sattva guna*. Without establishing *sattva guna* as the predominant quality, progress in Yogic practice cannot be achieved.

When one breathes primarily from the left nostril, *tamas* holds sway; when he breathes through the right nostril, a *rajasic* state is evident; and when the breath flows equally through both nostrils, he is in a *sattvic* state. With the help of *Pranayama* practice he can balance the breath and establish coordination between the mind and breath. The mind becomes calm and serene.

Transcending the *Gunas*

In order to overcome *rajas* and *tamas*, you should try to strengthen your *sattva* by cultivation of divine virtues, eating *sattvic* food, and by practicing japa, worship and meditation and control of senses and by studying spiritual books.

As *Atman* is beyond all the three *gunas*, after overcoming *rajas* and *tamas* through the force of *sattva*, you should go beyond *sattva* also, for *sattva*, like the other two *gunas,* is also a binding force. You should identify yourself with *Atman* and practice deep meditation and devotion. When you cross all the three *gunas*, then you attain freedom from the bondage of Karma and from the cycle of births and deaths.

The signs of a Yogi who has transcended the three *gunas* are described in the *Bhagavad Gita* as follows. When there is a divine call for him to do work for the solidarity of the world, he does not hate any work nor get attached to work; He just performs it as an instrument in the hands of God. He is also not attached to happiness and knowledge. He is free from likes and dislikes. He is entirely unconcerned whether the *gunas* come and go. He remains unshaken by them. He is a non-involved spectator. He abides in his own eternal Self. He is above the pairs of opposites. He maintains a balanced state of mind in pleasure and pain, in honor and dishonor. To him a clod of earth, stone and gold are the same. He is the same to a friend and a foe. He serves the Lord abiding in the hearts of all beings with unswerving devotion. He becomes fit for becoming one with Brahman and attaining liberation or release from the cycle of births and deaths. (14. 22–26)

6

Action and Inaction

Bhagavad Gita (Song Celestial) is a dialogue between Lord Krishna, an Incarnation of God, and Arjuna, a warrior prince. In it Lord Krishna expounds eternal spiritual truths and the rare secrets of Yoga and Vedanta. *Gita* forms part of the *Mahabharatam,* a great Epic of India.

In the eighteenth *sloka* (verse) of chapter Four of *Bhagavad Gita,* Lord Krishna says,

> He who sees inaction in action, and action in inaction, is wise among men; he is a Yogi and performer (i.e., attained the end) of all actions. (4.18)

One may wonder how can there be "inaction in action" and "action in inaction." This statement looks like a puzzle, and appears to be a total contradiction. It sounds like saying "walking without walking," "eating without eating." Lord Krishna Himself confirms the puzzling nature of these words – action (Karma) and inaction (Akarma), when He says, "Even scholars are confused as to what is action? what is inaction? Therefore I shall teach you the nature of action and inaction . . . . . " (4.16).

What do we normally mean by "action" and "inaction"? In the common usage "action" means "doing" or "performing" a work through the movement of the body, hands and feet, and "inaction" means "non-performance" or "absence of activity."

Inaction

Does inaction means "non-performance" or "mere absence of action"? Can a person achieve inaction by simply sitting quietly and not doing anything? A person may be sitting quietly and he may not do anything, but if he has the sense of "I, me, mine" and the sense of doership or if he thinks that he is the doer, he is ever doing action. This is "action in inaction."

His inaction also induces the feeling of egoism. The inactive person says, "I am sitting quietly. I am not doing anything." Inaction is wrongly attributed to the Self. "One does not achieve inaction," says Lord Krishna, "by non-performance of action, nor does one attain *siddhi* or freedom from action by mere renunciation of action." (3.4) Because even when one is sitting quietly, his mind will be going on thinking something or other. Thought is real action, and even breathing is action. Hence Sri Krishna emphatically states,

> "Verily none can ever remain for even a moment without performing action; for, everyone is made to act helplessly indeed by the qualities born of nature." (3.5)

Action and the idea of Doership

The confusion regarding the meanings of action and inaction arises out of the idea of doership. When we perform actions, we ordinarily take ourselves as the "doers" (*karta*), and enjoyers of the fruits of the actions. But are we really the doers? In the vision of Vedanta[1] and *Bhagavad Gita*, we are not the doers or actors. How do we, then, think that we do or act? We think so, because of our ignorance. Who is the real doer? It is our body and mind that perform actions. We wrongly identify ourselves with our body and mind and so think that we perform actions. The Upanishads declare that we are not the body and mind. We are the eternal Self or Atman or pure Consciousness or Awareness. The Self does not act. It is a silent witness or observer only. In its presence the body, the sense organs and the mind perform their respective functions.

A wise person, a sage, who possesses the Knowledge of Self, knows that only his body acts, and that as Self, he does not act at all. He perceives inaction or actionlessness, even when engaged in activities. He has no idea of doership. His actions are burnt by the fire of wisdom or the Knowledge of Self. This spiritual fire consumes the effects of all kinds of action, good and bad, and frees the enlightened sage from the bonds of action. Just as a seed burnt in the fire cannot germinate, so also the actions burnt in the fire of Knowledge of Self cannot produce future birth. Lord Krishna says in the *Bhagavad Gita,* "To one who is devoid of attachment, who is liberated, whose mind is established in knowledge, who works for the sake of sacrifice, the whole action is dissolved." (4.23)

An action done as worship of God, without expectation or attachment to its fruit, is no action at all.

An ignorant person sitting quietly thinks that he is not doing anything. But as he identifies himself with the body and mind, he is working through his mind. His wrong notion is similar to that of a person sitting in a moving train. The trees and buildings outside the track appear to him to be moving in the opposite direction. Moving objects that are very far away appear to be motionless. Even so in the case of I, an actionless Awareness or Self, sitting in the body, when the body and its organs act, it looks as though this Self acts, and when the body sits quietly, it is mistaken for inaction.

Renunciation of Action

Lord Krishna says, a person does not attain freedom from action by mere renunciation of action." (*Gita,* 3.4). What is meant by renunciation of action? Renunciation of action does not mean non-performance or giving up action. In fact, as already stated, none can ever remain even for a second without performing action; for everyone is made to act helplessly indeed by the forces (*gunas*) born of nature. The *gunas* of nature, as we know, are three: *sattva* (purity or harmony), *rajas* (passion or restlessness) and *tamas* (inertia or dullness). *Sattvic* action helps to attain purity. *Rajasic* and *tamasic* actions bind a person to *samsara* (cycle of births and deaths). (For details, *see* Chapter 5. Three *Gunas* (Modes of Nature), *above*).

With reference to *gunas*, action is of three types: *sattvic, rajasic* and *tamasic,*

> "Action performed as duty, without attachment, without love or hate, without desire for fruit is called *sattvic*." (*Bhagavad Gita*, 18.23).

The performer of pure action (*sattvic* action) experiences great joy. He wholeheartedly performs his duty or any other work, not caring for the reward but offering it willingly at the feet of the Lord. (*Gita,* 18.26).

> "Action done by one longing for pleasure or with egoism or with much effort is declared to be *rajasic*." (*Gita,* 18.24).

A *rajasic* (passionate) person performs various selfish actions. He can never work without expectation of a reward. He expects pleasure as fruits of actions. (*Gita,* 18.27).

> "The action performed under delusion and without regard to the capacity and consequences, loss and injury to others, is declared to be *tamasic* (dark)." (*Gita,* 18.25).

Tamasic action causes harm to others. A *tamasic* person acts blindly. He does not bother about his capacity to perform the actions or about their consequences. He does not discriminate between the good and bad. (*Gita*, 18.28).

Then what is the true meaning of renunciation of action? Lord Krishna states,

> "Verily it is not possible for an embodied being to abandon actions entirely, but he, who relinquishes the rewards of

actions, verily called a man of renunciation." (*Gita*, 18.11).

So the true meaning of renunciation is giving-up the notion of "I am the doer," and doing actions without attachment to the fruits of actions. Lord Krishna emphatically declares,

> "Thy right is to work only, but never with its fruits. Let not the fruits of action be thy motive, nor let the attachment to inaction." (*Gita*, 2.47).

Actions done with the expectation of reward bring bondage. It is the desires and attachments that are responsible for bondage and the consequent rebirths. Hence Lord Krishna exhorts us:

> "Without attachment do thou always perform actions that should be done, for, by performing actions without attachment man reaches the Supreme." (*Gita,* 3.19)

Performing actions for the benefit of others without attachment, i.e., selfless service is Karma Yoga. (For details, *see* Chapter 14. Karma Yoga, *below*). If you find it difficult initially to give up the desire for the fruits of your actions, then Lord Krishna advises you to "perform actions with devotion, for God's sake, holding Him as the final goal." (*Gita,* 11. 55). When you perform actions as offering unto the Lord, you will attain the purity of your heart and through it eventually Self-realization. (*Gita,* 3.19; 12.11). At the same time you would be able perform actions with devotion and utmost sincerity, as you are offering them unto the Lord. Then work becomes worship.

If you are unable to perform actions for God's sake, Lord Krishna prescribes another approach: "Do your work for your satisfaction, but dedicate the results to God." (*Gita,* 12.11; 18.11).

Service to God

What does "performing actions for the sake of God or dedicating their fruits to God" mean? It means service to God.

Does God need our services? No. Then what else does it mean? It means selfless service to other beings, because God as the Supreme Self resides in all beings. All beings and the entire universe are His manifestations. Just as both the ocean and the waves are the same water, the Lord and all beings are the same Self. The Self is indivisible like ether or space, and it is the same in all bodies. It is the same Consciousness in all beings. (*Gita*, 18.20). "It is one alone, without a second," declares *Chandogya Upanishad*, 6.2.1). "Though One, He roams in various forms." "The Soul in all indeed One. . . . . The diversity of souls is like the diversity of the reflections of the moon in the waves," says *Brahmabindu Upanishad,* (12). Saint Ramalingam of Tamil Nadu, India sings in praise of the Lord: "I am in all beings, all beings are in Me. Realizing this thou shall seek the good of all beings" so Thou said unto me, O! Lord of Truth.

Subramanya Bharathiar, a great poet of Tamil Nadu, India said,

> "All living beings are God only, nothing else. Not only living beings, but also all things that we see around are God."

Lord Krishna in the *Bhagavad Gita* declares,

> "With the mind harmonized by Yoga, the Yogi sees the Self in all beings, and all beings in the Self. He sees the same everywhere." (6.29)
>
> "He, who sees Me everywhere and sees everything in Me, never becomes separated from Me, nor do I become separated from him." (6.30).

Thus service to other beings is service to God.

Inaction in action

He, who performs actions without egoism and attachment to their fruits, really does nothing at all. Though he is ever engaged in activity, for he has realized his identity with the actionless Self (*Gita,* 4.20). His selfless action is dissolved (*Gita,* 4.23) and does not bind him, just as a roasted seed does not germinate. He is freed from the rounds of births and deaths. He is truly called a man of renunciation, a Yogi. (*Gita*, 18.11). He is not tainted by actions, just as a lotus leaf is not wet by water. (*Gita,* 5.10). The Yogi understands the secret of Karma or actions. He perceives actions from the state of inaction, at the same time enjoying inaction in the midst of actions. He thus sees inaction in action. All actions are equally welcome to the Yogi. He does not hate an unpleasant work, nor he attached to a pleasant one. (*Gita*, 18.10). He is free from worries, anxieties and fears. His mind is calm, and he enjoys supreme peace. (*Gita,* 5.13). He does not identify himself with the body, though he still possesses it. Though appearing to be active, he is free from the idea of "doer." He never forgets that the Self within is always actionless and at peace, though his body and mind are engaged in various activities. He does not dwell on the enjoyments of the past, takes no thought of the future, and is indifferent about the present. Completely free from the illusory notion of the physical individuality, he is aware of his identity with all beings.

References

1. Vedanta is a non-dualistic philosophy expounded by *Upanishadic* seers and sages of India thousands of years ago. *Upanishads* form the final parts of *Vedas* and embody the philosophy of Vedanta.

7

Fruits of Actions (*Karma-Phala*)

Karma and its fruit, action and its effect, are inseparable. Every cause is followed by its effect. No power on earth can stop it. Every action produces a two-fold effect. First, it comes back to the doer as reaction. Second, it may act on other people and theirs on the doer. When I do an evil act, then my mind is in a certain state of vibration, and all other minds that are in a similar state have a tendency to be affected by the vibration of my mind, depending upon the force of the vibration and the distance. When I do a good action, then my mind is in a positive state of vibration, and all minds with a similar state have a tendency to be influenced by my mind. That is why an evil doer generally goes on doing more and more evil. His actions become intensified. This is also true of the doer of good and his good actions will become intensified. So in doing evil we injure ourselves and others also. In doing good, we do good to ourselves and to others as well; and like other forces, these forces of good and evil gather strength from outside forces.

Motivation

It is our motivation, good or bad, that determines the fruits of our actions. Shanthideva, a *Bodhisattva*, said,

> Whatever joy there is in this world, all comes from desiring others to be happy, and whatever suffering there is in this

> world, all comes from desiring myself to be happy. (*Bodicaryavatara*)

As the Law of Karma is inevitable and infallible, when we harm others, we are harming ourselves, and when we bring them happiness, we are bringing ourselves future happiness. Lord Jesus told His disciple:

> He who kills a beast without cause, though the beast attacks him not, through lust for slaughter, or for its flesh, or for its hide, or for its tusks, evil is the deed that he does, for he is turned into a wild beast himself. Wherefore is his end also as the end of the wild beast.

Lord Jesus has thus lucidly said that those who kill animals for food or for other purposes shall suffer a similar end in the future.

Good, Bad and Mixed Actions

The results of various actions can be classified as good, evil and mixed. If the effect of an action is beneficial to oneself or to others, without injuring any living creature in any manner, then it is called good action. An action which causes suffering, sorrow or misery to oneself or to others is called a bad or evil action; while an action whose result is beneficial to some but at the same time is harmful to others is called a mixed one.

In this world of relativity with the limitations of time and space, it is impossible to find any action that is absolutely good or evil. The *Gita* says, "All actions are enveloped by evil, as fire by smoke." (18.48).

Relation between Action and its Reaction

There is causal relationship between the nature of actions and that of their results. Good actions yield good results, and bad or wrong actions bring bad results. All cultures share this belief. (*See* "The Law of Causation" in Chapter 9. Universal Laws, *below*). As you sow, so shall you reap." If you sow wheat, you will harvest wheat only and not rice. Every good thought, word or deed begets a good reaction in this life or next. Every bad thought, harsh word or evil deed comes back to harm you in this life or next.

Results of Actions

What are the results of good, bad and mixed actions?
Results of Good Action are:

1. Purification of the mind, i.e., the removal from the mind of its dross that is the effect of narrow selfishness and gross sensuality;
2. Happiness in the higher regions, during the period between the death and rebirth in this physical world;
3. Coming back as a human being again to earth with facilities for purification and spiritual growth. However, if you perform actions without attachment to their fruits and you have attained the Knowledge of Self or Supreme Devotion having your mind completely purified, you will have no more birth.

Results of Bad Action are:

1. The mind becomes more and more impure;
2. Suffering in the nether region or hell during the period between the death and rebirth on earth;
3. If the action is very bad, after suffering in the nether region, you take your birth in this world with subhuman nature; and as a subhuman being, and placed amidst very unfavorable environment.

Mixed actions are partly bad and partly good. For example, if you earn money by unlawful means and build a temple or hospital, it is a mixed action.
Results of Mixed Actions are:

1. The mind becomes pure in certain respects and more impure in others.
2. You suffer for some time in hell and enjoy for some time in the happy regions above.
3. Afterwards you ordinarily take birth on earth as a human being.

Meritorious deeds bring merit. The acts of charity and self-sacrifice bring name, fame and honor in return. When you love and respect a person wholeheartedly, you will be loved and respected in turn by the same person. When you tell lies, deceive others and injure them, you will degrade and degenerate yourself, and there will be many others to tell lies to you, deceive you and injure you. When you use kind and loving words to a person, he, in turn, will use kind and loving words to you. On the contrary, if you use harsh, rough and scolding words to a person, you will get harsh, rough and scolding words in turn from the same person or someone else. Even if you murder someone secretly or commit adultery in a secluded place, still you cannot avoid the karmic punishment.

Every thought, word or action is always stored as an impression in the subconscious mind. Later at an appropriate time, it comes back to the surface and yields its effect. So nobody can avoid the merits of a good and benevolent thought, word or deed, and similarly nobody can prevent the demerit of a sinful thought, word or act. A wrong doer may escape legal punishment, but he cannot escape the karmic effect.

Here is a true story that was reported in a magazine from India.

In Coimbatore of Southern India, there was a very rich man and a very poor man. Somehow they became very close friends. The rich man wanted to become even richer, so he used to lend money and make a lot of money on interest. One day the poor man needed some money, so he went to his good friend and said, I've never asked you for anything before, but now I need 5,000 rupees. Could you please lend it to me?"

Certainly, I'm glad that you're asking me. Here, take it."

"What is the interest charge?

"Oh, don't worry. There is no interest."

The poor man was quite surprised. "Oh, thank you," he said, "You are really a good friend." He took the money, and after a few months of hard working, he was able to pay back 2,000 rupees. And of course, he did not ask for a receipt because they were such good friends. Then after some months, he brought the other 3,000 rupees to pay off the loan in full.

His rich friend took the money and asked, "Why are you giving me only 3,000 rupees? You borrowed 5,000 rupees."

"Oh, don't you remember that I gave you 2,000 rupees some months back?

"Did you? I don't think so. I don't have any memory of that. Come on, you have to give me the full amount of 5,000 rupees."

"Brother, please, don't you remember when I brought the money, you even said, "I am so glad that you are able to make a payment so soon."

"No, I don't remember ever saying anything like that. I never forget money matters. If you had really given it to me, I would not have forgotten. You better give me the full 5,000."

"All right. I trust in the truth. The truth will take care of every thing I'll get the money. He was really disappointed, but went and sold everything he had, got 5,000 rupees and brought it to his friend. "This time," he said, "I want to make sure that you are going to remember this. Let's go to the temple. The priest will be doing the worship service to the deity. Right there, in front of God, I want you to say that you never received the 2,000 rupees from me. Once you say that, I'll give you the full 5,000."

"Sure, why should I hesitate since you never gave me any money."

So they went to the temple; the rich man said that he had never received the 2,000 rupees., and the poor man gave him the 5,000 rupees. Within two weeks, all of a sudden the rich man became partially paralyzed. Within another two weeks, many other complications set in. Within a month, he died. You may escape the legal punishment by spending a lot of money on lawyers, but you cannot escape God's punishment. What you have sown, you must reap.

When do Karmas bear Fruits?

When will an action bring its fruit in the form of either happiness or pain? A farmer reaps harvest only after several months. The time span may vary according to the nature of crops. Vegetables may give the yield in a few weeks; grains in five or six months; fruit trees like mango may take four or five years to bear fruits. Every crop takes its own time to give the yield. In the same way every action brings its effect in due course. How long does each action take to bear the effect? There is no definite answer. If you do some good today, someone will do good to you under similar conditions sooner or later. Our present actions may produce their effects the next moment, the next day, the next month, in a year, or in a future birth. There is no definite rule here. Every action takes its own time to bear its fruit. Until time, condition, circumstance and place are ready for the ripening of the fruit, the Karma hangs in the balance. We have a choice in doing good and bad Karma but we have no choice in the enjoyment of their fruits as and when we want them. Karma rests with us; the timing of the fruit rests with God. He determines when we should have it. If you reflect over all that is happening to you and others around you, over which there is no control, you will easily see the truth of this statement.

Karma and Rebirth

As per the effects of one's Karmas, one takes birth in a rich, middle or very poor family. A person of merit takes his birth with clear intellect and great ability in a learned, rich and prosperous family. One who is neither very sinful nor virtuous, takes birth in a middle class family. One who commits sins takes rebirth in a poor and starving family as a beggar or as dumb, deaf or lame or as a slave and illiterate. So the happiness and good fortunes or suffering and misfortunes that we see in this world are due to the effects of people's past Karmas.

The fructifying Karmas produce the body, its longevity, tendencies and the conditions of the present life. The span of life is generally determined at the time of birth. This may, however, be revised by one's subsequent Karmas. The practice of *Pranayama*, etc. prolongs the span of life, while the non-observance of rules of health shortens the life span.

Sometimes a large number of persons may perish simultaneously in a shipwreck, plane-crash, or in an earthquake. As we are living in this universe, so we are governed by its laws. Our lives, to some extent, are regulated by them. In us lie the dormant tendencies (impressions of the past Karmas) which may cause all sorts of suffering and all forms of death. The tendencies fructify when they are excited by a powerful external factor.

The Wheel of Action and Reaction

Everyone performs millions of actions in his or her lifetime and enjoys their fruits in the course of the present life or the next. While enjoying the fruits of past actions, he or she performs new actions, which bear fruits in the future. Thus the wheel of action and reaction goes on rotating and in this wheel, each soul is passing from one point to another on and on, age after age, taking birth after birth. Is there any hope of extricating ourselves from this wheel?

Ignorant people deny the existence of the Law of Karma. They say that all activity will end after the death of the body, nothing will remain and no further responsibility for the body's actions. But will the Law of Action and Reaction cease to function because these ignorant people do not believe it? No. Whether anybody believes it or not, it will continue to operate. Our belief or disbelief can never arrest the ceaseless operation of the Law of karma. Such being it nature and inevitability, how can we free ourselves from this Law, and attain eternal freedom? We can free ourselves from the clutches of this Law, when our Karma becomes Karma Yoga. (For details, see Chapter 14. Karma Yoga, *below*).

8

Karma and Character

Character

Our character is the aggregate of tendencies, the sum total of the inclinations of our mind. These are the result of previous mental actions such as desires, tendencies, thoughts, ideas and impressions. Our present character is the resultant of our past Karma or actions, both mental and physical, and our future will be determined by our present actions.

Conduct or behavior reveals our character. Conduct also molds our character. Cultivation of good conduct needs rigorous discipline and constant vigilance. We shall have to watch every thought, word and action. With all our good intentions, we may be carried away by the force of our previous wrong impressions, instincts and impulses. Good behavior indicates that we have a refined or polished, disciplined mind and spiritual culture.

The results of past actions are experienced as pleasure and pain. Both pleasure and pain or happiness and misery have equal share in molding our character. In some cases misery plays a greater role in molding character. If one were to study the great personalities of the world, it would be found, in most cases, that misery taught them more than happiness, poverty taught them more than wealth, and blames brought out their inner fire more than praise. (*See* Chapter 38. Purpose of Suffering, *below*).

Knowledge

Knowledge is inherent in us. No knowledge comes from outside; it is all within. Like fire in a piece of flint, knowledge exists in the mind. The external world is simply the suggestion, the friction that brings it out. What we say "learning" is really what we discover by taking the cover off our own soul which is a mine of infinite knowledge.

Will

A tendency becomes stronger each time the related action is repeated. In this way our character is shaped by the actions we perform. The actions depend on the will. Therefore, a strong will indicates a strong character, and a weak will a weak character.

Karma's Influence

Karma has a tremendous influence on character. The most common actions that a person performs will tell you his real character. All the actions are the display of his thought, the manifestation of his will; the will is caused by character and character is derived from Karma. The gigantic will of great souls like Buddha and Jesus could not be obtained in one life, for we know who their fathers were. Millions of petty kings like Buddha's father had been in the world. Millions and millions of carpenters like Joseph had come and gone. Had they produced any great soul like Buddha or Jesus? No. How do you explain the gulf between the petty king and Buddha, and carpenter and Jesus, whom millions of human beings worship as God? The gigantic will that manifested Buddha and Jesus must have been through ages and ages continually growing bigger and bigger until it emerged as Buddha or Jesus. "All this is determined by Karma. No one can get anything unless he earns it," says Swami Vivekananda.[1] Our Karma determines what we deserve and what we can assimilate. Our past actions are responsible for what we are today. Whatever we wish to be in the future can be produced by our present actions. So we have to know how we have to work. By knowing how to work we can obtain the greatest results. The aim of all work is simply to bring out the power of the mind, to wake up the soul.

Cause and Effect

Our character like Karma is subject to the Law of Action and Reaction, because it is the total result of past actions. In the chain of cause and effect, each effect is latent in the cause and each cause is latent in the effect. So every form of character is in itself a cause as well as an effect, just as a seed is the cause of a tree and the tree in turn is the cause of the seed. This great truth explains why one's character is good, another's bad or why one individual behaves in this way or that. Neither parents nor God is responsible for the differences in our characters.

Habits

Habit is formed by a repeated-action. Habit reflects one's nature. Control of habits is control of nature. Old bad habits can be changed into healthy, desirable habits through the force of a pure, strong will. A weak, idle person is a slave of habits. He always imagines that habits are innate and they cannot be changed in one's lifetime. This is a wrong notion. If you want to change old habits you have to struggle hard. The old habits will try to return, resist, persist and recur. A mental conflict will go on between the old impressions and the new impressions, between the old habits and the new habits. You must be careful and vigilant at all times. Be alert like the soldier on duty.

The old bad habit asserts: "O friend! You enjoyed several things through me. Why do you drive me off now? You are very cruel. I have a right to stay here."

The whole world runs through habits only. People cling to tea, coffee, cigarettes, movies, novels, gambling, playing cards, etc. through the force of habit. The habit does not leave easily. It resists.

While trying to get rid of an evil habit, if you are careless, the old habit will reappear. Do not relax your determination to get rid of it. Gradually it will die out, and the new, good habit will gain strength in the end. Be determined. Success is certain.

Do not become a victim to evil thoughts like wrath, passion, greed, pride and attachment. If you are swayed by them, they will drag you down from the path of virtue, and make you to do all sorts of wicked actions; selfishness and greed will cloud your understanding. You may not know what you are doing. So control your emotions and thoughts. Then only you will not do any wrong deeds. Practice regularly pranayama, meditation, Japa and vow of silence to control your emotions and thoughts.

Prarabdha Karma cannot be avoided. Endure them with poise, and take care of your present actions. With determination stick to the correct path. Place yourself in God's hands. Dedicate everything to God. The key to overcome the Law of Karma is to spiritualize all actions by doing everything for the sake of the Lord. Then you will attain eternal peace and liberation from Karma.

Reference

1. *Karma Yoga and Bhakti Yoga*, New York: Ramakrishna-Vivekananda Center, 1982, p. 7.

9

Universal Laws

Introduction

There is perfect order in the universe in everything. Every event of the world is governed by eternal, immutable Universal Laws. A knowledge of these Laws of Nature will help you to clearly understand the inner harmony and the logical order of the universe, and to realize the glory of the Lord, the Lawgiver.

The Universal Laws consist of (1) Law of Cause and Effect or Law of Causation, (2) Law of Karma, (3) Law of Action and Reaction, (4) Law of Compensation, (5) Law of Retribution, and (6) Law of Resistance. All these are complementary to one another and operate together.

You should have a comprehensive understanding of these laws and their operations. Only then you can live in this world smoothly and happily. There are positive and hostile forces in the universe. With a knowledge of the universal laws, you can utilize the positive forces and neutralize the hostile forces to serve your aims. Otherwise you will become a slave and be tossed hither and thither by the hostile forces.

The captain of a ship, who has a mariner's compass, who has knowledge of the sea, the routes and the oceanic currents, can sail smoothly. Otherwise his ship will be tossed here and there helplessly and be wrecked by dashing against some icebergs or rocks. Likewise, a wise sailor in the ocean of life, who has a thorough knowledge of Laws of Nature can sail smoothly and reach the goal of life.

Law of Cause and Effect

The Law of Causation is a universal law. It governs all the phenomena of nature. It keeps up the inner harmony and logical order of the universe. Not only the physical phenomena but also the deeds of human beings are subject to this law.

The laws of gravitation, cohesion, adhesion, attraction, and repulsion on the physical plane, and the law of likes and dislikes, the law of relativity, and the law of association on the mental plane—all operate in strict accordance with this law.

Life involves succession of events. Events are the effects of their causes. The sun shines, the wind flows, the tree blossoms and bears fruit, the mind thinks, feels and wills, the brain and other organs in the body work in accordance with the mighty Law of Cause and Effect.

The seed is the cause of the tree, and the tree in turn is the cause of the seed. The cause is found in the effect and the effect exists in the cause. This is the universal unending chain of cause and effect. The world runs on this basic law.

No event can happen without having a definite cause at its back. War, earthquake, volcanic eruption, thunderstorm, lighting, disease of the body, fortune, misfortune—all have definite causes behind them. There is no such thing as a chance or accident, even though we mostly do not remember the events of past life.

Law of Karma

The actions of human beings, like natural phenomena, are subject to the Law of Causation. Hence it is known as Law of Karma. Every action is bound to produce its reaction or result. Our health or illness, happiness or misery, wealth or poverty, intellectual brilliance or dullness, good tendency or evil tendencies—all are the effects of our past actions (Karmas). Neither our parents nor God is responsible for them.

Every action produces a twofold effect. First, it gives us an appropriate fruit. That is, good action produces good effect; bad action, bad effect. Second, every thought we think, every word we speak, and every action we perform leave an impression in our subconscious minds. What we are at present is the effect of the sum total of all the impressions of our past. This is really what is meant by our character. If good impressions prevail, our character becomes good; if bad, it becomes bad. Our character influences our motives and tendencies. (*See* Chapter 8. Karma and Character, *above*).

As you think, so you become. You create your own destiny. Cultivate good thoughts, you will become pure, an embodiment of good character. Do good actions always. Serve, love, and give. Live to serve others. Then you will enjoy peace and joy. If you cause pain to others, you will reap pain. If you give happiness to others, you will reap happiness.

When any evil thought arises, kill it by the sword of discrimination. Speak sweet and loving words. Speak the truth. Develop patience, mercy and universal love. Do not do any harm to anybody. Do everything as a form of worship to the Lord and do selfless service. Fix your mind on God. Then you become free from the operation of the Law of Karma. (*See* Chapter 14. Karma Yoga, *below*).

The Theory of Pre-ordination. Orthodox Christians and theologians believe that God fixes the destiny of a person before his or her birth. This theory of pre-ordination is not logical and not tenable. If it were true, then human beings would have no independence and freedom, and no moral responsibility. It would make God partial, unjust and whimsical. Why should God make one happy and another unhappy, one healthy and another unhealthy, one rich and another poor? Is He so whimsical and eccentric? Is he so biased? If God is all merciful, why can't He make all equal, noble and virtuous? Why is one born blind? Why should one suffer owing to the whim of such a Creator? Questions like these arise if you accept the theory of pre-ordination. This hypothesis does not stand the test of reason.

Inequalities of the World. The Law of Karma has been the basis on which the Hindus, Jains, Buddhists and Sikhs have built up their culture and the theory of rebirth. It is the proper explanation for the inequalities of the world, pleasure and pain, health and sickness, wealth and poverty and all other dualities. The Law of Karma is logical, sound and tenable. It is a law of perfect justice. H. P. Blavatsky,[1] in her *The Secret Doctrine*, considers the Law of Karma as "the unerring law which adjusts each effect to its cause, in the physical, mental and spiritual planes of being . . . intelligently and equitably."

Everyone reaps the fruits of his own actions. You are the maker of your own destiny by your thoughts, and actions. You are a free agent. You become a bad person by your bad habits, but you can change your thoughts, habits and tendencies, and thus can become a good person sooner or later. You have free will.

Frederick Lenz reports in his *Lifetimes true Accounts of Reincarnation,* "A large percentage of people who have had remembrances of past lives expressed that their actions in past lives affected their succeeding lives. They observed that when they did positive things in a past lifetime, they later reaped the reward for those actions; and when they performed harmful actions, they later had to pay the penalty." (Indianapolis, N.Y. The Bobbs-Merrill Company, 1979, p. 117).

What you are today is the result of your past actions. What you would be in future would be the effect of your present actions. *Bible* says, "God is not mocked, for whatsoever a man soweth, that shall he also reap." (*The New Testament: Galatians* 6.7–8). You take the physical body to reap the fruits of your Karma. If you give happiness to others, you will receive happiness. If you cause suffering to others, you will reap suffering. Lord Jesus says, "With what measure you shall mete, it shall be measured to you again." Sow a good thought and a good deed, you will reap a good harvest of peace and prosperity. Lord Jesus adds, "Do unto others as you would have them do unto you." He also exhorts: "Love thy neighbor as thyself."

Mysterious Nature of this Law. The Law of Karma is subtle and mysterious. Nobody knows the future. It is said that certain evil actions produce certain diseases. Yet it is difficult to say positively which particular bad action is the cause for a particular disease. If a person suffers from cancer, it may be the result of one single wrong action or a combination of several bad actions. Diseases and sufferings are karmic purgation.

God can never be unjust or partial. He never rewards one and punishes another. He never chooses one for suffering and another for happiness. God is not responsible for the differences in the conditions of people. Those differences are due to the differences in their past actions. (*See* Chapter 10. The Doctrine of Karma, *below*). Never blame God for your suffering. Correct your thoughts, habits and character.

Can one's Karma be taken over by Another

Saints and sages live in the world to alleviate the sorrows of mankind through either spiritual teachings or Yogic power or taking over others' Karmas on themselves. Paramahansa Yogananda,[2] in his autobiography entitled *The Autobiography of a Yogi*, writes:

> "By putting on the ailments of others, a Yogi can satisfy, for them, the Karmic Law of Cause and Effect. . . .
>
> "The spiritual law does not require a Master to become ill whenever he heals another person. . . . On rare occasions, however, a Master who wishes to quicken greatly his disciples' evolution may then voluntarily work out on his own body a large measure of their undesirable Karma.
>
> "Jesus signified himself as a ransom for the sins of many. With his divine powers, Christ could never have been subjected to death by crucifixion if he had not willingly cooperated with the subtle Cosmic Law of Cause and Effect. He thus took on himself the consequences of others' Karma,

especially that of his disciples. In this manner they were highly purified and made fit to receive the omnipresent Consciousness or Holy Ghost that later descended upon them." (*The Autobiography of a Yogi*, Los angels: *Self-realization Fellowship*, pp. 236–37).

Similarly the physical bodies of Sankaracharya, Paramahamsa Ramakrishna, Ramana Maharishi and other saints suffered greatly due to the Karmas of others which they took over. Only great saints are able to assume the Karmas of disciples and devotees.

Good and Evil. Only the Law of Karma can explain the mysterious problem of good and evil in this world. It can bring solace, contentment and strength to the afflicted. It gives encouragement to hopeless. It pushes him to right thinking, right speech and right action. If all people understand this law correctly and mold their life carefully, there will be heaven on earth; greed, jealousy, hatred, anger, and passion will vanish; virtue will shine everywhere.

The main idea of Karma, then, is not one of punishment for past mistakes and crimes, but one of learning lesson and redirecting the course of your life in the right path (*See* Chapter 18. Practice of Karma Yoga, *below*).

Your karmic journey ends when you completely pay off your karmic debts today, next year, next birth or after a hundred thousand lifetimes. That happens when you attain Enlightenment or Self-realization. Then you become united with God, the ultimate Reality. (For details, *See* Chapter 40. Liberation, *below*).

Collective Karma. Whatever is true in the case of an individual is also true in the case of a nation, for individuals make a nation. "As in small, so in great," says ancient Hermes.

The collective Karma of a race or nation is governed by the same law. Nations rise and fall, empires flourish and decline on the same principles underlying the Law of Karma. National calamities and mass sufferings and deaths cannot occur without sufficient cause. We may not be able to perceive the causes, but it is certain that nothing unmerited can happen to a nation. People's collective evil deeds, their religious, ethical, communal or color dissension, mutual hatred and persecution bring on them the wrath of divine justice and they pay for them in the form of large-scale suffering. Karma is insentient. There must be a dispenser to allot the fruits according to the nature of actions. A just overseer knows how much wages are to be paid to various workers in a contract job. Similarly the Lord allots fruits according to our actions.

Law of Action and Reaction

The grand Law of Causation includes the Law of Action and Reaction, the Law of Compensation and the Law of Retribution. Isaac Newton's Third Law of Motion states: "To every action there is an equal and opposite reaction." The Law of Karma is similar to this Law of Motion.

To every thought, desire, imagination or action of a person, there is an equal reaction. Virtue brings its own reward; vice brings its own punishment. If I bring joy to others or if I relieve the sufferings of others, I will get joy. If I hurt another person, or cause misery and pain to another, I will in turn get misery and pain. God never punishes the wicked nor rewards the virtuous. It is their own actions that bring punishment or reward. It is the Law of Action and Reaction that brings the fruits. No one else is to be blamed. The law operates with precision and accuracy.

The Law of Action and Reaction operates both in the physical and mental planes. A tennis ball strikes the ground and rises up with equal force. If I speak sweet loving words to anyone, he returns the feeling of love and speaks sweet words to me. When I do an action by error, am I still liable for the reaction? There is no escape, no matter how absent-mindedly I do it. He who understands this law will never do any wrong action, because he knows that it will react upon him and bring misery and pain.

Law of Compensation

The Law of Compensation operates everywhere in nature. For instance the seed breaks and a tree appears from the seed. The tree grows in accordance with the Law of Compensation. Fuel burns and destroyed, but heat is produced as a compensation. If there is an ebb tide in one place, there is flood tide in another place. If there is day in India, there is night in America. Calm follows a storm. Every effect has a cause. There is a perfect balance between the cause and effect. The Law of Compensation maintains the balance and establishes equilibrium in Nature.

If you do an evil act you will reap a bad fruit in compensation. Your suffering may appear to be unjust, you may think that you do not deserve it at all, but if you try to find out the cause of this suffering you will realize that it is a just compensation. The affairs of our life are so very intricate and our intellect is so feeble that we are not able to grasp the cause of a suffering or event.

If you take an individual life as an isolated event that begins with the birth of the physical body and ends with its death, you cannot find any correct explanation for the affairs of life. If you deny pre-existence and rebirth, then there will be no compensation for the virtuous person who has done noble deeds and for the wicked man who has committed crimes. The chain of cause and effect will be broken abruptly and there will be terrible injustice everywhere. This cannot be. If you connect your present life with the past and future, then there will be perfect compensation. A soul's life of countless births is a continuous stream. The physical body may change but the events and their compensation continue throughout. If a virtuous person who has not done any evil act in this birth suffers, it is due to some wrong act that he might have done in his previous birth. He will have his compensation for his good actions in his next birth. If a wicked man doing many evil actions apparently enjoys happiness in this birth, it is due to some good action performed in his previous birth. He will have compensation for his evil actions in his next birth. The Law of compensation embraces a wide range of the whole soul-life. Life does not end with the disintegration of this physical body alone. There is reincarnation. There have been countless previous lives also. (For details, *see* Chapter 29. The Doctrine of Reincarnation, *below*).

Law of Retribution

Every wrong action or crime brings its own punishment in accordance with the Law of Retribution. He who hurts another person hurts himself. He who robs another person robs himself. Every wrong act causes punishment first in the inner nature, and then externally in the form of pain, misery, loss, disease, etc.

Here is a story where a person escapes retribution because of his means, but in the end the law gets him. From the balcony of his bungalow by the riverside, the judge witnesses a ghastly murder. He clearly identifies the murderer and phones the police. A man is caught and the case appears before the same judge.

The judge is surprised to see that this is not the man whom he had seen! He imagines that the man will be freed, but to his surprise and horror, all the evidence piles against him to declare him guilty of the murder. The judge is a keen student of Karma and the law-codes laid down by Manu of pre-Christian era in his *Manu Smirti* in India. How could he sentence an innocent man for a crime he never committed?

To reconcile the reasoning of the Law of Karma the judge asks the man to come into his chamber. There he tells him that as he had actually seen the murderer, he , the accused, was not guilty. The judge expresses his wonder how fate finds him guilty beyond a shadow of doubt. He frankly tells the man that he can do nothing except pass the death sentence, and questions him if he had not committed a murder in the past. The man now admits that he did, but by spending money and giving gifts he was able to bribe his way to freedom on false evidence.

The judge tells him that he was now paying full penalty for the first crime even though he did not commit the second one. Now the Law of Retribution was in operation.

The Law of Retribution is just. You have to pay the price some day. No one can escape from the reaction for an act done earlier.

You should remember the Law of Causation, the Law of Action and Reaction and the Law of Retribution at every moment of your daily life. You should control your emotions and impulses through the practice of pranayama and meditation. Then only you will not do any wrong action. Life necessarily involves good and some evil. If you dedicate all your actions to God, you can free yourself from the contamination of evil.

Law of Resistance

Every thought, every action causes an impression in the subconscious mind. Whatever you see, hear, feel, smell or taste causes impressions. So a human being is a bundle of impressions (*samskaras*). It is these that bring a person again and again to this physical plane. They are the cause for the repeated rebirths. The impressions combine together through repetition and form habits. Habits develop into tendencies. The sum total of all the tendencies constitutes your character. If your character is pure and strong, your will also be pure and strong.

Control of habits is control of nature. Old evil habits can be changed into healthy desirable habits through the force of the pure irresistible will. The old habits will resist. So try resolutely again and again to change them by developing new good habits. Eventually the new good habits will stay. They will work themselves till they get perfect success in driving out the old ones. This is also another law of nature. Life is a mixture of divine and demoniacal nature. The fight between them is always going on in the body and mind. If you strive with determination the new good habits will establish themselves quickly. The pure, strong, irresistible will is bound to succeed ultimately. Its powers are ineffable.

References

1. Blavatsky (1831-1891), a Russian lady, was one of the founders of the Theosophical Society in 1875. She developed psychic powers and remained the spiritual head of the movement until her death. Her multi-volume work *The Secret Doctrine* is a major source book of modern esoteric studies.
2. Paramahansa Yogananda (1893-1952), one of the great sages of India, came to the United States of America in 1920 and founded Self-Realization Fellowship in Los Angels, California. He was one of the first Eastern sages to spread his teachings in the Western world.

10

The Doctrine of Karma

Introduction

One of the most fundamental doctrines of our world is the doctrine of Karma. It is found in most of religions and systems of philosophy. It is one of the most ancient doctrines that are common to Hinduism, Jainism, Buddhism and Sikhism of the East. The theory of Karma gives a logical explanation to the problem of suffering and happiness in the world of living beings. It is a moral Law of Causation that explains the causes and effects of actions. (*See* Chapter 9. Universal Laws, *above*). I is also connected with the doctrine of Liberation, for Liberation means complete freedom from Karma and its consequences. (*See* Chapter 40. Liberation, *below*).

The general conception of Karma is that good deed bear good fruits, and evil deeds bear evil results. The doctrine of Karma conditions the course of transmigration and influences the state of life in each existence. There is no escape from the results of Karma. The inevitability of this doctrine extends to all kinds of action, mental and physical. The principle of Karma is immanent in the world, and all beings are governed by it. It presupposes transmigration or rebirth. The results of all deeds of a person may not bear fruits in his present lifetime. In order to reap the results of remaining deeds he has to be born again. The Karma regulates not only the present but also the future;

the chain of moral causation links the past, present and future in a being's existence.

Karma creates the need for readjustments and inevitably leads to rebirth, an outlet for the dynamic factors that have been set in motion. The consequence of this principle is personal retribution; i.e., acts by which we injure others are inevitably bring back injury to ourselves, whereas acts by which we benefit others eventually bring benefit to us.

This doctrine was discovered by the astute ancient sages of India through the intuitive power of intense concentration of mind, and focussed on the perplexing problems of differences and circumstances of human beings. In that concentration, they came to discern a certain rhythm at work beneath the incessant flux of human beings' fortunes and misfortunes.

Supported by Scientific Theories

The doctrine of Karma is a perfect scientific law. Several great scientific discoveries lend support to the doctrine of Karma. They include: (1) the theory evolution of animal and human forms, (2) Newton's third Law of Motion, (3) the conservation or indestructibility of energy, (4) the theory of heredity and (5) the unity of universe.

The theory of evolution brought together all the myriad kinds of species in Nature into some kind of scheme of progressive improvement. It reveals that life is a continuation of all that has evolved before. It is a long series beginning with primal molecule and ending with the complex man. "Man is the epitome of the whole creation."

The doctrine of Karma and reincarnation teaches the gradual evolution of the germ of life or the individual soul through many lives and various forms. It thus supplements the evolution theory and completes the process of evolution. The evolution of the body depends upon the evolution of the soul. When these two are combined the explanation becomes perfect.

Newton's third Law of Motion states that for every action there is an equal and opposite reaction. The Law of Karma is exactly similar to this Law of Action and Reaction. Every mental or physical action of a human being brings him/her back an equal reaction. (*See* "Law of Karma" in Chapter 9. Universal Laws, *above*).

The Principle of Conservation of Energy reveals that no energy can be destroyed in the process of transformation. In the same way human thoughts and deeds are energies that are not destroyed but reappear in the form of their effects upon others and upon ourselves. They are seeds that sprout eventually into manifestation.

The next discovery, the Theory of Heredity, explains that the features of the physical body are inherited ones. But it cannot explain the variations in mental powers and outlook among the children of the same parents. The doctrine of Karma and rebirth alone can explain such variations. The mental characteristics are transmitted ones and derived from one's own past earthly life alone.

Newton's Law of Equal Return holds true in the world of ethics. Whatever we do to others is returned to us in the same way at some time. Life pays us back in our own coin. Our misdeeds come back to us as misfortune. The good deeds return to us as good fortune. We get what we give.

The Principle of Unity of the Universe reveals that the universe constitutes a single entity. The same principle indicates a soul's journey through various lives is one continuous process. Each appearance of life emerges out of what has somewhere gone before, because the present cannot be separated from the past.

Thus human life becomes an education of mind, character and capacity. This education develops over a long period of time in a series of related physical re-embodiments; each embodiment provides appropriate lessons through experiences and reflections generated in it. All living is learning. All reincarnation is education. Taking a new body is taking a new seat in life's school. The growth of mind and consciousness is the true biography of an individual soul.

The Doctrine of Justice

Karma is a doctrine of justice. In the world we come across all kinds of inequalities and diversities in the conditions and circumstances of people. One child is born with beautiful body and eyes; another is born blind. One is born in a wealthy family; another is born in a very poor family. One becomes a genius in a specific field; another is dull and mediocre. One lives long and happily; another dies at an early age leaving the dependent family or parents in the lurch. Are such inequalities awful products of mere chance or the unjust fiats of an arbitrary God? No. Neither chance, nor parents, nor God is responsible for such inequalities. They are merely the consequences of good or evil deeds performed by people in their past births. The reactions of past Karma can come into operation in the same birth or in a future birth. There is no escape from the retributive consequences of past Karma. Nor can we shift the blame for our present conditions and problems on our parents or God. We are personally responsible for our present fortune or adversity.

Freedom to shape our Future

Karma, however, does not doom us to fatalism. We have the freedom to shape our future destiny by cherishing good thoughts and performing virtuous deeds. (*See* Chapter 34. Destiny and Self-effort, *below*). We can learn lessons from past experiences and refine our thoughts, words and deeds. We can learn to build a balanced personality. We change our character, give up vicious desires, develop virtuous aspirations, and learn the art of right living. Karma provides us with assurance that no efforts would be wasted. Whether in this birth or in a later one we would enjoy their just fruits.

Karma never kills initiative but positively promotes it. What we do now will actively contribute to the making of our future, no matter what we have done in the past. We can change our own circumstances by our will power, for destiny is self-earned.

Lastly we have to learn through Yoga practice and

philosophic reflection the art of being unruffled. For, troubles and miseries will come, but as they come so will they go. Fortune is a turning wheel. Meanwhile our mind should remain calm and balanced.

Eastern religions as well as the pagan faiths of primitive Europe wisely appropriated the scientific doctrine of Karma. But for an apparent accident of history it might also have been a part of modern Christianity. It lived in Christian faith for five hundred years after Jesus. Then a group of men, the Council of Constantinople, banished it from the Christian teaching, not because it offended the ethics of Jesus, but because it offended their own petty personal interest. It must now be restored to the modern world. (*See* Chapter 11. Karma in the World Religions, *below*).

"In the past the nations of Christendom persecuted in the name of their faith, fought religious wars and undertook crusades against infidels and heretics; today they have ceased to be Christians in any thing but name," says the great philosopher Aldous Huxley, "and the only religion they profess is some brand of local idolatry, such as nationalism, state-worship, boss-worship and revolutionariness. From these fruits of historic Christianity, what inferences can we draw as to the nature of the truth?" (Aldous Huxley, *The Perennial Philsophy*, New York: Harper & Row, Publishers, 1945, p. 242). God is one and all religions are mere paths to reach Him. There will be peace and harmony only when religious leaders realize this truth. It is the duty of those who rule the nations to guide thoughts, to influence education and to lead religions towards this truth.

The safety and survival of Western civilization imperiously demand not only religious harmony, but also the restoration of the doctrine of Karma. When people learn that they cannot escape the consequences of their thoughts, dispositions and deeds, they will be more careful in their conduct and more cautious in their thinking. When they understand that human life is an evolutionary process of gradual growth toward

Self-realization, they will begin to assess their physical and moral values aright. A sound ethical life will follow naturally as a function of such understanding. The West has an urgent need for the acceptance of Karma and rebirth, because they make people and nations ethically self-responsible. In the highly materialistic world of today much is said about undesirable things but few talk about the ultimate goal of life and the relevance of the doctrine of Karma to it. Hence the urgency of popularizing the doctrine of Karma among people.

Molding Character

A believer in the doctrine of Karma is a free agent and knows that he creates his own destiny and molds good character by his thoughts and deeds. (*See* Chapter 8. Karma and Character, *above*). To quote Swami Abhedananda, a brother-monk of Swami Vivekananda,

> "He who obeys the Law of Karma is more moral and more virtuous than one who blindly obeys the Ten Commandments. He stands on a more rational ground than one who fears the punishment of God. He shrinks from doing anything wrong, not because it is written in a scripture, but because he knows that every wrong action will sooner or later react upon himself and will make him unhappy and miserable. He performs good deeds for the reason that they will bring good reaction in the form of happiness, peace, tranquility and higher enlightenment. What we call rewards or punishments of God are nothing but the reactions of our own mental and physical actions. The doctrine of Karma teaches that God never rewards virtuous nor punishes the wicked." (*Doctrine of Karma,* Calcutta: Ramakrishna Vedanta Math, 1989, pp. 15 – 16).

Lord Krishna, in the *Bhagavad Gita,* says,

> "The Lord accepts neither the demerit nor even the merit of

> any; knowledge is enveloped by ignorance, thereby beings are deluded." (5. 15).

The aim and purpose of human life is to attain the Knowledge of Self or God-realization. Right conduct is one of the indispensable means to that end. The degree of liberating knowledge attained is determined by the extent of virtue developed. As pointed out by Aldous Huxley, "The tree is known by its fruits; God is not mocked." (op cit., p. 242).

The collective conduct of a nation is a test of the religion prevailing in it; it is a criterion by which we may judge the practical effectiveness of that religion in helping individuals to advance toward the goal of human life.

11

Karma in World Religions

Introduction

There are various religions in the world. All of them recognize and accept the universal doctrine of Karma. The major religions are Hinduism, Jainism, Zoroastrianism, Buddhism, Judaism, Christianity, Islam and Sikhism. Of these, Hinduism, Jainism, Buddhism and Sikhism have originated in India, and the others in the West. We will now examine the doctrine of Karma in each major religion.

In Hinduism

Hinduism is "the oldest, the most spiritualistic, the richest and most complex . . . of all the world's great religions," says Archie J. Bahm in his book *The World's Living Religions*, New York: Dell Publishing Co. 1964). Hinduism is more a way of life than a form of thought. While it gives absolute liberty in the world of thought, it enjoins a strict ethical practice. It has emphasized more persistently the realization of the ultimate Reality as the goal of life than any other religion. It insists not on religious conformity but on spiritual and ethical outlook in life. One who does good can never comes to grief. (*Bhagavad Gita*, 6.40). In Hinduism practice precedes theory.

Hinduism is not a sect but a fellowship of all who accept the law of right and seek for the truth. It recognizes the four supreme ends: righteousness (*dharma*), wealth (*artha*), art and culture (*kama*) and liberation (*moksa*). The Hindu code of practice links up the realm of desires with the perspective of the Eternal.

God is conceived as God with attributes and also God without attributes. God is one. He has no name and form, but people worship Him in various names and forms. "Truth is one; sages call it by different names." (*Rig Veda*, 1. 164).

Hinduism accepts incarnation of God in human form. Lord Krishna says in *Bhagavad Gita*,

> "Whenever there is a decline of righteousness, O Arjuna, and rise of unrighteousness, then I manifest Myself." (4.7)

Hinduism firmly affirms that the various religions are different paths to the same God, just as there are different paths to reach the summit of a mountain. In fact, Hinduism shared her land for centuries with Parsees, Buddhists, Muslims, Sikhs and Christians.

Karma in Hinduism

No other notion from the sacred traditions of India has had more influence on the life of Indians and on world views than that of Karma, for in it lies the foundation of astute ethical, psychological and metaphysical doctrines. Karma is not a mechanical principle, but a spiritual necessity. God is its supervisor. (*Svetasvatara Upanishad*, 6.11). Justice is an attribute of God. Every action, every thought is weighed in the invisible but universal scale of justice. Divine law cannot be evaded. It is not imposed from without, but wrought into our nature. We carry with us the whole of our past.

The past is regarded as determined, but there is freedom for shaping the future. The *Bhagavad Gita* asks us to raise the self by the Self. It is never too late for the sinner to mend himself. The doctrine of Karma does not shut the gates of hope against despair and suffering, guilt and peril.

According to his deeds the embodied one successively assumes forms in various conditions, course and fine, in innumerable rebirths. *Katha Upanishad* states that a person who has no control over his mind, and is always impure, does not attain the highest state and undergoes the cycle of birth and death. (1. 3.7)

Personal Responsibility. The idea of Karma and the moral world it implies carries two important psychological corollaries. First it commits the Hindu who understands it to complete personal responsibility. Each person is the maker of his own destiny through his actions. Most people are unwilling to admit this. They prefer to blame some one for their difficulties. This is simply ignorance. Everyone gets what he deserves according to his deeds. There is no chance or accident.

Choice in decision-making. Second, as Karma implies a lawful world, it has been interpreted as fatalism. Though ignorant people succumb to this interpretation, it is untrue to the doctrine itself. The consequences of a person's past decisions condition his present lot, but the decisions are freely arrived at. This means that the career of a soul as it travels through innumerable human bodies is guided by its choices, deciding what it wants at each particular stage of its pilgrimage. These wants may be to seek sensual pleasure, wealth, fame, power or social dedication. Each desire that aims at the ego's gratification thickens the veil of ignorance that covers the individual self. When it becomes sick with personal attachments, dispassion dawns and turns inward, and at last by the Grace of indwelling Self or God, the embodied soul realizes its true nature and passes into complete fusion with God.

Pre-Vedic Asceticism

The figures of men seated in acetic posture of meditation or standing in yogic posture have been discovered among the antiquities of the Indus Valley Civilization. Dr. L. M. Joshi has pointed out that the ascetic sculptures of Harrappan origin depict the figures of *munis* and *sramanas* of pre-historic India. (*Brahmanism, Buddhism and Hinduism*, Kandy: Buddhist Publication Society, 1970, pp. 62–63)

The *munis* and *sramanas* were ascetics of pre-*Vedic* period. *Rig Veda* and *Brhmana* texts show that they were known to the *Vedic* teachers. (*Rig Veda*, x. 136. 2–4; *Aitrareya Brahmana*, vii. 13.7). The beliefs and practices of *munis* and *sramanas* were against the central philosophy of *Vedic Brahmanas*.

Jainism represents a continuation of this Pre-Vedic asceticism. Buddhism also springs from it (Dr. G.C. Pande, *Studies in the Origins of Buddhism*, Allahabad: University of Allahabad, 1957, p. 317)

Samkhya, Yoga, Jainism and Buddhism and ascetic ideas of old *Upanishads* were originally derived from the ideas of *munis* and *sramanas*. (Heinrich Zimmer, *Philosophies of India*, p. 281). These ideas included the doctrines of *samsara*, Karma, Yoga, *dhyana* and *moksa*.

In the *Vedas*

The term *veda* literally means systematized knowledge, and it is derived from the root *vid*, to know. The *Vedas* are the most ancient scripture. This scripture is, of course, "earlier than that of either Greece or Israel and reveals a high level of civilization among those who found in it the expression of their worship." (Nicol Macnicol, *Hindu Scriptures*, London, 1938, p. xiv). The *Vedas* are four in number: *Rig*, *Sama. Yajur* and *Atharva*. They contain mantras or inspired hymns uttered by the great *rishis* (sages). The *Vedas* were preserved by word of mouth for thousands of years before they were reduced to writing. They are a storehouse of theories about the nature of the cosmos, its evolution as well as the evolution of man. They reveal a high level of civilization.

The word *karma* occurs in the *Rig Veda*, but it means religious rites such as sacrifices. *Brahmanas*, one of the three divisions of the work portion of the *Vedas*, are concerned with practical, everyday things with the details of sacrificial rites and with specific duties and rules of conduct. It is believed that in the sacrificial rites is found the germ of the doctrine of Karma: "Thou cannot gather what thou dost not sow. As thou dost sow, so wilt thou reap."

In the *Upanishads*

The *Upanishads* are the concluding portions of the *Vedas*. They are metaphysical treatises replete with universal truths. They deal with the fundamental issues of philosophy. "In the whole world," says Schopenhauer, the renowned philosopher of the West, "there is no study so beneficial and so elevating as that of the *Upanishads*. They are the products of the highest wisdom. They are destined, sooner or later to become the faith of the people."

MaxMuller, who edited the fifty volumes of the *Sacred Books of the East* series, devoted the first volume to the *Upanishads*. In the Introduction he writes: "My love for Sanskrit literature was kindled by the *Upanishads*. . . . The earliest . . . will always maintain a place in the literature of the world, among the most astounding productions of the human mind in any age or in any country." (Oxford, 1879, I, pp. lxvii).

Among other things, the *Upanishads* teach the moral doctrine of Karma and the notion of rebirth. The doctrine of Karma governs this world of becoming. It is supreme in shaping our conduct and character. It is not external to us, but within us. It is the unfailing law of our being. Virtue brings its victory and ill-doing its retribution. The *Svetasvatara Upanishad* says God is the ordainer of Karma. (6.11). God is law as well as love. His love is through law. The working of Karma is wholly dispassionate and just. The *Brahadaranyaka Upanishad* asserts: "Truly. One becomes good through good action, bad by bad." (3.2.13). This represents the encompassing scope of Karma. From this notion arises the idea that one's worldly situation and personality are determined by one's thoughts, feelings, desires and deeds. One's desire influences one's will; one's will leads one to act in certain ways; and finally one's actions bring proportionate and appropriate results. What one is today is the result of one's past actions; and what he will be in the future will be determined by his present actions. The King of Death tells Naciketas, "Thinking 'this is the world, there is no other,' he falls again and again into my power." (*Katha Upanishad*, 1.2.6). He who is filled with selfish desires and attracted by worldly possessions becomes subject to the Law of Karma that leads him from birth to birth and so he is under the control of the King of Death. The only way to break this turning wheel of life and death (*samsara*) was to free oneself of the bondage of Karma.

If one misses the right path, he is not doomed to eternal suffering. He has chances of acquiring merit and advancing to life eternal. Until the union with the eternal Reality is attained, there will be a succession of lives which will give him scope to acquire enlightenment and attain eternal life.

In the *Bhagavad Gita*

Next to the *Upanishads, Bhagavad Gita* is another basic scripture of Hinduism. It is a part of the epic *Mahabharatam.* Aldous Huxley calls this ancient scripture*, Bhagavad Gita* as "the most systematic statement of the perennial philosophy." The *Gita* gives a complete philosophy of life, reconciling the secular and sacred, work and worship. The atomic scientist Robert Oppenheimer not only studied *Gita* but also learned Sanskrit in order to learn it in the original. Henry David Thoreau says in *Walden* (ch. 16) "in comparison with *Bhagavad Gita*, our modern world and its literature seem puny and trivial. . . . ." *Bhagavad Gita* contains the cream of the *Upanishads*. It is a universal Gospel. It teaches the Yoga of Knowledge, Yoga of Action, Yoga of Meditation and Yoga of Devotion. Even though *Gita* is an ancient scripture composed several thousand years back, it is relevant to all times and to all people. The central message of *Gita* is the harmonization of worldly life with spiritual life.

What is the nature of actions? "All actions," says *Gita*, "are wrought in all cases by the forces (*gunas*) of Nature only." (3.27). In reality, the *gunas* of Nature—*sattva, rajas* and *tamas*—perform all actions. The world is grown on the basis of Karmas. (15.2). It is the *gunas* that make everyone to perform actions. "Verily none can ever remain for even a moment without performing action; for, everyone is made to act helplessly indeed by the *gunas* born of Nature." (3.5). It is the bondage of Karma that binds a person to this world. The bondage of Karma is due to one's desire for objects of senses, passion and attachment to them. It leads to rebirth.

When do actions bind a person to worldliness? When he, deluded by egoism, identifies the Self with the body, mind and senses and thinks, out of ignorance, that he is the doer of all actions, then he is bound by his actions. It is the desire for the fruits of actions and not the actions themselves, that gives rise to the karmic process. Ignorant people perform actions with attachment to their fruits and thus bind themselves to the effects of their actions. (3.29). When actions are performed without desire or attachment to their fruits, they are no actions at all.

Can a person free himself from the karmic process by non-performance of actions? No. It is impossible for an embodied being to abandon actions entirely; but by relinquishing the idea of doership and the fruits of actions, he can free himself from the bonds of actions. (18.11)

Gita emphatically declares: "Your right is to work only, but never to its fruits . . . ; nor let your attachment be to inaction." (2.47). How can the renunciation of the fruits of actions be attained? The renunciation of the fruits of actions can be attained only through the Yoga of Devotion. Therefore, you should dedicate all actions and their fruits to God with mind centered on Him. (3.30). Consecrate all actions to God; then you are freed from the bonds of Karma. (9.27, 28) (*See* Chapter 39. Freedom from Karma and Rebirth, *below*).

Manu *Smrti* (the Code of Manu)

This is an important work of pre-Christian era on morality and law. It is a metrical work of 2,685 verses. It has exercised immeasurable influence on the life of the Hindus over the centuries. It deals with religion, law, custom and politics. It is essentially a scripture of righteousness (*dharma sastra*). It declares:

> Action , that brings from the mind, from speech and from the body, produces either good or evil results; by actions are caused the (various) conditions of men, the highest, the middling and the lowest. (12.3)
> Know that the mind is the instigator here even to that connected with the body . . . . . (12.4)
> Coveting the property of others, undesirable thoughts, adherence to false doctrines are sinful mental actions. (12.5)
> Abusing others, speaking untruth, talking ill of others, talking idly are evil verbal actions. (12.6)
> Taking what has not been given, injuring creatures, criminal sex with another person's spouse are wicked bodily actions. (12.7)
> One obtains the results of good or evil mental, verbal and physical acts. (12.8)

IN JAINISM

Introduction

Jainism originated in the prehistoric period. The long line of teachers who handed down the faith consists of twenty-four *Tirthankaras*, liberated saints. The last *Tirthankara* was Varthamana (also known as Mahavira), a contemporary of Gautama Buddha.

Jainism admits perception, inference and testimony as sources of valid knowledge. On the basis of these sources it forms its view of the universe. The physical world consists of four elements: matter, space, time and causes of motion and rest.

Jainism does not believe in God but the *Thirthankaras* are adored as ideals of life. It does not accept the authority of the *Vedas*.

Soul (*jiva*) exists in all living beings. The soul in its pure state possesses infinite perception, infinite knowledge, infinite bliss and infinite power. It is all perfect. Ordinarily, however, with the exception of a few released souls all other souls have their purity and power covered by a thin veil of *karma* matter. *Karma* matter has been accumulating in them from beginningless time, due to the forces of passion and desires.

Theory of Karma

In Jainism *karma* does not stand for deed, work and fate, but it is an aggregate of very fine and imperceptible matter that envelops the soul. It is a force that binds the soul to the consequences of good, bad and indifferent actions. The *karma* overpowers the innate qualities of the soul and binds it. It causes the reincarnation of the soul as god, human or animal. Entering into any state of existence, the soul assumes a physical body and gets the senses. Through the senses arise desire and aversion, and on account of desire karma clings to the *jiva* and the cycle of existence continues. (*Pancastikaya-samayasara*, 135–37)

Karma also determines (1) the length of life in any birth, (2) the specific body with its special qualities and faculties, (3) the nationality, family, social standing, etc., and (4) the inborn energy of the soul.

By our actions of mind, speech and body we are continually producing *karma* matter.

The *karma* of the past life of a soul generates in it certain cravings and passions that seek satisfaction. The cravings in a soul attract the particles of *karma* matter.

The body that we get through our parents is not a mere chance acquisition. Our past *karma* determines the family, in which we are born as well as the nature of the body—its color, stature, shape, longevity, the nature of sense organs and motor organs that it possesses. While all these, taken together, may be said to be due to *karma* in the collective sense, each of these taken separately may be said to be due to a particular kind of *karma.*

According as *karma* matter has been generated by good, bad or indifferent actions, it gives us pleasure, pain or feeling of indifference. Even the knowledge, that we are constantly getting by perception, inference, etc., is the result of the effect of *karma* matter. We just get that kind of knowledge and feeling that we deserved to have.

After the effect of a particular *karma* matter is once produced, it is discharged and purged off the soul. If no new *karma* matter were to accumulate, then the gradual purging off of the *karma* might make the soul free of *karma* matter. But as it were, while some *karma* matter is being purged off, other *karma* matter is continually pouring in, and so bondage and the cycle of deaths and births continues.

By intensive practice of ten virtues of self-control, truthfulness, purity, charity, renunciation of greed, asceticism, forbearance, patience, sincerity and non-injury, one can become unattached to all things and attain freedom from bondage. Emancipation comes only as the result of the final extinction of the *karma* matter. (For further details, see H.V. Glasenapp, *the Doctrine of Karma in Jain Philosophy*, Bombay: Jivan Lal Panna Lal Charity Fund, 1942).

In Buddhism

Introduction

Buddhism is based on the teachings of Gautama Buddha (sixth century B.C) of India. As a prince he was awakened to the awareness of human sufferings, and he wanted to find the means to overcome the sufferings. He spent several years in study, penance and meditation to discover the origin of human sufferings and the means to overcome them. At last he received enlightenment.

Buddha developed an Eightfold Path as a means for the eradication of suffering. The Eightfold Path consists of right views, right determination, right speech, right conduct, right livelihood, right endeavor, right mindfulness and right concentration. These eight steps remove ignorance and desire, enlighten the mind and bring about perfect equanimity and peace. Thus liberation from misery and rebirth is attained.

After Buddha's death, his followers modified his original teachings and formed two major divisions: Hinayana and Mahayana. Hinayana holds more rigidly to the original teachings of Buddha. It accepts Buddha as an enlightened teacher and *nirvana* as the goal of life.

Mahayana has integrated the teachings from other philosophical systems and holds the attainment of perfect wisdom as the object of *nirvana.*

The Doctrine of Karma

Karma is *Kamma* in Pali. It means "action." The word *karma* in Buddhist texts means will or volition, the intention or motive behind an action. It is the motivation behind the action that determines the karmic fruit. Every action produces an effective reaction.

The existence of everything is conditional, dependent on a cause. Nothing happens by chance. This is called the Theory of Dependent Origination. The Doctrine of Karma is only aspect of this doctrine. The present existence of an individual is the effect of his past, and its future would be the effect of his present existence.

What is that causes different characteristics and circumstances among people? Some are beautiful and others ugly. Some die young and others die old. Some are rich and others poor. These are produced by different types of actions.

Non-killing results in long life. Killing other beings results in short life. Non-harming brings health, while hurtful actions create conditions for illness. Anger and hatred are the conditions for ugliness, and loving care, gentleness and kind words create the conditions for beauty. Generous past actions create the conditions for wealth and those motivated by greed create the conditions for poverty.

We are the heirs of our own motives and deeds. So it is important to see what our motives and intentions are and to understand the results they condition. Reflections on the Law of Karma can bring a very strong motivation and inspiration to spiritual practice and to lead a virtuous life.

Karmic destiny unfolds for various people according to their actions. Here is a story. One man in Buddha's time, seeing a monk passing by, thought to offer him food. The man offered food to the monk but afterwards regretted having done so, thinking that it was a waste. The monk was an *arhant*, a fully enlightened being, and it is said that offering food to an *arhant* has a powerful wholesome karmic effect. As a result of that effect the man was reborn as a millionaire for seven consecutive lifetimes. But as the karmic effect of his having regretted his own generosity, he had a miserly disposition throughout those seven lifetimes and was thus unable to enjoy his great wealth.

The problems of present life are mainly due to the wrong actions of the past lives. Buddhism, however, does not explain how a continuity of cause and effect is maintained as between one life and a subsequent life. Hinduism avoids this difficulty by postulating a subtle body (*linga-sarira*) serving as the vehicle of mind and character. The subtle body carries over our Karma from one life to another life.

Buddhism takes the survival of personality for granted up to the time of attaining *nirvana.*

Karma, by itself without any desire, cannot produce any good or bad result. One attains liberation when desire or craving had completely ceased.

Karma in Judaism

Judaism is the religion of Isralites who trace their origin back to Abraham (1750 BC); the real beginnings probably are to be linked with Moses, "the Lawgiver." About 1300 B.C. some of the Isralite Hebrews were in Egypt serving as slaves to the Egyptians. To them came Moses (1300 B.C) with a twofold message: a god who revealed his name to be Yahweh (Jehovah) had appeared to him in the desert of Midan, directing him to go to Egypt and lead the Isralites out of bondage.

Jewish scripture is *Torah* which means "law" or "teaching." It consists of the first five books of the Old Testament.

Yahweh made a covenant with his people through revelation; the people also were held responsible for their actions and warned that disobedience would lead to adversity, but obedience would bring blessing.

The essential teachings of Judaism are:

1. The world was created by Yahweh at the beginning of time with three levels: the heavens, the earth and an underworld called *sheol.*
2. Although many gods might exist and be served by various people, for the true believer there is but one God, Yahweh, who is to be worshipped and obeyed to the exclusion all other gods. Yahweh is the creator of the world and its inhabitants; He is savior and judge.
3. Man's duty is to obey his creator; he also has freedom to choose to serve Yahweh or to disobey. He has only one life in which to be rewarded or punished.
4. Social morality and ethical living was stressed as part of Yahweh's requirements.

(For further details, *see* David C. Bradley, *A Guide to the World's Religions,* Englewood Cliffs, N. J.: Prentice-Hall, 1963)

The Doctrine of Karma

The idea of the doctrine of Karma is found in some passages of *Torah* (Old Testament). For example:

> "Whoever sheds the blood of man, by man shall his blood be shed." (*Genesis*, 9.6)

It is in Jewish mystic tradition called Kabbalah that the doctrine of Karma and Reincarnation is specifically dealt with from twelfth century onwards. Kabbalistic ideas are both fascinating and relevant to modern days. They also provide some startling similarities to the other faiths such as Hinduism and Tibetan Buddhism.

The Kabbalists have taught that every human soul is created by God (the *Ein Sof*) in order to fulfil a unique role in the divine plan, a notion that recalls the Hindu concept of one's *dharma.* Every soul is wholly unique and precious, and each has a vital part to play. Kabbalists have insisted that one single life time is seldom sufficient for the soul to complete its mission on earth, so that several incarnations—*gilgulim* in Hebrew—are almost always necessary.

References to reincarnation are found in the *Sefer Bahir* (Book of Brilliance) that first appeared around the year 1175 in southern France. About a century later, the *Zohar* (Book of Splendor) dealt more extensively with this doctrine.

With the spread of Kabbalah in Israel during the sixteenth century, this doctrine became a key element in the Jewish esoteric tradition.

The Kabbalah affirms the reincarnation of the soul in order to fulfill all of its unmet Commandments. The *Book of Splendor* specifically mentions several causes that necessitate additional lifetimes in the physical world. One of them is the failure to raise a child. Therefore, marriage inevitably involves reincarnation. Each spouse gets the one he or she deserves, and child-rearing is an important aspect of earthly existence.

In his book, *Sefer Ha Gilgulim* (The Book of Transformations) Chaim Vital promulgates the doctrine of Issac Luria that various people on earth are inwardly related to one another because of their joint origin in the same "family of souls." The early Hasidic leaders, a few hundred years later, stressed the same concept to their followers.

In the Jewish esoteric discipline, the goal of the transformation for each soul is to end its cycle of death and rebirth. This idea is similar to the concept of liberation of Hinduism and Buddhism. Our sojourn here on earth is meant to bring us closer to our Creator with joy.

Karma in Christianisty

Christianity is basically an historical religion, as it is founded in actual historical setting. It is based on the teachings of Jesus Christ. He inherited the Jewish vision of a God of infinite love and mercy. He taught the people to be perfect as the heavenly Father is perfect. His "Sermon on the Mount," "Lord's Prayer," and Parables contain the essence of his teachings.

Paul played a major role in spreading the wisdom of Jesus. His own ideas were incorporated in the Bible. In fact more than one third of the New testament (Bible) is devoted to the writings of Paul. Jesus emphasized love as against fear, whereas Paul appealed to both love and fear.

Man, created by God, fell by Adam's sin. The idea of "original sin" rejected by Jews and of no concern to Jesus, became a cardinal Christian doctrine due to Paul. Jesus, by sacrificing himself on the cross, paid the debt in full. All that any man needs in order to redeem himself is faith and adoring service to Jesus.

Over two thousand years, Christianity has spread all over the world by the work of missionaries.

Karma

The early Christian Church accepted the doctrine of Karma and Reincarnation which was expounded by the Gnostics and numerous Church fathers, including Clement of Alexandria, the Celebrated Origen (both third century) and St. Jerome (fifth century).

The ideas of the Doctrine of Karma and that of Reincarnation are found in numerous Biblical passages: "Whosoever sheddeth man's blood, by man shall his blood be shed." (*Gen.* 9.6); "all they that take the sword shall perish with the sword." (Matthew,

26.52); and so on. H. Spencer Lewis, in his book, *The Secret Doctrine of Jesus*, states that Jesus taught secretly the doctrine of Karma to his disciples. He also asserts that this doctrine is inferred in many parables given by Jesus to the public during his preaching.

Action is performed by body, speech and thought or mind, and every action brings an effect or reaction. Jesus Christ has referred to mental Karma in the Sermon on the Mount: "Ye have heard that it was said by them of old time: Thou shall not commit adultery. But I say unto you, that whosoever looketh on a woman to lust after her hath committed adultery with already in his heart." (Matthew 5.27-28).

If you study the Sermon on the Mount carefully, you see how the doctrine of Karma is the only explanation of the concept of Christian love as seen in verses from the Gospel of Matthew: "Ye have heard that it hath been said, Thou shalt love thy neighbor, and hate thine enemy. But I say unto you, Love your enemies, bless them that curse you, do good to them that hate you, and pray for them which despitefully use you and persecute you" (Matthew 5:43–44). Jesus was emphasizing that love, confined to neighbor or kin, in a reciprocal relationship, is neither good nor bad, but love returned for hatred eliminates a Karmic debt. By this act you become a deserving son of God. Jesus adds, "That ye may be the children of your father which is in heaven; for he makes his son to rise on the evil and on the good, and sendeth rain on the just and on the unjust."

The doctrine of Karma explains why reconciliation with your brother , to whom you are indebted, is the first step toward God-realization. Jesus remarks, "Verily I say unto thee, thou shalt by no means come out thence, till thou hast paid the uttermost farthing." (Fifth chapter of Matthew). He warns that that you cannot obtain life eternal, unless you have paid the karmic debt of the last farthing.

The Doctrine of Forgiveness of sins

Is the orthodox Christian teaching of forgiveness of sins

tenable? The Law of Karma holds: Every act, word or thought produces its consequences sooner or latter in the present or in the future life. Evil acts produce evil effects, good acts produce good consequences. This is strict and impartial justice. Supreme Power can have neither wrath nor mercy, but leaves every cause to work out its inevitable effects. Jesus said, "With what measure you mete, it shall be measured to you again." (Matthew, vii. 2). However, in the Church, Christians are promised that their sins will be forgiven, if they only believe in "precious blood of Christ," the blood offered by Him for the expiation of the sins of the whole of mankind. How illogical and most demoralizing is this doctrine of the Atonement? Again should the offender wait till the last day of his mortal life to repent? These are the assumptions of the Church.

Can the results of a crime be obliterated even if the crime itself is pardoned? Every good as well as evil action has its effect, as palpably as the effect of a stone flung into a calm water.

Karma in Zoroastrianism

Zoroastrianism was founded by Zoroaster (sixth century B.C). The most important scripture is *Avesta*. The chief deity is Ahura Mazdah, god of light and truth. Man has been created by God. He has both a body and a spirit or soul. He has freedom of choice. Man has only one life in which to determine his destiny. The righteous will be rewarded with a place in a heaven where he will share in God's blessed existence. The unrighteous will suffer terrible torments in an underworld. At death, each is judged and transported to his deserved abode. When the savior comes to inaugurate the Kingdom of Righteousness there will be a resurrection and a final judgement. At the end of a cosmic year (about twelve thousand earthly years), there will a general resurrection of both the good and the bad, and all will pass through a purging stream. To the souls of the righteous it will be as warm milk, to the wicked like molten metal. All sin will be burned away by the stream and all mankind will be forever with God.

Karma in Islam

Islam arose in the seventh century AD "Islam" means submission to the will of Allah. Islam is based on the teachings of Mohammed (571–632). Its scripture *Quran* represents Allah's complete revelation to Mohammed.

The five doctrines of Islam are:

1. There is only one God, Allah. He is all-seeing, all-knowing and all-powerful.
2. There are angels, chief of whom is Gabriel.
3. The *Quran* is Allah's final message.
4. There are twenty eight prophets of Allah, including Mohammed.
5. There will be a "last day." There will be a resurrection of the body, in a final judgment, and a final destiny in heaven or hell depending upon Allah's decision. Heaven is a man's paradise. Hell is the abode of those who oppose the teachings of Mohammed and the will of Allah.
6. *Kismet* (fate) is taught, but need not be accepted by the faithful. This asserts that all that happens is foreordained.

The five pillars of the Faith are the five duties to be performed. They are as follows:

1. To recite the *Shahadah*: "There is no God but Allah and Mohammed is the prophet of Allah."
2. To perform *salat* or prayers five times daily.
3. To give alms to the needy Muslims.
4. To fast during the month of *Ramadan*, the ninth month of the Muslim lunar year.
5. The *Haji*, the pilgrimage to Mecca at least once during a Muslim's life.

The universe is the creation of Allah. Mankind lives on earth, Allah in a heaven above the earth, and shaitan in a hell beneath the earth. All mortal beings will be judged someday and will enter either heaven or hell.

Islam proclaims a strict monotheism, with Allah as the sole authority. The purpose of man's life is to obey and serve Allah. Women are to be obedient to their husbands, who are to treat them with kindness.

The *Quran* contains all that is necessary to live a holy life.

On a Day of Judgment, all will rise from the dead and the records of each man's deeds will be read with consequent consignment to eternal heaven or hell.

Karma in Tibetan Buddhism

Buddhism existed on the southern and western foothill of Tibet almost from the time of Buddha. In the mid-seventh century Tibet became officially a Buddhist nation.

Tibetan Buddhism is tremendously rich in materials on death and dying, more than any other Buddhist country. Tibet was one of the most literarily prolific nation the world has known; the number of titles is measured in tens of million. Tibet produced a predominantly spiritual literature. Now the Chinese invasion has resulted in the destruction of thousands of monastic libraries in Tibet.

The doctrine of Karma and Reincarnation is fundamental to Buddhist thought. The word for Karma in Tibetan language is *las*, which means action. The Buddhist scriptures classify Karma into contaminated and non-contaminated. The contaminated Karma is the action of an ordinary person. It is of three types: positive, negative and meditative. These are the three roots of cyclic (*samsaric*) existence. Negative Karma results in rebirth in a lower realm; positive Karma produces rebirth in the human plane or the world of gods; and meditative Karma brings an higher state of existence. The non-contaminated Karma is the action of a saint who is free from delusion and abides in wisdom.

The doctrine of Karma is not fatalistic. The future is in our hands. Karma promotes self-responsibility in all our thoughts, words and deeds. Self-responsibility is primarily an attitude of discipline in action as a means of progress toward enlightenment.

The Tibetan people understand Karma to be a natural and just process. So Karma instills in them a sense of responsibility in whatever they do.

12

Karma in the Systems of Philosophy

Philosophy, in its widest sense, means "love of knowledge." Modern man knows much about the external world, but knows nothing about his real and internal nature. Prompted by external clamors and sophistication, he seeks happiness and peace from external objects and sensual enjoyments, and suffers from emotional problems and several psychosomatic diseases. This is due to lack of a philosophy of life. Life, without a guiding philosophy, is like a castle built on sand. Indian philosophy provides an effective philosophy of life, and opens the door to eternal peace and joy.

Karma in Indian Philosophy

Introduction

Indian philosophy, unlike modern Western philosophy that is primarily an intellectual pursuit, is based on knowledge of truth. It tries to seek answers to the fundamental questions of life: What is the purpose of life? What is the nature of the world in which we live? And so on. Indian philosophy is not a mere metaphysical speculation. It is a practical guide to the daily life. Its insights were directly experienced by ancient sages of India. Its theories and ideas are not limited to any particular era, culture or group. They are universal and are meant for one and all.

Indian philosophy is an integration of several disciplines like metaphysics, epistemology, logic, axiology, ethics and others. It holds a holistic approach toward life, aiming at a direct experience of the ultimate Reality. It provides an effective philosophy of life and opens the doer to eternal peace and joy.

The schools of Indian Philosophy are divided into two broad groups: Orthodox and Heterodox. The first group consists of six main philosophical systems: Nyaya, Vaisesika, Samkhya, Yoga, Mimamsa and Vedanta. They are regarded as Orthodox because they accept the authority of the *Vedas*. The three main Heterodox systems are Jainism, Buddhism and Carvaka. These do not believe in the authority of the *Vedas*. However, they do believe in the authority of their own spiritual leaders and founders.

The Doctrine of Karma

All the Indian systems except Carvaka believe in the theory of Karma and rebirth. Whatever action an individual performs, he has to reap its fruit – good or bad – in the future. When the fruits of some actions cannot be enjoyed in the present life, the person has to take another birth in order to enjoy them.

The unseen potency of an action requires some time before it could yield its fruit to the doer. This would often accumulate and yield the fruit in his next life. Only the fruits of those actions that are extremely wicked or particularly good could be reaped in this life. The nature of the next birth of a person is determined by the nature of his maturing actions of this life. A person has had an infinite number of past lives of varied nature and the instincts of each kind of life exist in dormant in his subconscious mind and thus whenever he has any particular birth in the human or animal realm, the special instincts of that life (*vasanas*) come forth. In accordance with these *vasanas* the person passes through the painful or pleasurable experiences as determined for him by his actions.

When once any actions become operative, they cannot be avoided. However, the dormant actions are destroyed once for all if the person attains the Knowledge of Self. But even such a liberated person has to pass through the experiences pertaining to ripened actions.

The Carvaka System

The Carvaka System believes in pure materialism. The origin can be traced to the Vedic period. It holds that only this world exists and there is nothing beyond. There is no future life. The postulates of religion, God, freedom and immortality are illusions. The highest end of life is enjoyment of pleasure.

The Carvaka System does not believe in the existence of a soul in man. When a man dies nothing is left of him to enjoy or suffer from the consequences of his actions hereafter.

The Samkhya Philosophy

The Samkhya System is considered to be the oldest of all philosophical systems. It is attributed to the sage Kapila. It is a system of dualistic realism. It admits two ultimate realities: conscious *Purusha* and the unconscious *Prakrti*. *Purusha* (Self) is ever pure and ever free, but it becomes the subject of pain and pleasure when it forgets its true nature and identifies itself with *Prakrti* (Nature). *Prakrti* is the material cause of the universe and it is composed of three *gunas—sattva, rajas* and *tamas*. (For details, *see* chapter 5. Three *Gunas,* above). Although the *Purusha* is in itself free and immortal, due to ignorance it identifies itself with the body, the senses and the mind, and thus experiences pain and suffering. Once it realizes its true nature through spiritual practice, it attains freedom from suffering.

In Samkhya the Law of Karma is autonomous and works independently of the will of God.

The Nyaya-Vaisesika Systems

The Nyaya System was founded by the sage Gautama (third century BC). It is a philosophy based mainly on logical grounds. All the systems of Indian philosophy use the Nyaya system of logic for philosophical reasoning and debates.

The Vaisesika System was founded by the sage Kanada (third century BC). It is allied to the Nyaya System. It is mainly a system of physics and metaphysics.

The Nyaya-Vaisesika Systems believe that the Law of Karma

is under the guidance and control of God; God creates the world in accordance with this law. The stock of merits and demerits of Karmas of the individual souls cannot by itself lead to their proper effects, because it is an unintelligent principle. It is God who controls our stock of merits and demerits of Karmas and dispenses all the joys and sorrows of our life in accordance with our Karma.

According to the Nyaya-Vaisesika Systems, the fruits of Karmas are regarded as similar to the fruits of trees that take some time before they can ripen. Even though there may be pleasures here and there, birth means sorrow for human beings, for the pleasure is followed by many sorrows. As there is no sorrow in a person who is in deep dreamless sleep, so there is no sorrow in the person who attains salvation. When once this state is attained all efforts cease forever.

The Nyaya-Vaisesika Systems hold that the will of God not only brings about the creation and dissolution, but also acts always among us in a general way, for without it our Karmas cannot ripen. The bondage of the world is due to the ignorance of taking body, senses and mind as our own Self. When once knowledge is attained, ignorance is destroyed and no pleasure will attract us. With the destruction of ignorance, there will be no attachment or aversion to things. Then the actions for fulfillment of desires cease, and with it rebirth and sorrow cease. Without ignorance and attachment, actions cannot produce the bondage of karma that leads to the embodiment and its experiences.

Yoga Philosophy

Yoga was practiced even in pre-Vedic period in India, But it was not formally systemized until it was codified by the sage Patanjali in his *Yoga Sutras* during third or second century BC. Yoga philosophy accepts the epistemology and the metaphysics of the Samkhya with its twenty-five principles, but, unlike the Samkhya, it admits the existence of God.

The Yoga System studies all aspects of human personality and teaches us how to control the modifications of the mind through the observance of ethical discipline, practice of meditation, detachment and surrender to God.

Karmas in Yoga are divided into four categories: (1) white—those that produce happiness, (2) black—those that produce sorrow, (3) white-black—actions partly virtuous and partly vicious, and (4) mental acts of self-abnegation and meditation that are devoid of any fruits as pleasure or pains.

All external actions involve some sins, for it is difficult to work without taking the lives of insects. All Karmas proceed from the fivefold afflictions (*klesas*), namely, ignorance (of our real nature), egoism, attachments to objects, aversion to unpleasant things, and desire for life. (*Yoga Sutras,* 2. 3). These five afflictions permeate our minds and induce us to perform actions and suffer.

The actions performed create *karmasaya* (the receptacle for the accumulated Karmas); our actions, dispositions (*vasanas*) and memories leave subtle impressions (*samskaras*) in the mind. They will bear fruits either in the present life or in a future lifetime. The dispositions and imprinted impressions serve as the source of the five afflictions. The afflictions tend to reinforce the ignorant notion that actions directed to some end are desirable, and in performing them people are trapped in the wheel of births and deaths. If a person dies before all of his accumulated Karmas are exhausted, his soul with the karmic residue and unfulfilled thoughts, desires and feelings enters such a new body that shall make it possible to experience their fruits. The Karmas of the present life thus determine the particular kind of future birth, the period of lifetime and the painful or happy experiences destined for that life.

Patanjali presents the Yogis with a set of practices for attaining freedom from the bondage of Karma. Those practices and selfless actions reduce the power of *klesas* and enable the Yogi to renounce worldly pleasures. He ultimately attains Self-realization. No new Karmas arise to him. The Knowledge of Self scorches the accumulated Karmas. Then his soul no longer needs a new body; it is liberated from afflictions, and it experiences eternal freedom.

Vedanta Philosophy

The Vedanta philosophy is the most comprehensive of the Indian systems of philosophy. It arises out of the *Upanishads* that mark the culmination of the *Vedic* speculation and are fittingly called the Vedanta or the end of the *Vedas*. The Vedanta was taught and practiced by the sages of the *Upanishads* and it was handed down through a long line of sages. Sage Vyasa codified these teachings in the *Brahma Sutras.* Gaudapada (seventh century AD) gave a systematic exposition of *advaita* Vedanta (non-dualism) in his *Mandukyakarika.* Sankaracharya[1] perfected the non-dualistic system in his commentaries on the *Brahma Sutras* and important *Upanishads*, and in his original works: *Vivekachudamani, Atma bodha,* etc. in seventh century AD. He was India's most celebrated teacher and is regarded as one of the greatest minds the world has known.

There are three main Schools of Vedanta System: Non-dualism, Qualified Non-dualism and Dualism. Of these systems, the *Advaita* Vedanta (Non-dualism), as interpreted by Sankaracharya has exerted the greatest influence on Indian life. According to this School of Vedanta, the supreme Brahman is One without a second. It is the only Reality. It pervades the whole universe and yet remains beyond. The world originates from this eternal Spirit, rests in it and dissolves in it. We perceive many objects on account of our ignorance that conceals the real Brahman from us and makes it appear as many objects. Brahman embodies within Itself the power of *Maya* that is the basis of mind and matter.

The main teachings of *Advaita* Vedanta are: Self-realization is the goal of life. The individual is essentially Brahman. The soul realizes its true nature when ignorance is destroyed by knowledge attained through intense practice of discrimination, dispassion and meditation. The realization of the truth "I am Brahman" is perfect wisdom or liberation from bondage.

One, who is ignorant of the real nature of the self, foolishly identifies it with world experiences and performs good and bad actions. He thus becomes subject to the bonds of Karma. But when he attains the Knowledge of Self he becomes free from the bonds of Karma and realizes his oneness with Brahman.

Karma in Theosophy

Theosophy is a part of a broader religious phenomenon known as Esotericism. It is concerned primarily with the knowledge of the hidden mysteries of divinity.

In 1875 a group of persons including the Russian lady H.P. Blavatsky inaugurated the Theosophical Society in New York City. Blavatsky who had developed psychic powers remained the spiritual head of the movement until her death in 1891.

In 1879 Blavatsky moved to India and established the international headquarters of the Society at Adyar, Madras. The Society now has branches throughout the world.

The Society's objectives are: to form a nucleus of the universal brotherhood of humanity without distinction of race, creed, sex, caste or color, and to encourage the study of comparative religion, philosophy and science. The Society attempts to direct individuals to the source of unity beyond all differences.

H. P. Blavatsky's multiple-volume *The Secret Doctrine* is a major source book of modern esoteric studies (Adyar (Madras): Theosophical Publishing House, 1978). She defines Karma as "the unerring law that adjusts effect to cause on the physical, mental and spiritual planes of beings" (*The Key to Theosophy*, Wheaton, Il.: Theosophical Publishing House, 1981, p. 121). She depicts it as a law of harmony that continually restores the harmonious state of the cosmos whenever it becomes disturbed. She declares, "Every creature is subject to karma." (*The Secret Doctrine*, 2.361)

The world of Being is governed by the Law of Karma. It is "the ultimate Law of the universe;" it "exists from and in eternity, truly for it is eternity itself." (*The Secret Doctrine,* 3.306)

Karma is an aspect of the Reality that comes into play as manifestation proceeds. Karma as the law of cause and effect is involved in all differentiation and all relationships, spiritual as well as physical. Blavatsky does not predict a one-to-one relationship between cause and effect. In her view Karma is not a mechanical linear system. Rather it works in an interconnected system in which everything affects everything else. The working of Karma is not linear but multidimensional like the weather at a given place.

Karma is involved in the vast sweeps of cyclic life. While the law of cycles sets manifestation going in recurrent patterns, Karma fashions the specific events within the cycles.

Individual Karma. It molds tendencies and determines events in our lives. Just as a stone falling into a pond produces waves, all our actions cause similar disturbances in our lives. All our deeds, thoughts, etc. react upon ourselves with the same force with which they were set in motion.

As human beings have reached higher levels of mind and become capable of choice, individuals become responsible for their actions in a way not possible among lower animals. With this responsibility came personal Karma. We ourselves are responsible for our lives. Our circumstances, character and personality are the outcome of forces we ourselves have set in motion. We are "under the empire of self-made destiny." Karma gives us back the effects of our own mental and physical actions. We reward and punish ourselves through the effects of our Karma.

However, as Karma gives us the consequences of our own actions, so it also works with our evolution and growth. Our lives give us feedback and we can learn from experience. If we consciously shape the future we can attain salvation.

Though we cannot erase the influences we generated in the past, we can influence the future course of our lives by taking care of the mode of our recent living. If we sublimate our harmful tendencies, eliminate defects and counteract negative elements, we generate new forces that alter the karmic outcome of past actions. In this effort right motives, feelings and thoughts are more important than even right action, for energies from higher planes are more powerful than physical energies. According to Blavatsky, It is a law of occult dynamics that a given amount of energy expended on the spiritual or astral plane is productive of far greater results than the same amount of energy expended on the physical objective plane of existence, (*The Secret Doctrine*, 2.369)

Thus love, compassion and other positive emotions are more powerful factors in fashioning our Karma. By shedding away the negative qualities like pride, possessiveness and selfishness, we may return to our native purity of the soul.

Karmic Interconnections. Blavatsky's exposition of Karma also includes group and national Karma. The strands of our individual Karma are interwoven with those of our nation and other groups with which we have strong ties. All social evils and social opportunities are karmic. Everyone participates karmically in the actions of our nation. As nations are interdependent in the world, each individual is in some ways karmically linked with all others, and we all share the outcome of world events.

Karma in Aurobindo's Integral Philosophy

Aurobindo (1872 – 1950) was a Yogi, nationalist, poet, critic, thinker and spiritual leader of India. Born in Calcutta, he was educated in England. In 1910 he moved to Pondicherry and established Aurobindo Ashram there. Spiritual evolution is the central theme of Aurobindo's philosophy. It is seen as a hierarchy of consciousness manifestation. Yoga is a means for quickening the process of the evolution of consciousness.

It is the spirit of balance and harmony that sustains the universe in its proper course. By harmonizing seemingly conflicting forces such as matter and spirit, body and mind, existence and essence, the Law of harmony provides the right kind of environment for the creative evolution. Integral philosophy contemplates the cosmic whole as a super-organic unity and self-harmonizing system of divergent forces imperceptibly blending with one another within the limits of an all-controlling moral order.

Integral Yoga is the practical application of the integral worldview. It lays its major emphasis upon the need for total integration of personality with a view to perfecting the art of harmonious living in tune with the creative urge of Being.

Aurobindo's Integral Yoga seeks to incorporate the essence and processes of the traditional Yogas, blending their methods and fruits into one system. It seeks an integral and total change of consciousness and nature, not for the individual alone but all of humanity and the entire cosmos.

Integral Yoga shares with Theosophy the universality of spiritual outlook. Its special emphasis is on the evolutionary potentials of the emerging New Age—Supramental Age. Integral Yoga is dedicated to the out-flowering of the Divine in global humanity. Therefore its keynote is the integration of the spiritual values of the world's major mystical traditions.

Its karmic significance is that if we learn to cooperate consciously with the creative force of planetary evolution, then our age-old dream of the kingdom of heaven on earth can inevitably come true. That is, a unified world order based on truth, justice and love can emerge.

So the focus of integral self-discipline lies not on individual mystic Self-realization only, but rather on the desirability of harmonizing the individual Self-realization with the evolutionary perspective. The Self-realized Integral Yogi would joyfully cooperate with the process of evolution toward the emergence of a new global society.

Self-development through spiritual practice brings in supreme knowledge, Divine love, eternal joy and peace. Here the Law of Karma operates on the evolutionary level. The fundamental laws of science such as the law of conservation of energy, the law of cause and effect, etc. are expressions of the eternal righteousness on the scientific level. They constitute the intellectual aspect of the Law of Karma. Nothing happens in this world without a definite cause.

An active principle of cosmic justice controls the operations of Nature and the human destinies. Herein lies the specific meaning of the Law of Karma: As you sow so shall you reap: like action, like consequence. Mahatma Gandhi laid special stress upon this implication of the Law of Karma: Violence begets violence, hatred begets hatred. So love alone can save the humanity from the self-destructive vicious circle of mutual hatred.

We as humans hold in the depth of our being a profound spiritual perfection. This is our distinctive human essence. There is a constant interaction between the forces of the past and the future, between Karma and our essential essence, between our sensual desire and spiritual aspiration.

The more our knowledge expands the more we learn to make a

judicious adjustment between the karmic dynamism of the past and the creative urge for self-development. The motivation flowing from such interaction ultimately determines our course of evolution.

Karma and Western Psychology

The doctrine of Karma reached its zenith within the cosmological and psychological worldview of Hinduism. Yet the emergence of spiritual and transpersonal ideas in the contemporary Western psychology offers an opportunity of gaining new insights into this ancient doctrine.

C.G. Jung (1875–1961) was a famous psychologist of twentieth century. India had a major influence upon Jung's thought. Although many Hindu and Buddhist concepts fascinated him, it was the doctrine of Karma and rebirth that played a central role in the development of Jung's thinking to the end of his life. (*See* C. G. Jung, *Memories, Dreams, Reflections*, ed. By A. Jaffe, New York: Vintage Books, 1965). After his break with Freud in 1910, one of the major sources Jung turned for support and new insight was Eastern religion. During the period from 1920 to 1940 the *Upanishadic* notion of Self (Atman) played a major role in the development of Jung's concept of "Self." (See C. G. Jung, "Psychological Types," *Collected Works*, 6, Paras 188 and 189, Princeton University Press)

Later, though he turned to the Western alchemy, the Eastern concept of Karma and rebirth continued to reappear in Jung's thinking. The main basis of Jung's understanding of Karma probably came from his in-depth study of Patanjali's *Yoga Sutras*. During this period Jung gave a detailed commentary on the *Yoga Sutras* including a thorough discussion of Karma in terms of *klesas*, previous lives and unconscious potentiality for this life.

Karma, he says, is essential to a deeper understanding of the nature of the arch type. "There is a rich world of arch type images in the unconscious mind and arch types are conditions, laws or categories of creative fantasy, and therefore might be called the psychological equivalent of the *samskara*." (C. G. Jung, "Psychological Commentary on Kundalini Yoga," *Spring*, 1975,

p. 8). The influence of Karma theory of the *Yoga Sutras*-type is especially evident in the way Jung described arch types as at first latent seed (*bija*) state that later actualized *samskaras* that have sprouted and flowered.

In Jung's early thinking, there is no personal inherited Karma as such, there is only the collective inherited Karma of one's ancestors, the arch types, that one creatively individualizes in one's personality development.

During the last years prior to his death Jung seemed to soften his earlier rejection of the notion of personal Karma and its psychological function in rebirth. The problem of Karma and one's rebirth has remained obscure to Jung due to the lack of empirical evidence. Later he got the evidence in a series of dreams that described the process of his reincarnation. After this experience he viewed differently the idea of reincarnation, very close to the traditional Indian thought. For Jung, motivation for knowledge is the Karma that leads to a series of reincarnations; once a complete understanding is attained, there would be no need for any further rebirth.

Transpersonal Psychology. Transpersonal Psychology is the most recent development in modern Western Psychology. Through it, the door is opened wide for the direct exposure of modern psychology to the Hindu and Buddhist notions of Karma and rebirth. The Eastern dogma or predisposition (paradigm) that sees Karma serving as a filtering device (*Yoga Sutras*, 1.1, 2) has helped to focus attention on the theories of constructive and /or reductive nature of cognition. While modern scientific psychology has tended to adopt stimulus-response models that assume that we cognize what exists, Karma theories of the Jaina, Buddhist and Hindu traditions presuppose that our ordinary awareness is a construction and not a mere registration of the external world. It is our past personal and cultural patterns of behavior that construct the karmic filters through which our present experience is passed. This Eastern paradigm provided support for some philosophers and psychologists who saw the mind functioning as a reducing valve. Within certain limitations we are able to reprogram and reconstruct our awareness in line with our motivations. Karma suggests that the roots of habitual responses may be more deeply rooted in the psyche than modern psychology suspects.

While the current work in American psychology parallels Karma theory in understanding ordinary consciousness as a constructive process, the Eastern paradigm has clearly taken the lead in analyzing the ways in which the various filtering categories of the mind can be rendered inactive or even completely rooted out through the practice of meditation.

The strongest influence from Karma theory via the Transpersonal psychologists to modern psychology has been focused on Eastern methods of meditation.

As per Patanjali's Yoga, karmic patterns established in this and previous lives are being de-conditioned and their filtering activity negated. *Yoga Sutra* 2.52 states that the regulation of breathing removes the veil that covers the discriminative awareness, and *Sutra* 2. 54 refers to "the withdrawal of senses" from the perception of worldly objects.

Today, Karma theory is reaching out through the ever widening circles of Transpersonal Psychology to such diverse areas as neuro-physiology, learning theory, perception, motivation, cognition, altered states of consciousness, psychotherapy, parapsychology and psychology of religion. In effect some basic assumptions of modern scientific psychology are being challenged by those of Karma and rebirth.

Reference

1. Ernest wood in his *Vedanta Dictionary* (New York: Philosophical Library, 1964, pp. 171-73) suggests that Sankaracharya lived within a century after Buddha.

13

Philosophy of Right and Wrong

Meaning

Right (*dharma*) and wrong (*adharma*) are both relative terms. It is very difficult to define these terms precisely. The sage Kanada (Third Century BC), the exponent of Vaiseshika Philosophy says in the opening *Sutra:*

> "That which brings supreme bliss and exaltation is right (*dharma)*. That which elevates you and brings you nearer to God is right. That which takes you down and away from God is wrong. That which is done in strict accordance with the injunctions of the scriptures is right, and that which is done against the injunctions of the scriptures is wrong." (*Vaisesika Sutras*, 1)

To work in accordance with the Divine Will is right, to work in opposition to the Divine Will is wrong. It is very difficult for a common man to find out what exactly will be the Divine Will in certain actions. Hence wise sages declare that people should consult scriptures and realized persons. A realized sage can readily find out the Divine Will by hearing the inner voice.

Conscience

But an ordinary person may not be able to do this by consulting his conscience only. Conscience is not an infallible guide. It changes according to the stage of his development. The voice of conscience alone is not sufficient to guide you in understanding the laws of God, right and wrong, and good and evil. The scriptures and realized persons only can truly guide you in the discharge of your duties properly. That is why in the *Bhagavad Gita* Lord Krishna emphatically declares:

> "He who, having cast aside the ordinances of the scriptures, acts under the impulse of desire, attains neither perfection, nor happiness, nor the highest goal." (16. 23)
> "Therefore let the scriptures be thy authority in determining what ought to be done or what ought not to be done; knowing what has been declared by the ordinances of the scriptures, thou ought to act in this world." (16. 24)

If you cannot understand the scriptures, then strictly follow the words of a Guru in whom you can place absolute faith and confidence. If there is fear, doubt, pricking of the conscience and uneasiness of mind, know that you are wrong. If there is joy, exhilaration and satisfaction, understand that you are doing a right action.

Easy Way

There is an easy way to find out what is right and what is wrong. That work which gives elevation, joy and peace to the mind is right; that which brings depression, pain and uneasiness to the mind is wrong. Selfishness clouds understanding. Therefore if you have even a tinge of selfishness, you cannot find what is right and what is wrong. A very pure and sharp intellect is needed for this purpose.

Lord Krishna describes in the *Bhagavad Gita* the nature of *sattvic, rajasic* and *tamasic* intellects in the following verses:

> "That intellect, which knows the path of work and renunciation, what ought to be done, fear, and fearlessness, bondage and liberation, is *sattvic.*" (18.30)
> "That intellect, by which one incorrectly understands *dharma,*

> *adharma*, and also what ought to be done, and what ought not to be done, is *rajasic*." (18.31)
> "That intellect which, enveloped in darkness, views *adharma* as *dharma* and all things perverted, is *tamasic*." (18.32)

The *sattvic* or pure intellect knows what ought to be done and what ought not to be done at particular places and times. It knows the actions that produce results which are prohibited by the scriptures.

The *rajasic* intellect is unable to distinguish between right and wrong or unable to understand the difference between righteous actions and unrighteous actions.

The *tamasic* intellect regards righteous acts as evil and considers right things as false. It looks upon virtues as vices. It views everything in a perverted vision.

In the *bible* it is said: "Do unto others as you would have done unto you." This gives the gist of right conduct. Non-injury is the highest virtue. If you are well established in non-injury in thought, word and deed, you can never do any wrong action. Naturally, Patanjali in his *Yoga Sutras* has given non-injury (*ahimsa*) great prominence. Non-injury is the first *Yama* or self-restraint to be practiced by a spiritual aspirant. To give happiness to others is right; to cause misery and pain is wrong. Stick to any rule that appeals to your reason and conscience, and follow it with faith.

Before you act you must stop to think, to reflect upon its effects, your surroundings and your motive. When you earnestly do what you recognize as your duties, you will progress and enjoy peace and joy.

In Japanese Buddhism, which began in the twelfth century, great emphasis is laid on right action, for Zen Buddhism is not a theoretical philosophy but a way of action, a philosophy to be practiced in daily life. To attain the experience of enlightenment, which is the goal of Zen Buddhism, sitting in meditation is necessary, but the practice of meditation alone is not the total substance of the Zen Buddhist's life. Indeed meditation serves to develop wisdom, but we must be able to give concrete expression to the wisdom, and to do so we have to cultivate right action. We have to work, to act with love, kindness and respect for others, to do our part to change our world into a better world. The Zen way is not to withdraw from life into an isolated utopia, but to get into life and change it from the inside by right action. When taking care of our daily affairs, we should distinguish the good from the evil, and practice the former and abstain from the latter. But what is good and what is evil? In Zen Buddhism an action is considered good when it brings happiness and well-being to oneself and others, evil when it brings suffering and harm to oneself and others. We must not create suffering to others. Because we ourselves and others are not different, and all are in reality extension of each other.

Zen introduces a very unique concept into its notion of virtue. This is the concept of the "deed of no merit." An illustration may explain what this deed is. If a person goes to church, the priest or minister may announce to the congregation that he has some plans for the future and ask for donations to implement the plans, in front of him and the congregation, one may raise his hand and say, "I donate $ 1000." This may come very easily to him. But it is quite a different matter when a starving person begs him for a few dollars when nobody else is watching. Many people like to do good, provided that they can at the same time receive some honor. Even Jesus, though he urges his disciples not to let their left hand know what their right hand is giving, comforts them by saying, "The Father who seeth in secret shall reward thee." This is not a deed of no merit. As long as the thought of any reward , whether open or secret, is there, the deed is still based on expectation. For a deed to be totally pure, it must be done without any thought of reward, whether worldly or divine. It is this kind of pure deed is called a "deed of no merit." And because no merit is sought, it is indeed a deed of infinite merit.

For a deed to be pure, it need not necessarily be a grand one. What is important is the motive behind it and not its magnitude. If the motive is pure the deed is pure; if the motive is impure, then, no matter, how grand the deed is, it is still impure.

On the day when Buddha was to enter *Parinirvana* (leaving

the body), all his disciples and devotees journeyed to his place in the hope of seeing him for the last time. Many of them made long pilgrimages over the difficult Indian terrain. Because it was their last chance to see Buddha, the disciples and devotees brought with them the best gifts they had to offer to Him: flowers, fruits, incense, clothes, lamps, etc. They burnt incense and lit lamps, praying for Buddha remain alive until all arrived. As the crowds gathered around Buddha, by the night fall, thousands of lamps burning together created an ocean of light which dispelled darkness.

At the moment Buddha passed away, suddenly weather changed. A storm struck up with a strong wind that swept across the crowd. The wind blew out all lights except one small lamp far behind in the corner. This small lamp remained lit even though the wind was blowing heavily . All the people gazed at it with astonishment and wonder. When the storm was over, it was discovered that the small lamp was brought by an old lady. This lady was very poor. She did not have anything to eat or drink all the way from her distant place. She had only one small coin with her, and though she was hungry and thirsty, she used her coin with deep devotion to buy a small lamp with oil and wick to offer it to Buddha. This was the lamp that remained burning through the wind and storm.

Evolution of the Concepts of Right and Wrong

In the process of evolution, man is the highest of all living creatures. Through a further process of evolution, a love of self produces the sense of right and wrong and also the sense of duty. In the initial stage human beings live on the animal plane and identify the soul with the body. At this point the self is the center of all things. Then the individual begins to call that which is beneficial to himself right, and that which causes him pain and suffering wrong. Moved by the love of self, he first takes care of the lower or narrow limited ego without recognizing the self of others. At this stage of development, the individual seeks only his own pleasure and gratification and avoids that brings him discomfort and suffering, as we find in savage tribes. By degrees, when the spiritual nature begins to unfold, the individual learns to respect the rights of others who are closely related to the self. He now feels that he should not do anything that injures his nearest of relative. This is the beginning of the sense of duty. Henceforth, the ideas of right and wrong are no longer confined to the motives of self-preservation and self-gratification, but include the selves of those related to him by family ties.

Next, if the individual comes into contact with neighbor who brings comfort or happiness into his life, he develops for the neighbor the same feeling that he bears toward his relatives. This is the origin of duty toward and concern for friends and neighbors. At this stage of development the concepts of right and wrong goes on widening as the process of spiritual evolution progresses.

At the matured stage of spiritual development the individual realizes the oneness of all beings – the Self in him is the Self in all beings. Then the concepts of right and wrong acquire spiritual connotation. That which contributes to Self-realization or God-realization to oneself and others is right, and that which takes one away from this highest goal of life is wrong.

14

Karma Yoga

What is Karma Yoga?

We have learnt that the Law of Karma is an unerring Law of Cause and Effect. Everyone has to reap the fruits of his actions during this life or in future lives. No one can escape from the reactions of his actions nor can he resort to inaction with a view to avoiding the bondage of Karma, "for everyone is made to act helplessly indeed by the forces (*gunas*) born of Nature (*Gita,* 3.5). Is it then possible to free oneself from Karma while continuing to do actions? Yes. It is possible for one who has become perfectly unselfish, and has no thought, word or deed for himself. If he works for others or the world or God alone, then there is no "himself" in him. Thus he becomes a non-doer though his body or mind acts. Then his Karma (action) becomes Karma Yoga.

Karma Yoga, therefore, is a system of discipline aiming at the attainment of freedom through selfless service. It is the knowledge of the secret of work. It makes a science of work. It shows how best to use the work itself as a means of freeing oneself from the bondage of the world.

> "Karma Yoga *ondre nammai kakkum ennum Vedam*," said the great saintly poet Subramanya Bharati of Southern India. It means that Karma Yoga alone can save us. Swami Sivananda used to say, "Serve, Love." Serve with love, because without

love you cannot serve. Karma Yoga is service for the joy of serving.

Karma Yoga describes the method by which the individual soul can free itself from the binding force of the Law of Causation and attain to perfect freedom. It is doing selfless service to living beings without any attachment and sense of doership.

Selfishness

We generally have an eye on the rewards of our efforts even before we start any work. The mind is so framed that it cannot think of any work without expecting a reward of some sort for it. This kind of thinking is due to the *rajasic guna* or restlessness and passion.

The *rajasic guna* creates selflessness and attachment to the fruits of work. A selfish person has no ideal apart from satisfying his selfish desires. He is petty-minded. He is greedy. He always calculates: "How much can I get for this work?" He will weigh the work and the money in a balance. He is motivated by money. He will not be willing to do even a little extra work.

A selfish person has a very narrow vision, a small grove. He dwells within this small grove. His love is confined to his own body and to those closely connected with him. He knows no generosity.

Selfishness is the curse of human life. It veils our understanding. It is the root cause of all our suffering.

The feeling of "I and mine" makes you attached to the objects of senses and crave for possessing them. With the sense of possession comes selfishness, and selfishness makes you slaves of the objects of senses. The more you say, "I and mine," the more the slavery grows, the more the misery increases. Therefore Karma Yoga asks you to give up the sense of "I and mine," and not to identify yourself with the objects of the world. Never say "mine:" "my house, my car, my body, my spouse, my child." Any thing that you say "mine" is, like a mine, explodes and causes suffering to you. Nothing is yours. Everything in the world comes and goes by the laws of Nature. Any thing that comes to you is a gift from Nature or God. Just use it, but do not get attached to it. Attachment is a chain that binds you and brings misery.

So Karma Yoga says: cultivate discrimination and develop dispassion towards things; do not allow the mind to get into the whirlpool of selfishness. Hold your mind free. Then go out into the world and work as much as you can. Live in the world like the lotus leaf in water. Water cannot wet or stick to it. So live like it. This is dispassion (*vairagya*) or non-attachment.

Non-attachment

Non-attachment does not mean renunciation. The person, who gives up living in a house, wearing fine clothes and eating good food, and goes into the forest, may be the most attached person. His only possession is his body with a loincloth. His body and his loincloth may become everything for him, and while he lives he will struggle to preserve it. Here is a story to illustrate this point:

A Sadhu and his Loin Cloth

A sadhu under the instruction of his *Guru* (teacher) lived in a small hut at a distance from a village. He began his spiritual practice in that hut. Every morning after bath he would hang his wet loincloth on a tree by the side of the hut for drying. He would visit the neighboring village to beg for his daily food. One day on his return from the village he found that the rats had cut holes in his loincloth. So the next day he had to go to the village for a fresh one. A few days later rats again damaged his loincloth spread on the roof of the hut to dry. The sadhu felt annoyed and was wondering, "where shall I go again and again to beg for a loin cloth?"

All the same he visited the village and represented to the villagers the mischief done by the rats. They said, "who will supply you with cloth every day? Just do one thing: keep a cat. It will keep away the rats." The sadhu got a kitten in the village and brought it to his hut. From that day onward the rats ceased to trouble him and he was happy. He now began to tend the useful little creature with care. He was feeding it on the milk begged from the village.

After some days, villagers said to him: "Sadhuji, you require milk everyday. Who will give you milk all the year round? Please keep a cow. You can drink its milk and also give it to your cat." After a few days the sadhu procured a milch cow and there was no need to beg for the milk any more. However, the sadhu found it necessary to beg for straw for his cow. He had to visit the neighboring villages for the purpose; but the villagers said, "there is lot of uncultivated land close to your hut; just cultivate it and you shall not have to beg for straw for your cow."

Guided by their advice, the sadhu took to tilling the land. Gradually he had to engage some laborers and later on found it necessary to build barns to store the grains in them. Thus he became in course of time a sort of landlord. And at last he had to take a wife to look after his big household. He now became a busy householder.

After some time his *Guru* came to see him. Finding himself surrounded by goods and cattle, the Guru felt puzzled and inquired of a servant, " a sadhu used to live here in a hut; can you tell me where he has moved?" The servant did not know what he has to say in reply. So the *Guru* ventured into the house where he met his disciple. The Guru said to him, "My son, what is all this?" The disciple, in great shame, fell at the feet of his *Guru* and said, "My Lord, all for a single piece of loin cloth!"

Attachment to one thing will lead to another and go on multiplying and plunge you in deep worldliness. No escape from it. So keep away from attachment to anything.

Verily, attachment has no reference to things. It is all in the mind. The binding link of "I, me and mine" is in the mind. If we do not have this link with the objects of senses, we are non-attached wherever we are and whatever we may be. One may be on the throne and perfectly non-attached, like the king Janaka; another may be in rags and still very much attached.

Non-attachment does not mean carelessness or non-interest in the work you do. You should have greater interest in every work you do. You should do it skillfully with one-pointed attention and devotion and at the same time with perfect dispassion. Then there is no worry, no anxiety. When there is no mental disturbance, you can do a work perfectly and with greater joy. Perfection in action is Yoga.

Giving up attachment

How can the state of non-attachment be attained? There are two ways of giving up all attachment.

One way is to depend on your own will, the discriminative faculty of your mind. Thinking that you are non-attached, you should have to work for the sake of work, without any selfish motive in mind. Of course this is a very difficult way.

If you are a believer in God there is another way, which is much less difficult. Work for God's sake and offer the fruits of the work to Him. Then work becomes worship. Whatever you see, feel, hear or do is for him. Sri Krishna, in the *Bhagavad Gita*, says:

,

> "Whatever you do, whatever you eat, whatever you offer in sacrifice, whatever you practice as austerity, O Arjuna, do it as an offering unto Me (Lord). Thus shall you be freed from the bonds of action . . .." (9. 27, 28)

Everything—our body, mind, everything around us, nay the universe itself—is a manifestation of God. Everything belongs to God. So is it not foolish to think, "this is mine," "that is mine," "I have done this," and so on. We are God's instrument. He works through us. Let us understand this and realize that the so-called "my work" is really God's work and its fruit belongs to Him. Let our body and mind work incessantly as per His will, and let us find ourselves free and at peace. Only our body and mind works, our real "I," the Self within, is a silent witness, observer. It is ever free and established in peace and bliss.

This is the proper attitude for doing work. If "we" work in this way, we shall never have any sense of doership and never be attached to anything.

> "He, who performs actions without attachment, resigning them to God, is untainted by their effects as the lotus leaf by water." (*Gita,* 5:10)

Such actions are not only service to God or His creation, but also are actions prompted by God's will, executed for God's sake by His own energy channeled through us. God is everything. Can we live even for a moment, breathe for a moment, if this all-powerful One does not will it? "He is the ever active Providence. All power is His and within His command. Through His command the wind blows, the sun shines, and the earth moves. He is the All in all; He is all and in all. We can only worship Him."[1] So work for God's sake and dedicate its fruit to Him. Then alone will come perfect non-attachment and freedom from bondage. This freedom is the goal of Karma Yoga.

Sacrifice

Sacrifice is the law of life. What does the Cross teach us? Sacrifice. What does a flower teach us? Sacrifice. The tree sacrifices its flower to produce a fruit. A candle burns itself away to give us light. The very air we breathe sacrifices itself to us. The air that goes in contains a lot of life; we breathe it out as carbon dioxide by burning the air breathed in. Without the air's sacrifice we cannot live.

So we live by sacrifice and should live to sacrifice. If we do not sacrifice anything, all the elements that sacrifice themselves for our sake will have a debit account in our name. So we are indebted to the very Nature. God or Nature has given us the life-breath, food, water and sunlight, and knowingly or unknowingly we are using them constantly. In return for all these gifts, we should lead sacrificial lives. The entire Nature demonstrates the benefit of sacrifice. Look at an apple tree. It gives us thousands of fruits. If you ask the tree, "Hey, how many fruits do you give in a season?" You might hear the following:

"Oh, several thousand."
"Ah, do people come and beg you for them?"
"No, I don't wait for that. I just give."
"Without their asking?"
"Yes, that is my nature. I find it a joy to give that way."
"Suppose nobody comes to take them?"

> "That is their business. I don't want to eat my own fruit, so I just drop them?"
>
> "But your apples are so delicious. Don't you at least try one?" If you have the ears to hear, you would hear the tree laughing at you. "Oh, don't think I'm like the human beings who eat their own fruits. Only human beings run after their fruits, and that is why they are so unhappy."

The tree not only gives fruits to those who praise it, but even to those who stone it. Throw a stone at an apple tree, you will get even more fruits. Throw a stone at a person and you know what you will get! So who is greater, the apple tree or the human tree? So do not expect anything. If you make an appointment for some result, you must be ready to face disappointment. Ask for nothing; just serve. That way you will retain your peace. Peace is always in you; it is not something to come from outside. As long as you do not disturb it by your expectations and anxieties it will be there.

Selfless service is what is called renunciation or dedication. When you renounce the attachment and expectation for the fruit of your action, you retain your peace. That is the forbidden fruit. Let us remember that. If ever God commanded Adam not to eat the fruit, it is not just that once upon a time in the Garden of Eden an apple was forbidden to that one man. No, we are all Adams and we are all planting trees – every action is a tree and every action bears its fruit. We are asked not to eat that fruit instead, offer it to others. The same message is given in the *Bhagavad Gita*; "Thy right is to work only, but never to its fruits." (2. 47). If you want to be happy in life, you have to renounce the fruits of your actions. The *Gita* asks, "How can there be happiness without peace?" (2. 66). What is the way to that peace? Dedication, sacrifice. What is sacrificed is, in the last analysis, the sense of "I and mine" or ego, and its offshoot, attachment. When this is transcended, every action is turned into a sacrifice. Then our entire life, our very living itself will be for the sake of others.

Non-attachment to work

By doing selfless service and dedicating its fruit to the Lord, as we have seen, we cultivate selflessness. The second important requirement of selflessness is to be unattached to the work we do.

Many people get attached to the work they do. They like certain types of work and take interest in them. They dislike other kinds of work. When conditions require them to leave the work that they like, they become unhappy. They also begin to take undue responsibilities on their shoulders and suffer and labor under care, worries and anxieties. This is not Yoga at all; there is attachment to the work.

How does a Karma Yogi deal with work? He tries to do each thing as it comes. Having done it or being forced to leave it to go to another duty, he takes it up in the same spirit. He concentrates fully and calmly on each duty as it presents itself. He is neither excited in doing a work as it comes, nor feels unhappy when he has to leave it. He also does not attempt to do several things at a time.

This is non-attachment to work. How can this be developed? Consider every work that comes to you as God's work. If conditions warrant you to stop any work on hand, take it as God's will. Nothing is yours. Allow the pure Divine energy to work freely through you as if you were an instrument, with no sense of doership.

This state is like the flute in the hands of Lord Krishna. It is a hollow reed. He could use it any way he likes to produce the sweetest music. Similarly keep your "body-mind flute" hollow by emptying it of your egoism. Then the Lord will play sweet music through you as His choice instrument. Then you will feel lightness in your work. You will be rid of all kinds of anxieties. You will be as free as a bird.

Do not have even the subtle attachment such as, "May God be pleased!" Just work for the sake of God. Then everything, even eating, walking, talking or breathing will become Yoga and worship. This is the essence of Karma Yoga.

Purification of the Mind

What is the object of doing a selfless service or a work without attachment? By doing service or working without attachment, we purify our mind. Egoism, hatred, jealousy, pride and all other negative qualities vanish. In their place, humility, pure love, patience, tolerance, kindness and mercy are developed. When mind becomes pure, everything becomes pure. This purification of the mind is the main purpose of Karma Yoga. In Karma Yoga we have great opportunity of cultivating good qualities and getting rid of our bad traits.

The narrow outlook makes us to feel separate from others. Through service the sense of separateness is destroyed. By serving all with pure love, we begin to feel oneness with all. Eventually we attain the Knowledge of Self and realize the One God who dwells in all.

Once on the banks of the river Ganges, two girls were drowning. Two young men at once jumped in the river and rescued them. One man asked one of the girls to marry him. The other man said, "I only did my duty. The Lord gave me an opportunity to serve and purify myself." The latter had purity of heart through this action, while the former became more impure through the same action, because of his selfish motive. Therefore if service is to purify the mind, it must be done without any selfish motive. If the motive is pure, then the mind will become pure.

The Features of Karma Yoga

The features of Karma Yoga are described below:

No Loss. Nothing is lost in Karma Yoga. Even if you do a little service to the sick or to the poor or to the helpless old people or orphans, it brings its own benefit. Do the service without expectation of anything, even thanks. Rather be thankful to the served for the opportunity given to you. Service to others is service to yourself. It purifies your heart and prepares your mind for the reception of Self-knowledge. The subtle impressions of your selfless actions and humility are imbedded in your subconscious mind. The force of these impressions will propel you to do more service. It will also develop compassion, love and spirit of service in your heart. "He who performs his bounden duty without caring for the fruits of his actions, is a renouncer and a Yogi." (*Gita,* 6.1).

Here is a story of a Yogi who was meditating on the banks of a river. He saw a scorpion falling into the water before him. He scooped it out, only to have it bite him. The scorpion fell into the river again. Once more the Yogi rescued it, only to be bitten a second time. The sequence was repeated twice or more. A bystander, who was watching this, asked the Yogi, "Why do you keep rescuing that scorpion when the only gratitude it shows is to bite you?" "It is the nature of scorpions to bite, and it is the nature of a Yogi to help others when he can," was the reply.

Expression of Divine Love. Service is a natural expression of love. It is a manifestation of Divine Love. It expands your heart and widens your vision. It reveals to you the identity of humanity and all living beings, for the Self in you is the Self in all beings. Identify yourself with all; love all. Feel that you are one with the whole universe. See God in all. "God pervades all beings", says the *Ishavasya Upanishad* (1.6). "I am the Self of all beings," says Lord Krishna in the *Bhagavad Gita* (6.30). It is only when you serve the Lord in all, you serve selflessly (without any selfish motive). Only then you serve all with equal vision and balanced mind.

Humility. Be ever ready to serve others. Unselfish service will bring name and fame. Name and fame will destroy you. Develop humility and feel you are nothing. Get immersed in that attitude and in the joy of serving. Never feel you have helped others. Cheer up the distressed; encourage the dispirited. Wipe the tears of the afflicted and remove the sorrow in him or her. Be a light to those who lost their way. Do service to the best of your ability and leave the rest to God. Do all your actions dispassionately. Do not be hurt by remarks, criticism and insults.

Do not consider any work as dignified or menial. All works are sacred. Study the autobiography of Mahatma Gandhi or the biography of Mother Teresa. They annihilated their little "I" through various kinds of service. Gandhi never made any difference between menial service and dignified work. Scavenging and cleaning of the lavatory was the highest Yoga and worship for him. Mother Teresa gave up teaching service for serving the poorest of poor, the sick, the destitute, the lepers and found in them Jesus Christ.

Inaction. Karma Yoga aims at inaction. This means not inactivity, but freedom in action or the transcendence of egoistic motivation. When the illusion of the ego or doership is transcended, then action occur spontaneously by the modes of Nature. In Karma Yoga there is no sense of doership (*See* Chapter 6. Action and Inaction, *Above*).

When actions are done without the sense of doership and without any attachment, then the actions cease to be ours and cease to bind or affect us with their reactions. Nature and her modes (*gunas*) weave the web of her actions, but without affecting the grief-free, self-existing peace. All is transmuted into Divine actions. Devotees of God who live in God and for God do their work joyfully for Him, beyond the restlessness of the mind and the false notion of the ego.

Service to Saints. Service to your Guru or a saint is the highest form of Karma Yoga. It will purify your heart quickly. You will draw inspiration from Him. His association will be like a fortress for you. You will not be affected by evil influences. You will get rapid spiritual progress.

Perfection. Do everything perfectly. Selfless service should be more perfect than any personal work. Karma Yogi works with more zeal than an ordinary person. Because he is doing it as a service to God. If you are cooking your own dinner, it can be just anything. But if you cook for some honored guest, you do it with great care and dedication. There is a joy in doing something as an offering. You will never get that joy when you do it just for yourself.

Humanitarianism

Our emotions outside our family circle take two noble forms of expression: love of God and compassion for suffering humanity. All religions of the world in their well developed forms are but the expressions of love for God.

Compassion for suffering humanity moves larger hearts very powerfully. Measures to alleviate the sufferings are then evolved. Mahatma Gandhi was extremely pained at the wretched conditions of the Indians in South Africa. This moved him to dedicate his life to ameliorate their conditions and restore their self respect. This ultimately led to a great spiritual fight against the South African Government itself. This fight gave birth to the Satyagraha movement. This great act of humanitarianism won the approval the whole world. Mahatma Gandhi has been recognized as one of the greatest Karma Yogi of the World. In achieving the freedom of India from the most powerful British empire, purity of mind in the form of observance of truth and non-violence was more important to him than freedom itself. He never forsook his firm adherence to truth and non-violence even when he encountered serious tests.

Humanitarianism by itself cannot be called Karma Yoga. It may be done for the sake of name and fame. But if it is done with firm selflessness in mind all the time and with the observance of moral virtues, then only it becomes Karma Yoga.

Test Yourself in the Field

It is in Karma Yoga than in other Yogas you see your weaknesses while serving others. The world is like a mirror. It shows your ugly spots. You see your limitations and drawbacks. You test yourself in the field. You find your angularities and moods better than when you are alone. Through service you can learn to recognize your weaknesses and work to correct them.

You should analyze your motives. If you have some sort of emotional or psychological problem, come back, sit down quietly and analyze the problem: "I went to serve him, but got annoyed when he did not thank me. Why should I expect him to thank me? That is not right. Next time I will render service without any expectation." In this way you can correct your angularities, and develop the habit of serving without any thought of yourself.

The flower does not know it is giving fragrance. Does it ever say, :I want to give a nice smell. Here is a nice person, I want to be extra nice to him." A candle does not think about giving light. It does not worry if you do not appreciate its nice flame. Did you ever hear a candle saying, "Hey, You look! I'm wasting my time. I'm melting away for you! Come read something with my light." No. It is just serving. You should serve like it.

The *Bhagavad Gita* exhorts you to work, but do not expect the result. When you expect it, you build tension and become upset. If you do not get the expected result, you become frustrated and angry. If you do not want anything from anybody, you are freed from these tendencies.

In the beginning all your actions may not be pure. Some may be with expectation of reward. You must be vigilant in scrutinizing your motives while performing actions. You must be ever introspective. Make concerted efforts in avoiding expectation. When you heart becomes purer and purer through constant service, your actions will become selfless.

Karma Yoga and Jnani

Sri Ramana Maharishi was a great Jnani. He attained the Knowledge of Self through the Path of Wisdom. His views on Karma Yoga are as follows:

> There is neither doership or doer for a Jnani. So he has no Karma. That is, a Jnani performs no action, though he is seen doing things. The radio sings and speaks, but if you open it, you will find no one inside. Similarly, the Jnani's body works like the radio, but there is no one inside as a doer. His Self is a silent witness only.

The Jnani can live and act without the mind, although living and acting require the use of the mind. The potter's wheel goes on turning round even after he has ceased to turn it after the pot is finished. In the same way, the *Prarabdha* Karma which created the body will make it go through whatever activities it was meant for. But the Jnani goes through them without the notion of doership. It is hard to understand how this is possible.

The Jnani knows that he is not the body and that he is not doing anything even though his body is engaged in some activity. This explanation is for the onlookers who think of the Jnani as one with a body and cannot help identifying him with his body.

Sri Ramana Maharishi stressed that to be successful the Karma Yogi must be free of the notion that he is helping others, and that he must also be unattached and indifferent to the consequences of his action. These conditions are met if all actions were performed without the sense of doership. He should act without thinking that he is the actor. Actions will go on even in the ego-free state. Each person has come into manifestation for a certain purpose and that purpose will be accomplished whether he considers himself to be the actor or not. Karma Yoga is action without the sense of doership.

It would take countless lives to exhaust the *Sanchita* Karma. But it is burnt up by one little spark of Jnana, just as a mountain of gunpowder will be blown up by a single spark of fire. It is the ego that is the cause of all the world and of the countless sciences whose researches are so great as to baffle description. But if the ego is dissolved by wisdom, all this immediately crumbles and the reality of Self alone remains. (*Source*: David Godman, ed., *The Teachings of Sri Ramana Maharishi,* London: Arkana Paper packs, 1985)

Reference

1. Swami Vivekananda, *Karma Yoga and Bhakti Yoga*, New York: Ramakrishna-Vivekananda Center, 1962, pp. 98- 99.

15

Components of Karma Yoga

Karma Yoga is a science of work. It has several aspects. They include:

- Knowledge of the power of words
- Self-abnegation
- Working for work's sake
- Harmonizing actions with life's goal.

Knowledge of the Power of the Words

One of the aspects of Karma Yoga is to know the relation between thought and word, and what can be achieved by the power of the word. In every religion the power of the word has been recognized. In some of them creation itself is said to have come out of the word. For example, the *Rig-Veda*, the foundational scripture of Hinduism, says, "In the beginning was Brahman, with whom was the word; and the word was truly the Supreme Brahman." Echoing this statement, almost exactly, *Bible*, the scripture of Christianity, says, "In the beginning was the word and the word was God." The *Mandukya Upanishad* declares:

> "OM, this eternal word is all this. What was, what is and what shall be, and what is beyond is OM." (1)

Apart from the word's higher philosophical and religious value, sound-symbols play a prominent part in the drama of human life.

When a singer sings with devotion inspiring devotional songs, the vibrations of the air caused by her singing go into the ears of the listeners, and touch their nerves and kindle their devotion to God. One woman is weeping out of sorrow; another woman comes along and speaks a few gentle words to her. The soothing words control the emotions of the weeping woman and she begins to smile. Think of the power of the word! One person calls another an idiot. The latter clenches his fist and gives a blow in the face of the first person. Look at the power of the word! The words are as great a force in common life as they are in higher philosophy. Time and again we manipulate this force without thought and without consideration. To know the nature of this force and use it well is a part of Karma Yoga.

Self-abnegation

What is the end of selfless work or work done for others? The main effect of selfless work is self-purification. By means of constant effort to do good to others, we are trying to forget ourselves. This forgetfulness of self is a great lesson to be learnt in life. Ignorant people foolishly think that through selfish action they can make themselves happy; but after years of struggle and frustration, they find out at last that true happiness consists in killing selfishness. No one can make us happy except ourselves. Every good deed, every act of service, every act of charity, every thought of compassion takes so much of self-importance away from our little selves and thus purifies us. The highest state of purification is self-abnegation, where there is no "I," but all is "Thou." Whether we are aware of it or not, Karma Yoga leads us to that end.

There are two tendencies in doing work: *pravritti* and *nivritti*. *Pravritti* means: "revolving towards," and *nivritti* means "revolving away from." *Pravritti* is the tendency of accumulating everything in one center, i.e., one's own self. When this tendency begins to break and is replaced by *niviritti*, then begins morality and religion. Both *pravritti* and *nivritti* are of the nature of work; the former is evil work, and the latter is good work.

> "*Nivritti*" says Swami Vivekananda, "is the fundamental basis of all morality and religion and the very culmination of it is entire self-abnegation, readiness to sacrifice mind and body and everything for another being. When a man has reached that state he has attained to the perfection of Karma Yoga."[1]

When a Karma Yogi reaches the state of perfect self-abnegation, nothing will work upon him. He is neither happy nor unhappy when acted upon by the external world. There is neither good nor evil for him . Good or ill fortune causes no change in his mind; in all conditions he remains the same. Here is a story of Suka:

In the ancient days, there was great sage called Vyasa in India. He is the author of the *Vedanta Sutras* which deals with the philosophy of Vedanta. He was a holy man. His father, grand father and great-grand father had tried to become perfect men and had failed. He himself did not succeed fully, but his son, Suka, was born perfect. Vyasa taught his son wisdom, and after teaching him the knowledge of Truth, he sent him to the Court of King Janaka. Janaka was a great king. Although a king, he had no body-consciousness. The boy Suka was sent to him for learning. Janaka knew that Vyasa's son was coming to him; so he made certain arrangements beforehand. When the boy presented himself at the gate of the palace, the guards took no notice of him. They only gave him a seat, and he sat there for three days and nights, nobody speaking to him. Suka was the son of a very great sage, and he himself was a most respectable person. Yet the low, vulgar guards of the palace would take no notice of him.

Then suddenly, the ministers of the king came and received him with all honors. They conducted him into a splendid guesthouse and gave him the most fragrant baths and wonderful dress and for eight days they kept him there in all kinds of luxury. The solemnly serene face of Suka did not change even slightly. He was the same in the midst of this luxury as when waiting at the gate.

Then he was brought before the king in the Royal Court. The king was on the throne, music was playing, and dancing and other amusements were going on. The king gave him a cup of milk, full to the brim, and asked him to go seven times round the hall without spilling even a drop. The boy took the cup proceeded in the midst of the music, dance and attraction of the beautiful faces. He went round seven times, and not a drop of the milk was spilt. His mind was not attracted by anything. And when he brought the cup to the king, the king said to him, "What your father has taught you, what you have learnt yourself, I can only repeat. You have known the Truth. Go home."

A Karma Yogi should have such a control over himself and remain unperturbed by good or evil. His mind should be so balanced as not to allow anything to work upon him as good or evil.

Working for Work's Sake

We can attain freedom from the Law of Karma by working for work's sake and not for fulfilling selfish desires. But is it possible to work for work's sake? Of course those who work for personal ends such as name, fame or money will say that it is impossible to do so. However, there are some people in every country who work without personal motive and desire for return. They work as if they were paying off a debt that they owe to parents, to society and to humanity. If we can work with this idea, all that we do is merely to cancel our debt to the universe, then we can work for work's sake. When we pay off a debt, do we think of getting something in return? No; we do our work, cancel our obligation and think no more about it. All of us owe something to state and country, to our families and neighbors and to our spiritual teachers. We are guarded and protected by the state and we enjoy social amenities. So we are in debt to the society. How can we pay off that debt? By being good members of the society, by doing what we can to serve others and by making every effort to fulfill our obligations to the community.

We must recognize the rights of others and not perform any act that may infringe upon those rights. We must not injure our neighbor since we do not wish to be injured by him. By being good members of the family and by bringing up our children in the right way, we pay our debt to parents and ancestors. By studying and following the teachings of great saints and spiritual teachers we pay our debts to them. The debt that we owe to our higher Self can be paid by realizing our true nature, and by freeing the soul from the bondage of Karma and of the world. This is, of course, the ultimate aim of life. If we keep these ideas ever in our minds, we will work without seeking any reward, and all work performed in this spirit will purify our souls.

There is another awareness that will also strengthen the idea of working for work's sake. All the forces that we are using in our organism, physical and mental, do not really belong to us. Is the air in our lungs ours? No. It belongs to Mother Nature. Every force operating through the machinery of our bodies is a force of Nature, and the Cosmic mind is acting in our minds. Nothing is ours. Therefore, Lord Krishna says in the *Bhagavad Gita:*

> "All actions are wrought in all cases by the forces (*gunas*) of Nature only. He whose mind is deluded by egoism thinks, 'I am the doer'." (3.27)

So long as we identify ourselves with our bodies out of ignorance of our true nature, and call ourselves doers, players or actors, we must reap the results of our actions. The moment, however, that we realize that our bodies and minds belong to Nature and that the knower of mind, senses and body is our true Self, then we let the body and mind work with the full awareness that we are neither actor, worker, nor doer, and we remain untouched by the consequences of our actions. The true Self is not the doer, but a silent witness only. Work can go on for its own sake, but the Self is not bound by it. The wise persons realize this and remain free from the attachments that proceed from ignorance. Such were Krishna, Buddha, Christ, Ramakrishna and similar others. Realizing the oneness of the individual soul with the Universal Spirit, they worked for work's sake, without thought of reward. Anyone who will work in like manner will remain in peace forever.

Harmonizing Actions with the Life's Goal

What can we do to harmonize all our actions with the highest goal of life? It is by finding "That" which, in the midst of our varied actions of the mind and body, remains always inactive, that we reach the final goal of life. Until we find "That," we will be forced to go on reaping the fruits of our actions and facing suffering and misery. "That" something , which is beyond all activity, is called Atman (Self). It is the knower in us. If we observe our internal process while we are doing anything, we will discover that the knower is constant. When we hear a sound, we know that we hear; when we see a flower, we know that we see; but the knower of the flower is not different from the knower of the sound. It is always one and the same. It does not change. It is not bound by the conditions that govern the changeable. If it were otherwise, there would be no way of differentiating changeable from the unchangeable.

The changeable is subject to time, space and causation, while the unchangeable is beyond them. Time and space are conditions of forms of thought. One thought following another gives us a conception of intervals that we call time. When two ideas rise simultaneously, what separates them is space. These ideas of time and space are subject to change, because our thought, on which they are based, is continually changing. Anything, that takes form in the mind and is conditioned by time and space, must change, but the knower, not being a condition of mind or limited by time and space, does not change.

When the knower is identified with the changes of the mind, it becomes knower and thinker. When it is identified with the sense perception, it becomes knower and perceiver. When it is one with the conditions and activities of the being, it becomes the physical person.

The knower as Atman is the permanent source of intelligence, above mind and beyond thought; i.e., in reality it is neither thinker nor actor. As knower we can not have desires or passions, for they are purely mental conditions. When we identify ourselves with the mind and body, we appear to be doers and we seek the results of our work. But the moment that we realize that our body is a part of the universal body, our mind a part of the Cosmic mind and that our souls are intimately connected with one another as parts of one universal soul, all activity assumes a new meaning for us, and it becomes impossible for us to act from selfish motives or to do wrong actions. It is only when, out of our ignorance, we identify our true Self or Atman with the limitations of the mind and body, that we become selfish and do things that bring us suffering and misery. The light of the true knowledge dispels the darkness of ignorance and reveals the true nature of our true Self.

This knowledge is the highest. It makes us realize that the knower is separate from the objects known but one with the Universal Knower (*Paramatman*). Paramatman manifests through each individual form. This highest knowledge of Oneness resolves the issue of the multiplicity of phenomenal objects into that underlying One Reality commonly known as God. Everyone has to arrive at the knowledge of Oneness. Since ages great saints and Yogis have realized the Oneness of existence and attained liberation and bliss. What is possible for one is possible for others. So everyone can realize it by practicing Yoga.

Reference

1. *Karma Yoga and Bhakti Yoga,,* New York: Ramakrishna-Vivekananda Center, 1982, p. 73.

16

Pre-requisites of Karma Yoga

Introduction

Karma Yoga, like other kinds of Yoga, requires disciplined life and cultivation of virtues. The practice of Karma Yoga without the cultivation of virtues may lead to egoism. Therefore, an aspirant has to examine his way of life, his mental outlook and attitude in terms of the requirements of Karma Yoga. Its pre-requisites are:

- Sound health
- Free from diseases
- Moderation
- Right outlook
- Austerity
- Transcending egoism
- Mastering the mind
- Control of senses
- *Brahmacharya* (Celibacy)
- Transcending the pairs of opposites
- Right attitude towards action

Sound Health

In order to practice Karma Yoga, you should have a healthy and strong physical body. The body is a boat to cross the ocean of worldly existence, and it is an instrument for doing virtuous deeds and selfless service. How can an unhealthy and weak person serve others? So you should take great care of the body, but you should not have any attachment for it. You should never feel: "This body is mine." Nothing belongs to you. Your body is an instrument in the hands of God. You should be ever ready to sacrifice your body for a noble cause. Practice regularly *pranayama* (breathing exercises), *asanas* (Yoga postures) and physical exercises in order to maintain sound health. Eat nourishing vegetarian food, observe the laws of health and the rules of hygiene and inhale pure air.

Free from Diseases

Sound health implies being free from diseases of the mind and body. All physical diseases take their origin in the diseases of the mind. Such modifications of the mind as hatred, anger, anxiety, worry, depression, stress, etc. corrode the mind and react on the body and cause various physical disease like blood pressure, ulcer, cancer, diabetes, etc. Good mental health can be maintained by practicing meditation, celibacy, moral disciplines and right conduct.

Moderation

Moderation in diet, work, rest and sleep is essential for a Yogic life. Buddha, after passing through severe austerities, adopted and taught a moderate path. Lord Krishna says in the *Bhagavad Gita:*

> "Yoga is not for one who eats too much, nor for one who does not eat at all, nor for one who sleeps too much, nor for one who does not sleep at all." (6.16)
> "Yoga becomes destroyer of pain for one who is moderate in eating and recreation, who is moderate in sleep and wakefulness." (6.17)

Moderation in eating, working and sleeping is indispensable for maintaining sound health.

Right outlook

Just as a farmer prepares his land before sowing seeds for raising a crop, you have to develop right outlook, genuine love and devotion to God and toward all beings. Develop a universal love that will keep the "field" of your mind fit and ready to receive the spiritual seed. Do not neglect this virtue. A peevish, complaining and unsociable being can never become a Yogi. So you have to be all loving and become a living channel for carrying the message of love and friendship to all beings. It is only by wholehearted devotion and sincere love that perfection is attained.

Austerity

Austerity is one of the purifying practices that prepare you for Yoga. It means giving up your dependence on external comforts, luxuries and addictions, and freeing the mind from the demands of the senses and endless desires. However, it does not mean self-torture. It just involves simple living with moderation in eating, sleeping and working. It also involves mental purity by avoiding unnecessary talking, meaningless discussion, impure thoughts and reading bad literature. Without regulating physical and mental habits, the mind cannot become a useful tool for Yoga.

Transcending Egoism

Egoism is the feeling of "I, me, mine." This prevents you from realizing your true nature. It is the ego that is the basis of all mental dramas: desires, attachment, aversion, selfishness, bondage of Karma and so on. It creates all kinds of problems, worries, anxieties, delusion and fear. It disturbs your mental peace. It is not easy to overcome egoism. It veils your eyes and you forget your real nature of divinity. By self-analysis, scripture study, deep devotion and surrender to God, you have to overcome your ego. Read the life stories of great sages and saints and learn lessons from their lives.

Mastering the Mind

At times desires, expectations, disappointments, anxieties, worries, memories of past enjoyments, reaction to current situations, loss of things to which you are attached and such others make your mind restless. Such states need not discourage you. They are common to most of us. Do not let your mind mislead you. Make a firm resolution to regularly practice Yoga. Sometimes you may feel motivated and encouraged. But at other times you may feel discouraged. You may even feel that you cannot succeed in Yoga. Do not allow such depressing states of mind make you to discontinue. Keep trying. A voracious horse kicks, rears and attempts to throw away the rider, but if the rider manages to stay firmly in the saddle, then the horse quiets down, knowing it has found its master. The mind behaves in the same manner. It will try to dislodge you, but upon finding that you cannot be shaken off, it will become your slave.

Control of Senses

The senses bring you in contact with external objects and thereby desires are created. *Bhagavad Gita* brings out the all-devouring nature of desire in the verses 36–43 of the third chapter. The cause of all sins and wrong actions in this world is desire. Desire forces you to work for its fulfillment. It is your greatest foe in this world. Desire enshrouds wisdom, just as smoke envelops fire. It can never be satisfied nor cooled down by the enjoyment of objects. It flares up more and more when it feeds upon objects of enjoyment, just as fire blazes forth more and more when fed with oil and wood. Even if all the objects of the world and all the beautiful things were to pass into the possession of a person deluded by desire, they would fail to give him or her complete satisfaction.

The senses, the mind and the intellect are said to be the seat of desire; through these it deludes you by veiling your wisdom. Therefore Krishna in the *Bhagavad Gita* advises that the senses first be controlled and then desire be killed. Indeed it is difficult to conquer the incomprehensible desire. Nevertheless you can conquer it by cultivating will power, discrimination and dispassion.

Brahmacharya (Celibacy)

Swami Sivananda points out in his *Karma Yoga* that the practice of Karma Yoga is not possible without *brahmacharya* (Divine Life Society, Fremantle Branch, 1985, p. 54).

According to Ayurveda, semen is the last *dhatu* (element) that is formed out of marrow. From food, chyle is produced. Out of chyle comes fat; out of fat comes marrow; out of marrow comes semen. These are the seven *dhatus.* There are three divisions in each *dhatu.* Semen nourishes the physical body, heart and intellect. One who uses his physical body only but keeps the intellect and heart undeveloped cannot expect to attain perfect *brahmacharya.* He can have *brahmacharya* of the body only but not of the mind and heart. The semen that belongs to the heart and mind will certainly flow out. If you do not develop the heart and do not practice physical exercise as well, you will have mental *brahmacharya* only. That portion of the semen that goes to nourish the heart and body will flow out.

The worldly life is dominated by sex and ego. Ego is the basis. Sex hangs on the ego. If the ego is destroyed by enquiry of "Who am I?," the idea of sex takes its heel by itself. Most people have become a slave to sex and ego on account of ignorance. The dawn of knowledge of Self destroys these two enemies of the Atman (Self).

The sexual energy is transformed into spiritual energy by pure thoughts and spiritual practice. It is flown upward into the brain and becomes *ojas* energy. Indeed this process of sublimation is a very difficult one; yet it is most essential for you as an aspirant.

Brahmacharya is a basic pre-requisite for you. The practice of celibacy does not lead to any undesirable results as imagined by Western psychologists. On the contrary it gives you inner strength, invigorates the mind and the nerves. It conserves your physical and mental energy. It bestows vigor and vitality. A perfect celibate can shake the world, can stop the ocean like Lord Jesus, and can command Nature and the five elements like Jnana Dev of India.

It is possible to practice celibacy by leading a well-disciplined life, studying spiritual books, practicing meditation and by eating pure and moderate diet. You are the eternal, pure, perfect and free Self. Feel this. Assert this. You will succeed in maintaining celibacy and transforming sexual energy into spiritual energy.

Transcending the Pairs of Opposites

Happiness and sorrow, pleasure and pain, success and failure, good and evil, gain and loss, life and death are the obverse and reverse of the same coin. They are the pairs of opposites. Good cannot exist without evil. Life cannot exist without death. They are relative terms. Pleasure and pain, life and death are linked together inseparably. Ignorant people want absolute happiness in this world. This is simply impossible. Evil exists to glorify good. Hatred exists to glorify love. Falsehood exists to glorify truth.

Transcending the pairs of opposites is essential for you as an aspirant of Yoga. Go beyond pleasure and pain, honor and dishonor, praise and censure and rest in non-duality.

Right Attitude toward Action

The following attitudes are appropriate for the practice of Karma Yoga:

1. Attitude of Equanimity
2. Attitude of Selfless Service
3. Attitude of God's Instrument
4. Attitude of serving the Lord in all

You can choose any of the above attitudes that is appropriate to your background and outlook.

Equanimity. Worldly people are generally elated by success and depressed by failure. Elation and depression are the attributes of the mind. But Karma Yoga requires an attitude of equanimity at all times, in all conditions and all circumstances. The attitude of equanimity ensures lasting peace of mind. Make conscious effort to keep a balanced mind in success and failure, in honor and censure, profit and loss, and in praise and blame.

People have likes and dislikes toward work. In general, they like white-collar jobs and dislike manual work. They take interest in what they like and get attached to it. They are unwilling to leave it when conditions warrant it. Such attachment and aversion are not Yoga. In Karma Yoga there is no attachment or aversion to work. All work is sacred. No work is superior or inferior. Every work is divine work. You should be ready to do any kind of work without any sense of superiority or inferiority. You should be ready to start or stop a work if God wills.

Do not allow egoism to creep in. Egoism blocks the free flow of energy. At the end of the day make a mental review of the actions performed. In how many cases, have you allowed selfishness to creep in? Close review will reveal to you the subtle forms that selfishness assumes. You must gradually endeavor to eradicate them.

Merge your will in the Divine Will. Work for the fulfillment of Divine purposes. Do not have any personal expectation. Have a poised mind in the midst of changes in the world. Work for the welfare of the world in unison with the Divine Will. Lord Krishna says in the *Bhagavad Gita:*

> "Perform action, being steadfast in Yoga, renouncing attachment, balanced in success and failure. Evenness of mind is Yoga." (2.48).

Merit and demerit do not affect the Karma Yogi who works with evenness of mind; he neither exalts over the good fruit of an action nor worries over the bad fruit of the other. As he dedicates every action to God, he performs it as efficiently as possible. In the *Bhagavad Gita* Lord Krishna says:

> "Endowed with wisdom (evenness of mind), one casts off in this life both good and evil deeds; therefore devote thyself to Yoga; Yoga is perfection in action." (2.50).

A Karma Yogi has no sense of agency (doership). He renounces the fruits of actions. He performs all actions for God's sake without desire for their fruits. With pure reason and resting in the Self, a Karma Yogi is aware that all actions are done by the forces (*gunas*) of Nature. He is aware that God really works through his body. He gets illumination and becomes free from bondage of cycle of births and deaths and attains liberation. Lord Krishna says in the *Gita,*

"The wise, possessed of knowledge, having renounced the fruits of their actions, and being freed from the fetters of birth, go to the place beyond all evil." (2.51)

Balance of mind brings out lasting peace and happiness to a disciplined person. It is indeed a rare gift. It can only be attained by protracted selfless service with equal vision, self-control and by cultivating Divine virtues such as compassion, love, devotion to God, serenity, tolerance, endurance, etc. The sensual pleasure is nothing when compared to the bliss enjoyed by a Yogi who has serenity and a balance of mind. So serve, love and give. The more willingly you serve, the more happier you will be.

Selfless Service. Another attitude is the attitude of selfless service. It is the attitude of serving without expectation of the fruits. Lord Krishna says in the *Bhagavad Gita,* "Thy duty is to work only, but never with its fruits. Let not the fruits of action be thy motive, nor let the attachment to inaction." (2.47)

The attitude of selfless service arises out of the knowledge of our real nature. Our real Self is not a doer. It is only a knower, a silent witness. Only the body and the mind driven by the forces (*gunas*) of Nature work. The forces of Nature cannot affect a Yogi who has the knowledge of the Self, for he has gone beyond them. He works for the sake of service without any attachment either to the work or to its fruit. Hence it is selfless service. (For further details, *see* Chapter 21. Selfless Service (*Nishkama Karma*), *below*).

The Attitude of Instrumentality. If you are of devotional temperament, then work with the feeling, "O Lord, I am an instrument in Your Hands; You work through me. Everything is Thy Will. I am Thine. All is Thine. Thy will be done. Thou art everything. Even a leaf cannot move without Thee. I live for Thee alone. I work for Thee alone."

Surrender yourself to the Lord, and dedicate all your thoughts, words and deeds at the Lotus Feet of the Lord as worship unto Him. Become a flute of an empty reed in the hands of the Lord. Remain ever absorbed in God. See God in all beings and by serving them you are serving God. The great ancient saint Thirumular of Southern India beautifully describes how service to humanity is service to the Lord, in his sacred text of *Tirumantiram:*

PadamadakoyilBhagavarkontreyil
Nadamada koyil nambark ankaka
Nadamada koyil nambarkon treyil
Padamada koyil Bhagavarka thame. (1857)
This verse means: Offering given to the towered temple
Reaches not the noble walking temples.
Offering given to the noble walking temples
Reaches surely the Lord in the towered temple.

The offerings of such things as fruits, milk, honey, cooked food, etc. made to the deity in the temple do not reach the needy persons, but the things offered to the needy people reach the Lord. Thus service to humanity is service to God.

The Attitude of Oneness. The world is a manifestation of God. This awareness makes you to feel the oneness of all beings. The Self in you is the Self in all beings. So by serving others you are serving God. When you serve with this attitude, then you will have no feeling of superiority or inferiority, no feeling "helping" others, and no feeling of separateness. You will find the oneness in the midst of diversity. Your work becomes God's work. You will have no strain or burden in rendering service. God serves God.

17

Qualities and Qualifications of a Karma Yogi

In this Chapter we shall consider the qualities and qualifications you have to possess as an aspirant of Karma Yoga in order to succeed in your efforts.

The basic requirements of all paths of Yoga are the same. An aspirant in any path of Yoga should have aspiration, faith, sincerity, purity, dispassion, concentration, serenity, energy, courage, patience, perseverance, etc.

Aspiration

As an aspirant of Karma Yoga, you should have sincere aspiration to become a good Karma Yogi. Without sincere aspiration no mission can be accomplished. Keen interest and aspiration are absolutely necessary to do anything with determination and perseverance, overcoming obstacles, if any, that might come in the way.

Faith

You should have absolute faith in yourself, faith in God, faith in the scriptures and faith in the words of your spiritual preceptor (*Guru*). Such faith is essential for perseverance in doing useful service to suffering beings.

Self-control

You should have perfect control over your emotions, your words, your taste and your senses. You should not make thoughtless remarks; you should avoid idle and loose talks, and you should be indifferent to sensual enjoyments.

Sociability

You should have an amiable, loving and sociable nature. You should be able to move and mix with everybody without distinction of caste, creed or color. You should be able to adjust yourself to the habits and ways of those to be served.

Tolerance

You should be tolerant. Sometimes someone may make offending remarks or even use harsh or insulting words. Unless you possess tolerance you cannot maintain a cool and balanced mind in such situations. One who is easily irritated and easily offended over trifling things is absolutely unfit for the path of Karma Yoga.

Forbearance

You should be able to bear insult, disrespect, dishonor, harsh words, censure, heat and cold and the pain of illness and physical exertion. Then only you could maintain balance of mind when you come across unpleasant situations while doing service to others.

Endurance

You should have power of endurance. You should have ability to bear the strain of physical efforts in saving and protecting people in danger. You should have patience and perseverance. You should not feel discouraged by failure. Failure is a stepping stone to success.

Humility

You should be humble and free from hatred, jealousy, harshness, etc. You should speak sweet words. You should be absolutely fearless. You should be polite, courteous, kind and helpful at all times.

Universal Love

You should have pure and universal love to serve all. "Love thy neighbor as thyself" says Jesus Christ. Where there is love, there is peace, joy, compassion and sacrifice. God is love and so is the human soul, being a spark from the same essence. St. John says, "He that loveth not, knoweth not God; for God is love."

Equal Vision

You should have equal vision. You should realize the oneness or unity of the Self everywhere. You should feel that all beings are one with the Self and that you own Self and the Supreme Self are identical. *Bhagavad Gita* declares,

> "With the mind harmonized by Yoga he (Yogi) sees the Self abiding in all beings and all beings in the Self; he sees the same everywhere." (6.29)
>
> "He who, through the likeness of the Self, sees equally everywhere, be it pleasure or pain, he is regarded as the highest Yogi." (6. 32)

The highest Yogi sees that whatever is pleasure or pain to himself is also pleasure or pain to all other beings. Therefore you should not harm anyone. You must wish the good of all. When you are established in the unity of the Self, you would see equally everywhere.

Non-injury (*Ahimsa*)

Ahimsa means non-hurting any living creature in thoughts, words and deeds. On the positive side, *ahimsa* leads to a spontaneous love toward all creatures. The Self in all beings is one and the same. By hurting anyone you are hurting everyone. Cultivate positive thoughts, love and compassion.

Truthfulness

You should speak the truth. Truth is the greatest of all virtues. If you are true to yourself, then you cannot be false to others. Your thoughts, words and actions should move in unison. By deceiving anyone you first deceive your own Self. Ram cannot cheat Ram" says Swami Ram Tirath, a saint of India.

Simplicity

You should reduce want and control the senses and lead a simple life. A person who indulges in luxury, becoming a slave of his senses, cannot be able to serve others. Such a person wants everything for himself and wants to exploit and dominate others.

Calm and Balanced Mind

You have to maintain a calm and balanced mind. Serenity is attained by the eradication of desires and cravings. To become free from the bondage of actions, an attitude of equanimity is essential. You must take pleasure and pain, gain and loss, success and failure, honor and dishonor as same. You should develop such a balanced state of mind by continuous effort.

Carefulness

You should be careful in doing any work. The whole heart, mind, intellect and soul must be on the work. Do everything diligently and perfectly. Do not do things in a hurry-scurry, in haste or flurry. Do every work with a cool, unruffled mind with full concentration.

Dedication

Complete dedication to service is needed. Devote heart and soul in the service rendered, and dedicate it to the Lord as a form of worship. You should feel that you are serving the Lord.

Dispassion

This is the most important virtue to be possessed by you as a Karma Yogi. You should work with total dispassion, without any attachment either to the work or to its fruits. You should have no desire for name, fame, appreciation, admiration and not even an expectation of thanks or gratitude. Then only you can attain to freedom from the Karma. For details, *see* chapter 39. Freedom from Karma and Rebirth, *below*).

Devotion to God

This is an added qualification of a Karma Yogi. This makes it easier to develop such essential qualities as humility, dedication and dispassion. A true devotee offers his thoughts, words and deeds to the Lord as a form of worship. Such dedication frees him from the bondage of Karma.

Steadfastness

You, like the Yogis of other paths, should be steadfast in practicing your chosen path. Steadfastness means perfect devotion and sticking to the path, without any wavering or oscillation of the mind. You must have a firm unshakeable conviction that steadfastness will lead you to the goal and attainment of eternal freedom and supreme bliss. Mahatma Gandhi was steadfast in Karma Yoga. He never deviated from his ideal. Steadfastness is a *sine qua* non for success. Only a steadfast person can apply his full heart and soul to the work on hand. Steadfastness develops willpower. It enables you to overcome stumbling blocks on the path of realization.

Knowledge of Senses and Organs of Action

A Karma Yogi should have a knowledge of the nature and functions of the senses and organs of action (*indriyas*). The real senses are in the astral body. They are very subtle. They have corresponding centers in the brain. They are moved by *prana* (life force). The senses of action are located in the vital sheath of the astral body. What you see outside—mouth, hands, feet, the organ of reproduction and anus—are mere external instruments.

The organs of action are the five soldiers. The commander-in-chief is the mind. The mind extracts work from these soldiers when it desires to get sensual objects for its gratification. The five organs of action cannot work independently without the influence of the mind. It is the mind that really works through these organs. It is the mind that really plans, schemes and directs all activities. Egoism is the doer and enjoyer, but through delusion the individual soul appears to be the doer and enjoyer. Therefore it reaps the fruits of actions in the form of pleasure or pain.

First, you perceive sensual objects through senses of perception—seeing, hearing, smelling, tasting and touching. You are attracted to the objects. Then comes attachment. From attachment springs desire to possess the objects for your enjoyment. The desire prompts you to exert to obtain the objects. Thus desire is the motivating force that prompts the mind to action.

If you can stop the thoughts, the fire of desire will be extinguished by itself, just as a lamp is extinguished when the supply of oil is withdrawn. The senses of perception and the thoughts should be controlled. The mind should be firmly fixed on the Lord. Only then you will become a true Yogi. Destroy attachment. Then the longing and preference for objects will die.

A Karma Yogi must not be carried away by emotions. He must calm down the bubbling emotions and impulses and purify them. He must destroy all vain thought and conserve energy. He should observe silence for two hours daily and six hours on Sundays and holidays.

Self-delusion

Mere physical control of the organs of action will not do. You must not think of the sensual objects. If your mind constantly thinks of various kinds of delicious food when you observe fasting, you will not get the benefits of fasting. You will be regarded as a self-deluded person or hypocrite. Lord Krishna says in the *Bhagavad Gita*,

> "He who, restraining the organs of actions, sits thinking of the sense-objects in mind, is of deluded understanding and a hypocrite." (3.6)

You must utilize the energy that is conserved by the control of the mind and organs of actions for higher purposes at the altar of God.

> "But whosoever, controlling the senses by the mind, engages himself in Karma Yoga with the organs of action, without attachment, (he) excels." (*Gita,* 3.7)

Perform right actions without attachment. This is the secret of Karma Yoga. Sri Krishna declares in the *Gita:*

> "The world is bound by actions other than those performed for the sake of sacrifice; do thou, therefore, perform actions for sacrifice alone, without attachment." (3. 9)

Do not become a pseudo Karma Yogi by giving charity or feeding some poor people or giving donation to a school or building a temple for the sake of name, fame and publicity. Care not for those little perishable things. Become a true Karma Yogi by doing selfless service with devotion to God.

Knowledge

You should have a working knowledge of Raja Yoga, psychology, physiology, family medicine, hygiene and Vedanta. Then you will be able to render service in different situations.

Conclusion

Even if you possess only a few of the above qualities and qualifications, you need not be discouraged. Plunge yourself into the service of God with devotion and dispassion. Start earnestly rendering selfless service, the other qualities will come to you by themselves. Draw inspiration from the example of leading Karma Yogis. (*See* Chapter 41. Some Karma Yogis, *below*).

Negative qualities to be avoided

The old impressions of vanity, cunningness, crookedness, pride, arrogance, petty-mindedness, self-esteem and speaking ill of or belittling others may still be lurking in your mind. You cannot shine unless you remove them completely. Success in Yoga is impossible without removing such negative qualities. You should take care to avoid the negative qualities:

1. *Irritability.* If you are easily offended by trifling things, you would lose the opportunities of service when they come. Cultivate adaptability and amiable and loving nature. Then the bad quality of

irritability would disappear. Do not get offended if your bad qualities and defects are pointed out. Thank those who point out them, and make sincere efforts to eliminate those bad qualities and defects.

2. *Self-assertive nature.* All of us have built up a personality from time immemorial. Our self-assertive nature compels us to dominate others. We do not wish to listen to the opinions and arguments of others, even though they may be sound, logical and reasonable. We assert and say, "what I say is correct." And defend it. This is a very dangerous habit. Try to see things with an open mind and learn from others' ideas and experiences.

3. *Faultfinding.* This nature arises from the self-assertive nature. We jump at once to find faults in others. We do not see the good in others. To remove this weakness develop pure love and liberal outlook, and look at the good side of others.

4. *Vain discussions.* We often waste our time and energy in vain discussions and arguments. The mind is agitated and the blood pressure goes up. Let us learn to mind our own business, and get fully involved with our spiritual practices. Then there will be no time to waste in useless discussions.

5. *Lust, Greed and Anger.* As Lord Krishna says in the *Bhagavad Gita* (16.21), these three constitute the gateway to hell and cause self-destruction. When these evil modifications of the mind arise, you would lose your balance of mind, discrimination and poise and tend to commit all kinds of evil crimes. Lust, greed and anger denote self-blindness and ignorance. They are the enemies of peace, devotion and knowledge. Seek the company of sages, receive spiritual instructions from them, study scriptures, contemplate on their messages and practice them. Then you can succeed in abandoning these evil tendencies, and become fit for rendering selfless service.

18

Practice of Karma Yoga

Karma Yoga, like other paths of Yoga, has to be strenuously practiced. As said by Swami Vivekananda, first you have to hear, then think, and then practice. First, you have to hear about it and understand what it is. Several things that you do not understand will become clear to you by constant hearing and thinking. It is difficult to understand everything at once. Every knowledge is within us. No one is ever really taught by another; each of us has to teach himself. The external teacher offers only the suggestion, that arouses the internal teacher. The latter helps us to understand things. Then things will be made clearer to us by our own power of perception and thinking; the clear ideas take deep root in the mind and grow into intense power of will.

Out of that will comes tremendous urge for working. This will flow into every vein, nerve and muscle, until the whole body is transformed into an instrument of Yoga of Selfless Service.

Then the desired self-abnegation and utter unselfishness is duly attained. This attainment does not depend on any dogma or doctrine. Whether you are a Jew, or Christian or Hindu, it does not matter. Are you unselfish? That is the question. If you are unselfish, you will attain perfection.

Much wealth not required

The practice of Karma Yoga does not require much wealth. What is required is a willing heart to serve humanity. A teacher can give free tuition for poor pupils and give them free books. This is Karma Yoga for him. A doctor can serve the poor without any fees and give them free medicine. This is Karma Yoga for him. A lawyer can plead for poor people without accepting any fees. This is Karma Yoga for him.

Serve and nurse the poor sick persons who live in your neighborhood. Go to the hospital and serve the sick persons with a loving heart. Pray for their speedy recovery. Study the scriptures of their religion in their presence. There are many such opportunities for service.

Service need not be Spectacular

To do service you need not have to do spectacular deeds. You can even begin with small acts of service. For example: when you walk, you should look down at your feet. There are many tiny living beings that crawl on the ground. If you are careless in walking, you may kill an ant or some other tiny creature. So look down and be careful when you walk. This is difficult to do because there is nobody to check on you and blame or praise you. There are people who do good things when they are in the company of others but not when they are alone. Karma Yoga teaches us to do good even when we are alone. When you see a broken bottle or a nail on the street, you should remove it so that it cannot hurt anyone. Walk carefully and take a longer step to save an ant on your path. You can serve the poor, the needy and the sick in many small ways. Giving need not have to be material. A smile, a kind word, a compassionate thought can be more important than material gifts. In serving you must not discriminate between great and small, but simply serve all. The value of your service is based on quality, not on quantity.

Alternate Routes

Karma Yoga has alternate routes. It can be practiced under the mode of either *Bhakti* (Devotion) or *Jnana* (Knowledge).

The goal of life is to transcend the finite self. This can be done either by shifting the center of interest and affection to a personal God or by identifying oneself with the impersonal Absolute (Brahman) that resides at the core of one's being. The first is the way of a *Bhakti*, and the second is the way of a *Jnani.* Work can be a vehicle for self-transcendence by either approach. For every action performed there is a corresponding reaction upon the doer. Every action performed for one's personal sake thickens one's ego and insulates it further from God. On the other hand, every act done without any personal motive purifies the heart.

Through Bhakti Yoga

The best way for the emotionally inclined person to perform actions selfless is to bring his affectionate nature into play and work for God's sake instead of his own sake. Lord Krishna in the *Bhagavad Gita* says:

> "He who performs actions, without attachment, resigning them to God, is unstained by their effects as the lotus leaf by water." (5.10)

Such a person is as active as before, but he works without a sense of doership, and without any expectation of reward. His work becomes worship and a service to God. God is the doer, he is a humble instrument in His hands. Performed in this spirit, actions lighten the ego instead of binding it. Each task becomes a sacred offering to God without thought of any personal benefit. Lord Krishna in the *Bhagavad Gita* declares:

> "Whatever you do, whatever you eat, whatever you offer as sacrifice, whatever, you give away, whatever austerity you practice, O Son of Kunti, do that as an offering to Me. Thus

shall you be free from the bondage of actions that bear good and evil results." (9.27–28)

Such a devotee "has no desire for the fruits of his actions," echoes the *Bhagavatam*, "he would always prefer Divine service." He surrenders the fruits of his actions to God and takes all that happens in his life as coming directly from Him. God's Will is his will. Surrendering himself to the Lord of all, he remains untouched by the vagaries of life. He has no anxiety for the outcome of his deeds. He forsakes every claim on his acts, so they leave no impression on his mind to produce future effects, good or evil. In this way he works out the accumulated impressions of previous deeds without acquiring new ones. The selfless Karma Yogi is completely at the disposal of others. He has no sense of possessiveness. Therefore he does not exist.

How to Practice

1. Cultivate the awareness that all creation is a temple for God. You can start with—your spouse, children or employer, for example—whom you can always try to see in this light. Or you can try to maintain this attitude with everyone you deal with. Or you can try to retain this awareness toward everyone and everything.
2. Have this attitude toward yourself, too. For example: when you take bath, feel that you are washing the Lord's temple. When you eat, feel that He is seated within and you are feeding Him. That way, even caring for your bodily needs becomes an offering to God.
3. Develop the awareness that God is present, watching all that you do. You can speak to Him internally as you go on doing your daily tasks.
4. After doing every work, take a moment to mentally offer it to the Lord. Before retiring at night, offer all that you did during the day.

5. Respect the work of all people. Everyone has his own capabilities and is given a job to perform. All are equal in God's eyes.

Through Jnana (Knowledge)

A Karma Yogi, whose disposition is more reflective than emotional, adopts knowledge approach to work. For this too the key is working unselfishly, but the psychological framework is different. He seeks to find the infinite Being at the center of his self.

This approach to work consists in discrimination, i.e., drawing a sharp distinction between the unreal and the real, the not-self and the eternal Self that stands apart from it. This requires a sharp and subtle intellect. Working with an expectation of a reward inflates the ego and binds the doer to karmic effects and veils the real Self from him. But working with the spirit of complete detachment, the Karma Yogi identifies himself with the true Self. Then he has no sense of doership. Though his body and mind works, because of his dissociation from them, he does nothing at all. In the *Bhagavad Gita* Lord Krishna describes it thus:

> "This body, O Arjuna, is called the Field; he who knows it called the Knower of the field by the sages. The great elements (earth, air, fire, water and ether), egoism, intellect and also the unmanifested Nature, the ten senses (organs of action and senses) and one (the mind) and the five objects of the senses (taste, sound, touch, form and smell), desire, hatred, pleasure, pain, the body, intelligence and fortitude—the field has thus been briefly described with its modifications." (13.1–6)

All of this has nothing whatsoever to do with the Self, the Knower of the Field. The field and its modifications like egoism, desire, hatred, pleasure, pain, etc. alone are changing and the Knower of the Field is a witness and unchanging. So to practice

Karma Yoga with the approach of Jnana requires a sharp and subtle intellect. It is indeed an incredibly difficult task to rely totally on this power of intellect; but for those who can practice it, the reward is by far the greatest.

How to Practice

1. Cultivate the attitude of the witness. Designate certain times of the day, before meals, for example, when you stop for a few moments and examine the contents and attitude of your mind. Mentally detach yourself from all sense of doership.
2. Before retiring, practice introspection. Review the day's activities, and note what sorts of circumstances caused you to lose witnessing attitude.
3. As you go about your daily activities, remind yourself that everything you see has a beginning, middle and end, and therefore, is not Real.

Though the conceptual framework of the above two approaches to the practice of Karma Yoga differ sharply, they aim at the same result. Both are designed to starve the egoistic personality to death by deflecting it from the fruits of the actions on which it feeds. Neither gives any hold to that native egoism which the world considers indispensable for competing successfully in the struggle for existence. Both types of Yogis aim at transcending existence for oneself. The bhakta does it by giving his heart and will to the Personal God. The jnani does it by cultivating discriminative knowledge.

Combining Karma Yoga and Raja Yoga

Raja Yoga is the path of Concentration and Meditation. Based on ethical perfection, it offers a systematic approach for gaining control over the mind. It is suitable for people who like to apply their willpower in dealing with life's situations and who wish to learn about all aspects of their minds. The Raja Yogi seeks togather and direct all his mental energy to the task on hand; so he can clearly understand it and accomplish it most efficiently. Raja Yoga is common to all other paths of Yoga.

How to Practice

1. Keep you mind focused on task before you. Do not daydream, dwell on the past, or plan for the future. Fulfill the duty of the moment with all your concentration.
2. Do your best and leave the rest. Apply yourself as best as you can, and do not get excited or anxious over the results.
3. Observe the types of activities you usually do well and those where you often make mistakes or get disturbed. Analyze and find out your strengths and weaknesses.
4. Repeat a holy mantra as you do your work. That way, though part of your mind will be engaged in the work, another part of the mind will be absorbed in the divine vibration of the mantra. Of course, if you need your full attention for a given task, you can leave the mantra for a while, and then return to it when the job is done.
5. To expand your capacity for service and to help develop your will power, do one thing that you do not want to do, and do not do one thing that you do want to do. Try doing this every day, or at least once a week.

Whatever approach or combination of methods you use in developing yourself as a Karma Yogi, it is helpful to remember Swami Sivananda's inspiring advice:

> "Do it now. Not tomorrow or the day after, but now itself. This is one of the most important rules of Karma Yoga. Opportunities come and go. You should be ever alert and vigilant and utilize every opportunity for service.
> Every minute is precious. Even a single minute should not be wasted. Keeping the body and mind fully engaged is the best panacea for all physical and mental ills. Exert yourself from this very second."

The Highest Service

The root cause of human sufferings is ignorance. Most people are not aware of their real nature. Out of ignorance they identify themselves with their bodies and minds and consequently undergo all kinds of sufferings and tribulations. They are bound by their actions, and are subject to the wheel of births and deaths. If you could remove this ignorance in ordinary people, that would be the highest service rendered by you to the humanity. Attain the knowledge of Self from your spiritual teacher, and with his blessings, as his instrument, disseminate that knowledge to the seekers.

Services like feeding the hungry, nursing the sick, giving charity to the poor, etc., though important, do not remove their misery permanently. They give just temporary relief to them. Spiritual service alone—imparting of knowledge of the Self—gives eternal freedom from suffering to the people.

Perseverance and Enthusiasm in Service

It is not easy to attain perfection in Karma Yoga. But if you have an iron will and a strong determination, nothing is impossible. Work hard for a long time with perseverance and patience.

Do not be discouraged by repeated failures. Know the causes of such failures and carefully avoid them in future. In your weakness lies your strength. Stick firmly to your convictions, ideals and practice, despite repeated failures. March boldly on the path. Say, "Come what may, I will surely come out with perfect success in this spiritual struggle. Failures or slips cannot in any way affect me." With that determination you are bound to succeed in any endeavor.

Nothing is lost when the candle burns. You do not lose anything in Karma Yoga. Even if you do a little service it brings its own reward. It purifies the heart and prepares it for the higher knowledge. Compassion, love and mercy are developed. The impressions of these virtues and good actions are recorded in the subconscious mind. At some time in the future they will rise up and urge you to do good actions.

Lifelong Practice

Practice Karma Yoga till the end of your life. Then only you are safe. Is there any greater Karma Yogi than Lord Buddha or Mother Teresa? They live in our hearts because they spent their whole life in serving others. You can also become a Buddha or Mother Teresa if you get established in selfless service with the right attitude.

Practice what the great Himalayan Sage Swami Sivananda says: kill ambition, kill desire for life, kill desire for comfort, but work and serve diligently and carry out the will of God. Work for fulfilling the Divine purpose. Work with all sincerity and devotion, but without any personal motive. You will be free from the bondage of Karma.

19

Obstacles

Introduction

There are several obstacles to the practice of Karma Yoga. They include pride, self-assertion, intolerance, anger, worry, hypocrisy and unhealthy and undesirable habits. Subtle forms of these obstacles lurk in the mind. They operate as oceanic undercurrents. A Karma Yogi has to equip himself with wisdom, will power, dispassion and discrimination in order to overcome the obstacles that stand in the way of his daily work.

Pride

Pride is a quality of rajasic mind. It is inveterate. It manifests again and again. It asserts whenever opportunities arise. By consciously cultivating humility and self-surrender to God, pride can be overcome.

Self-assertion

This is another quality of rajasic mind. It is difficult to eradicate a self-assertive nature. The person of self-assertive nature wants to dominate over others. He does not want to hear even the reasonable opinions and logical arguments of others. He will never admit his mistakes. He will try to justify his whimsical views by crooked arguments. This is a dangerous nature. The self-assertive person should change his attitude. He must develop the attitude of looking at things from the viewpoints of others. He should cultivate the habit of carefully listening what others say before giving his opinion.

Intolerance

An aspirant who finds it difficult to adjust to the ways and habits of others cannot be able to practice Karma Yoga. He is intolerant. He thinks that his ways of living alone are right. He jumps at once to find faults in others. He cannot see the good in others. He should eradicate this negative quality by developing tolerance, adaptability and patience. He should recognize the diversity in the ways of living among people.

Vanity

The undesirable negative qualities of vanity, crookedness, arrogance, etc. of the previous life may be still lurking in your mind. You cannot make any progress unless you eradicate them by consciously cultivating positive qualities of simplicity, straight forwardness, gentleness, etc.

Annoyance and Irritability

Every slight annoyance and irritability affect the mind. As an aspirant you should not allow these evil feelings to manifest in your mind. They should be nipped in the bud through the cultivation of forgiveness, love and sympathy for others.

Anger

The emotion of anger is a terrible barrier to the practice of Karma Yoga. It affects your health also. A terrible fit of anger shatters the nervous system and blood circulation. If you have no self-control, the emotion of anger will throw you out of gear like a turbulent horse that carries away the rider along with it. Cultivate self-restraint, mercy, love and compassion in order to control the emotion of anger, and to enjoy peace.

Worry and Depression

Worry and depression weaken the physical system and cause mental stress. Eradicate worry and depression by vigilant introspection and meditation. Cultivate equanimity, cheerfulness, and overcome the pairs of opposites like pleasure and pain, success and failure, etc.

Thoughtless Words

Thoughtless loose talks will not be relished by others; such talks even hurt the feelings of others. Think before you speak. Speak measured words. Give up idle talks. Do not assert your rights. Think more about your duties and not about your rights.

Clamor for Fashion

Clamor for fashion is an obstacle to Karma Yoga. Only a simple dress is appropriate for a Yogi. Beware of the disastrous effects of fashion. Fashion consists in half-nudity. It excites passion. It leads to overspending beyond one's means. It involves enormous waste of money. If the money wasted on fashion is utilized in charity and service, poor people will be benefited.

Can a fashionable dress and use of cosmetics give real beauty? No. It is only an artificial decoration. Divine virtues only can bring you everlasting beauty, respect and honor.

Fashion is a terrible curse. It infuses evil thoughts, lust, greed and devilish tendencies. Root out this desire for fashion. Do not waste your time, energy and life in vanity, in running after fashionable dress. Wear simple dress. Cherish noble thoughts. Simplicity will bring piety. You will be free from worry and anxiety. You can devote more time to spiritual pursuits and service.

Smoking

"One who smokes is unfit for the practice of Karma Yoga," says Swami Sivananda, Master of many great monks. If you are smoker you become dull when you cannot get a whiff of smoke. You cannot work in the absence of cigarettes. You waste your money that can be well utilized in the service of others. Researches have found the disastrous effects of smoking on health. It poisons the system and causes killer-diseases like lung cancer and heart disease. Nicotine of cigarettes affects many of your brain's hormones and nervous system. It stimulates your sympathetic nervous system and causes your body to produce more stress hormones. Nicotine increases the risk of sudden cardiac death. It paralyses your lungs' natural cleaning mechanism. It weakens your immune system. No wonder over 350,000 people dies prematurely in the United States each year from smoking-related diseases; 30% of cancer deaths alone are due to smoking. Chronic bronchitis and emphysema account for another 60,000 smoking-related deaths. Smoking also substantially increases the risk of stroke, peripheral vascular disease, osteoporosis, glaucoma, larynx, pancreas, cervix, peptic ulcer, asthma, gum disease, etc. Infants and children of smoking parents have a higher incidence of respiratory illnesses. Should one buy such serious diseases and health disasters by resorting to this evil habit? (For further details, *refer* Dean Ornish, *Dr. Dean Ornish's Program for Reversing Heart Disease*, New York: Ballantine Books, pp. 307-11)

It is not difficult to give up this evil habit. With one strong powerful will it can be abandoned entirely. Will strongly, "I will give up this intolerable habit this very second." You will succeed. The attempt to give up gradually will not produce lasting result. Develop your will; avoid bad company; enjoy the company of good people and saints. Practice yoga asanas and meditation; give up meat-eating and take healthy vegetarian food. All bad habits will take their heels. There is nothing impossible under the sun. Where there is a will there is a way.

Meat-eating

This is an elder sister of the evil habits of smoking and alcoholism. Meat-eating is highly harmful to health. It brings a host of ailments like heart diseases, diseases of kidneys and other diseases. Human beings constitutionally are not made for eating meat. Killing of animals for food is also a great sin. Instead of killing the egoism and the sense of "I, me and mine," ignorant people kill innocent animals to satisfy their tongue and palate. Most inhuman habit indeed!

Meat-eating and alcoholism are closely allied. To meat-eaters celibacy and mind-control are absolutely impossible. Mark how meat-eating tiger is ferocious and grass-eating cow and elephant are peaceful and mild!

Non-injury (*ahimsa*) is the greatest of all virtues. It is the first virtue that a spiritual aspirant should possess. We should have reverence for life. The prophets of Jainism and Buddha practiced non-injury as an important virtue for attaining perfection.

Pythagoras, the Grecian sage, preached, "Do not kill or injure any creature. Beware of defiling your bodies with sinful food! There are cereals, there are fruits, bending their branches down by their weight, and luxurious grapes on the vines. There are sweet vegetables and herbs that the flame can render palatable and mellow. Nor are you denied milk or honey, fragrant with the aroma of the thyme flower. The beautiful earth offers you an abundance of pure food and provides for meals obtainable without slaughter and bloodshed."

Dr. J. Oldfield, a senior physician of Lady Margaret Hospital, writes: "The products of vegetable kingdom contain all that is necessary for the fullest sustenance of human life. Flesh is unnatural food and therefore tends to create functional disturbances . . . .

Flesh-eating is one of the most serious causes of the diseases that carry off ninety-nine out of every hundred people that are born." In large meat-eating countries cancer mortality is very high. Vegetarians keep up sound health till old age. In the present century Dr. Dean Ornish, a disciple of Sri Swami Satchidananda, has found, on the basis of his research studies made from 1977 onwards, that non-fat vegetarian diet along with non-smoking, practice of Yoga asanas, pranayama and meditation and group support reverses heart disease without drugs or surgery (For details, see Dean Ornish, *Dr. Dean Ornish's Program for Reversing Heart Disease,* New York: Ballantine Books, 1990).

Go to a slaughter-house and butcher's shop and see the agony of the animals at the time of their being killed; your heart will melt; you will determine to give up meat-eating. Always think of the evils of meat-eating and the benefits of a vegetarian diet.

Gambling

Gambling is another dreadful curse. It tantalizes, tempts and deludes. It has broken the hearts of many. People become bankrupts by indulging in gambling. Bad habits like gambling lead to wrong thinking. The intellect becomes clouded and blunt. Discrimination fails. An enormous amount of money is wasted uselessly in gambling and drinking. All vices cling to gamblers.

It is very difficult to get a human birth. Human life is meant for God-realization. Do not waste this precious life in drinking, gambling, smoking and meat-eating. You will carry the impressions of these evil habits to your future births. Even God cannot help you.

Give up these evil habits from this very second. Arise, awake. "Become a virtuous person. Do good actions. Sing God's name, a potent antidote for all evil habits. Study religious books. Seek the company of sages and devotees, and all evil habits will be eradicated. Serve, love, give. Purify. Concentrate. Meditate. . . . May the Lord, the indweller of your heart give you strength to overcome all evil habits. May His blessing be upon you."[1]

Reference

1. Swami Sivananda, *Karma Yoga*, Fremantle: the Divine Life Society, Fremantle Branch, 1985, pp.154-5).

20

Duty

Introduction

Activities of mind and body are the mark of life. They find expression variously in the day-to-day work of our life. The work can be divided into three kinds according to the motive that inspires it. They are:

1. The first kind of work consists of all activities that are performed for the preservation of the body, and for the gratification of the senses. They are mainly guided by motives of hunger and procreation. These are cravings of animal nature. As the scale of evolution rises higher, these motives become more clearly defined, and they reach their culminating point in human being. The human being is the highest form of all living beings.
2. The second kind of work includes all actions done from a sense of duty.
3. The third kind of work embraces all that is done freely out of love.

When the basic motives of hunger and self-preservation are inspired by a love of self, they produce the sense of duty. This love of self is very limited at the outset when the human beings live on the animal plane and identify soul with body. At this stage, one's self is the center of all things. The individual takes care of himself without recognizing the self of others. At this stage of development he is concerned only with his own pleasure and pain. When the moral nature begins to unfold, he learns to respect the rights of those who are closely related to him. He now feels that he should not do anything to injure those related to him by family ties. This is the beginning of the sense of duty toward the family. Gradually this extends to neighbors and friends who are helpful to him.

Definition of Duty

Every day our duties vary according to our situations, When we go to our office or work place, official duties claim us; when we return home, household duties arise. Each situation brings with it a feeling of ought, and this feeling is the sense of duty in us. So duty is purely subjective. **It is the feeling of obligation to do certain acts under certain circumstances.** Duty creates a kind of bondage between the individual and his environment. As the nature and circumstances of each vary, so will the duties vary.

Relative

Duty, in its essence, is relative. What is duty for one person may not be duty for another person, and what is duty at one stage of life may not be duty at another stage. When a boy started going to school he assumes the duties of the student life; when he marries the duties of family life begin, and when he becomes a father, duties to his children bind him. He also has duties toward his country. Life is a continuous process of evolution and progression; higher duties evolve out of lower ones.

The idea of duty is different in different nations. The Hindu says what is in the *Vedas* is his duty; the Christian says what is in the *Bible* is his duty; the Muslim says what is written in the *Koran* is his duty; and so on. But the scriptures vary. However, the underlying spirit of all the scriptures is the same. That may be summed up in the admonition, "Do not be selfish, be unselfish." **Any action that is unselfish, and leads us toward God is good; any action that is selfish and makes us go downward is evil.** Not injuring any living being in thought, word and deed is virtue; injuring any being is sin. This idea is universal and common to all in every country and in all ages.

Duty and Stages in Life

The stages in life (*ashramas*), according to the Hindu system of morality, are four: *brahmacharya* (studentship), *grihastha* (householdership). *Vanaprastha* (forest-dwelling or seclusion, and *sannyasa* (renunciation). Each order of life has its own duties. The four stages are meant to shape life in a progressive process of development and steady growth.

Studentship. Manu Smriti, the ancient Indian scripture of moral code, describes the life of a student:

> "Let the student ever engage in the study of *Vedas* (Scriptures) and in doing service to his preceptor (*Guru*). Let him refrain from wine, meat, tasty dishes, perfumes, garlands, company of opposite sex, and from injury to sentient creatures. Let him give up lust, anger, greed, dancing, singing and playing on musical instruments, dice-play, gossip, slander and untruth.
>
> "Let the student always sleep alone and let him not waste his seed; he who from lust destroyed his seed, destroyed his vow. He should develop the spirit of service, humility and obedience. He should mold his character properly. He should be chaste in thought, word and deed."

The main features of the life of a *brahmachari* (student) are:

- Study of scriptures
- Service to the teacher
- Leading a pure and simple life
- Refraining from wine, meat, smoking, spicy food, perfumes, garlands and company of opposite sex
- Refraining from gambling, gossip, slander and untruth
- Avoiding bad company
- Practicing non-injury
- Giving up lust, anger and greed
- Strict celibacy and sleeping alone
- Cultivating the spirit of service, humility and obedience
- Molding good character

- Chastity in thought, word and deed.

If a student has taken the vow of life-long celibacy, he need not enter the stage of a householder. He can devote his whole life to spiritual pursuits.

Householder. After finishing the studies, a student enters the order of householder when he is ready for that stage of life. The order of the householder is the highest, as it supports the other three orders. If one leads a well-regulated householder life, there is no need for *sannyasa*. Marriage is no hindrance to spirituality and God-realization.

A householder helps the monks and the poor, and nurses the sick. One-tenth of income should be set apart for helping the poor. The householder should be devoted to God with an aspiration for God-realization. He must work incessantly, and perform all duties, giving up the fruits of his actions to God. He must earn a living by honest and fair means.

Non-injury is the highest virtue. But it cannot be strictly practiced by a householder. If a vagabond enters the house and tries to molest a lady, a householder cannot keep quiet. He will give the vagabond a good thrashing and protect the lady. When someone is in danger, it is the duty of a householder to save the life of that person by resisting evil.

Knowing that his parents are the visible representatives of God, the householder must please them always. He must treat them with respect, love and sweet words.

Both husband and wife must love each other and be devoted to each other and always maintain perfect chastity. They should not touch another woman/man even with his/her mind. They should help each other in spiritual development. They must share the family responsibilities and bear adversities and problems with poise.

Both the husband and the wife must observe moderation in food, sex, dress and recreation. They must be pure in heart and lead a simple life with noble aspirations. As soon as one or two children are born, the husband and the wife must live as brother and sister, and lead a spiritual life.

They should bring up their children with love and educate them and help them to settle down in life.

If they have sufficient means, they must help relative and friends and poor people in distress.

They must pay reverence to the good people and ignore the wicked. They must do charity and contribute to the construction and maintenance of public amenities and fulfill citizenship responsibilities.

They must cultivate divine qualities like mercy, love, purity, truthfulness, non-injury, prudence, honesty, compassion, generosity, patience, tolerance and right judgement.

After fixing up their children in life, a householder can become a *vanaprastha*, either alone or with the spouse. They can stay in a solitary place or in an ashram, and do spiritual practice and service.

Vanaprastha. A vanaprastha is free from attachments and anxieties and concentrates on spiritual practices. This is only a preparatory step to *sannyasa.*

Sannyasin. The glory and freedom of a *sannyasin* can hardly be described. He/she only can cut off all sorts of attachments. He/she wears orange robe. The very color of the orange robe gives strength and purity.

If a person is endowed with spiritual tendencies and if due to some obstacles he/she was not able to realize the goal of life, he/she is again born in this world in good environment and continues spiritual practice. Only when there are subtle desires, one has to enter into the household life. If one has discrimination, dispassion and intense yearning for liberation, he/she takes *sannyasa* even while he/she is a *brahmachari.*

General Duties of a Person

You have certain duties and responsibilities according to your station in life. You have to evolve morally and spiritually by performing your duties in the right manner, living according to the divine law and rules of conduct. Acquire a thorough knowledge of right and wrong and act rightly. (*See* Chapter 13. Philosophy of Right and Wrong, *above*).

Do service to the society according to you outlook and capacity; serve the country and the world as well.

Some persons earn money by taking bribes and by other illegal means. When their conscience pricks them, they feed some poor people and feel that they have done a great duty. This is their idea of duty. Poor deluded souls! May God give them right understanding!

Morality and duty vary according to the circumstances. The Ruler will fail in his duty, if he does not punish the wicked. To kill a person who is taking away the lives of many is non-violence. However, a *sannyasin* should not defend himself even when his life is in danger. He is one who has no body and identified himself with the Self.

Morality and duty are relative terms. They vary according to the state of life, evolution of the individual, time and circumstances. Marriage is a contract in the West, whereas in India it is a sacrament or holy act. The duty of a soldier differs from that of a *sannyasin.* To kill an enemy is the duty of a soldier. To practice non-injury in thought, word and deed is the duty of a *sannyasin.*

Do your duty satisfactorily in accordance with your stage of life, without attachment. Dedicate it to God. Evolve quickly in spirituality. Keep the ideal of life before your eyes always. Attempt to realize the ideal with tenacity and attain success with God's Grace. The *Bhagavad Gita* says,

> "He from whom all the beings have evolved and by whom all this is pervaded, worshipping Him with his own duty, man attains perfection." (18.46)

You and the whole of creation have evolved from the Supreme Lord. The whole universe is pervaded by Him. By worshipping Him through the performance of your own duty, you attain Self-knowledge or perfection.

Unselfishness: Divine Love

When we begin to feel for other beings in the same way as we do for ourselves, then we begin to rise above the limitations of the narrow self, and at that very moment we have taken our first step toward unselfishness. **The end is reached when we realize that all living beings are equal to ourselves.** Jesus said , "Love thy neighbor as thyself," and "Love thy enemies;" but He did not preach,

"Love all living beings," as did Buddha. When a goat was going to be killed, Buddha came forward and offered his own life for saving the life of the goat. The goat's life was saved, and the man, who would have killed it, afterwards became Buddha's disciple. When we begin to cherish all living beings as we cherish ourselves, then the sense of "I ,me and mine" (or egoism) vanishes, and we see all creation as one on the spiritual plane. Therefore *Bhagavad Gita* says,

> "He, who sees the same Divine Self (Lord) abiding equally in all, does not kill the Self by the self, and so attains the Supreme Goal." (13.28)

This realization of oneness of the Self (Spirit) is the highest ideal of life. "It is the climax of unselfishness, says, Swami Abhedananda, brother-monk of Swami Vivekananda, "and it is identical with Divine Love, because God loves all creatures equally. His love indeed shines alike upon all,"[1] as does the light of sun upon all.

When this love or feeling of oneness awakens in us, we rise above all duty, and work through love. Love is a higher motive than a sense of obligation. All work performed through this higher motive of love becomes worship of the Lord.

With the awakening of this love, comes all knowledge. Divine Love and Divine wisdom are one and the same. They awaken God-consciousness and lead us to the experience of the oneness of all beings. One who sees oneness becomes one with God, as declared by Jesus, "I and my Father are one."

When we realize our oneness with God, and reach that state of God-consciousness, all our desires and duties are fulfilled, all the knots of our heart are cut asunder, all doubts cease forever. (*Mundaka Upanishad,* 2.2.8). We then transcend all the Laws of Karma.

Reference

1 *Doctrine of Karma*, Calcutta: Ramakrishna Vedanta Math, 1989, pp. 103–4).

21

Svadharma (Own duty)

Introduction

We have been created and prepared for special work. Each one is great in his or her own place. The world needs everybody and everything. Even a blade of grass is not unwanted. It has a purpose. God has never created anything that will be useless. So let us not try to imitate and compete with others and say, "I must become this, I must become that." Why can't you become you? Here is a story.

The clock

Once I heard some strange sounds coming from inside a clock. I was curious to see what was happening, so I peeked inside and this is what I saw.

The main wheel was criticizing a small wheel saying, "You silly fellow, running so fast. Look how majestically I move."

Then, the little wheel pointing to the balance wheel said, "Well, look at that fellow over there. At least I am better than he is. He just goes one way, changes his mind, goes the other way, changes his mind, and goes back again."

"Yes," agreed the main wheel, "You do seem better than he." And both laughed at the balance wheel.

The little balance wheel listened carefully to their conversation and thought, "well, if they both think my work is so clumsy, why should I do it? I will strike." And with that he stopped moving.

Suddenly, the main wheel and the little wheel also came to a standstill. The little wheel asked the big one, "Are you moving?"

"No. How about you?"

"No. How about others?"

"We are still."

"Let us call for an urgent meeting," said the main wheel.

Then, the balance wheel laughed and said, "Don't you see that we are all interconnected? We all do our own jobs, but there is one common purpose for all of us to show the time. We are equally important in our respective places."

The main wheel and the little wheel realized their mistake and asked the balance wheel to forgive them and resume his job. That he did, and all the parts started moving harmoniously, and the clock hummed happily as it gave the time.

Nobody is inferior; nobody is superior. There is a common plan and we are all just playing our part. If we keep this truth in mind and play our part well, then life is beautiful and smooth.

You do not need to copy someone else. If it is your temperament, it will come automatically. Everyone has something special. Each person is unique. Nobody can occupy your position. Do not put yourself down. If you believe in the Cosmic Will, you will discover that an unseen Hand operating through you.

A sensible person will attain perfection in his or her own duty and make it a worship. Whatever you do should be a sort of worship or service. That is the sensible way to live. The Bhagavad Gita says,

"Each person devoted to his own duty attains perfection. . . ." (18.45)

"He who from whom all the beings have evolved and by whom all this is pervaded, worshipping Him with his own duty, man attains perfection." (18.46)

"Better is one's own duty, though imperfect, than the duty of another well performed. He who does his duty ordained by his own nature incurs no sin." (18.47)

How do we know our own duty?

Svadharma

Svadharma or your own duty is determined by your temperament, inclination or disposition. According to that, you take birth in a particular family. It is not that you consciously choose your parents, but it is decided by your mental impressions of your previous actions. The Cosmic Law decides, "You have learnt certain lessons from the previous class. Now, for further study, go to this class."

When you follow your svadharma, you go into your work like a duckling into water. You are naturally drawn to a particular field or profession. But when you want to change, you use your ego.

"I do not like this. That person seems to have a better job. I also want to do what he does." But what will you gain? You have brought certain inborn tendencies with you. You have prepared for a particular situation, and if you change, you lose all that.

A carpenter's son, for example, can almost automatically become a carpenter. He does not have to consciously learn everything step by step. But if he decides that carpentry is no good and that poetry is much nicer, he has to begin anew. It is like leaving a well-built home and going out to build a new one. If you do that, probably very soon you will want another even better home, because it is based on your egoistic choice, not nature's choice.

But if without your even knowing, you are transformed into something different, then that is part of nature. It is not that you choose to reject this and accept that, but rather the outcome of this is that. You might have been a bitter fruit yesterday, but today you are sweet. The nature pushes you up. May be you are a carpenter, and you move into a yoga community. You start doing your carpentry as Karma Yoga and at the same time, go deeper into the Yoga practices. After awhile you might be called on to share what you have learned and become a Yoga teacher, but it is not that you reject the carpenter's life.

If you try to avoid your nature and do something else, it will be temporary. If it is your Svadharma to do something, eventually you will be drawn back to that. Even at the Ashram, many people think, "Oh, as soon as I move in, I will just sit and meditate for fifteen hours a day and probably just eat fruit and milk." But if they are carpenters, within a couple of months they will be doing some carpentry work; if they are gardeners, they will be working in the garden, as their Karma Yoga.

You revert because when you see things, you are prompted to do them. Something tells you, "Hey, I can do it; I should do it." If you are an accountant, you will start doing the books and end up as the Ashram accountant. But this accounting is different from the accounting you did before. The work is the same, but it elevates you to a different level. You are not doing it as karma, but as Karma Yoga. Before you were working; now you are worshipping while doing the same work. You do not need to change the work, just change the attitude. Have the worshipful attitude and do your own work. You have to learn to grow from where you are, not to simply stop your old life and begin something new.

Work without Attachment

To perform your duty properly, you must do it with dispassion. Once you lose yourself in attachments, you are affected by them and cannot function properly. If an electrician puts on gloves before handling a live wire, he can use it and not be affected by it. Mental detachment is a kind of insulation. You insulate yourself with the attitude that, "Nothing belongs to me, but I have certain duties in life." A bank teller handles millions of dollars. If he identifies himself with the money, he would call himself a millionaire. He never identifies himself with it, but at the same time, he has a duty toward it.

Detachment in action does not imply irresponsibility. Whatever you do, you are totally responsible for it. You have even more responsibility in selfless action than in selfish action. In selfish action, if you are irresponsible, it is your loss. But in serving others, if you are irresponsible, many people lose.

Detachment keeps your mind calm and serene. The moment you show any attachment, you put tension in the mind. An eminent surgeon can perform any kind of operation with ease, but for even a small operation on his wife, he gets nervous and calls in another doctor. A shaking hand can never perform an operation. An action is an operation, and you cannot operate on anything if you shake, mentally or physically. People are nervous because they are selfish. A selfless person need never be nervous.

All our mental disturbances are caused by selfish attachments. If you are not selfish, you will never be anxious or worried over anything; there will be no need to hate anyone or to be jealous, angry or disappointed. That is why all the religious scriptures say, "Do not possess anything; lead a detached life."

Say, "All is Thine," instead of, "Everything is mine." If you put a lot of "mines" around you, they will wait to explode. Your peace is constantly in danger of being disturbed. So change all the "mines" into "Thine," and you will be safe.

You may wonder, "If I am not to be attached to things and people, why should I do anything? What benefit is there in having or doing anything?" Here we should know that things are with us for our use, not to possess.

A secretary in an office is given a table, typewriter, pen and paper. She will say, "This is my typewriter." But when she is fired, can she take the typewriter and go? No. In the same way, we are all hired here to do certain jobs. In this big "office," God is the Manager. He gives us typewriters, cars, houses, spouses, children, and experiences according to our Karma. But when the time comes for us to be "fired," when the Divine Manager feels we have finished our jobs, we have to leave everything and go.

Has anybody taken his car to the burial grounds? You cannot take anything with you. You came alone and you go alone. In between many things are given to you. If you just use them and then let them go, your mind will never be disturbed.

Anybody who does his duty in life, renouncing all selfish attachment, as a service to God and humanity, is called a saintly or holy person, because his mind is always calm and clean. He is always happy. So lead a detached, dedicated life. Do your duty well, but never expect any reward for your actions. By loving service you can conquer the whole world. You can be a good friend to all. You can always be happy.

To attain liberation or Self-realization, everyone need not become a renouncer and go to a secluded place like a forest or a cave and do tapas or practice intense meditation. If you have an active temper, do your own duty without attachment, you will attain liberation. The following story of a pious woman and a butcher will illustrate this.

A Pious Woman, a Butcher and a Yogi

Once a spiritual seeker named Kausika was meditating under a tree when he felt something fell on his shoulder. He wanted to know the cause of the disturbance and looked up to see a bird sitting on the branch above. It was the bird's excreta he had felt. Immediately he became angry. "How dare you do this!" he exclaimed as he glared at the bird. And as he stared flames leapt from his eyes and burnt the poor little bird. "Aha," he thought, "I have really attained some special powers. My meditation has been fruitful."

At noon, as was his habit, he walked to the nearby village to beg for his meal. He stood before the house where he often got alms, but that day his tone was a little different. He called, "Give me some food!" Immediately the woman inside noticed the change. "Excuse me, sir, I'm busy right now, but I will come as soon as I can."

"Does not this woman know who I am?" thought Kausika. "How dare she make me wait!"

After a short while the woman came to the door with the food. "You know, sir," she said, "I'm not a bird for you to burn."

He almost fainted. "What did you say? How did you know what happened in the forest? I haven't told anybody."

"You don't need to. You reflect yourself clearly in my mind."

"You are not an ordinary housewife. What kind of sadhana do you practice? Do you have a special mantra? You seem to have much greater powers than I."

"I don't know any mantras. I'm just a housewife. I always take care of my sick husband who is bedridden. When you came I was attending him. That is why I asked you to wait. I'm doing my duty in taking care of my husband. God placed me in this position and I'm fulfilling my responsibilities as best I can. That is all there is to tell."

"Is that all you do? I want to know more."

"Please, I'm not a scholar. I can't say anything more. If you want, go to the next town and seek a butcher there by the name of Vyadhan. He will tell you more."

"A butcher? You really want me to go to a butcher?"

"He is the one to answer your questions."

Kausika was really curious by now and so he journeyed to the next town. As he approached the butcher shop, he saw a big fellow with a huge knife, chopping and bargaining, haggling with customers over every penny. "He looks and sounds like a demon," thought Kausika. "How is he going to teach me anything?"

He was considering leaving when Vyadhan looked up and called to him. "Ah, so you have come. The lady in the next village sent you. Please have a seat. I will finish my job soon and then we can talk."

Kausika was stunned. The butcher seemed to know everything. So he sat quietly waiting. He saw that Vyadhan was not an easy businessman to deal with. He was strict with his price; he never gave way to anybody. When everything was finished, he closed the shop and called to Kausika, "Come on, let's go home."

On the way, Vyadhan purchased some vegetables. "Please sit," he said, "I will just cook these vegetables and feed my parents. They're old and blind, too. I need to take care of them. But as soon as I am finished, we can talk."

A little while later Vyadhan returned and said, "Now let me make something for you to eat and then we'll talk."

"No, I am not interested in eating. My hunger is different. Please feed me with your wisdom instead. I don't understand anything. I used to think that by sitting under a tree and repeating a mantra I was doing sadhana. And I did get something from my practice. But you people are doing all kinds of things. You are a butcher and she is a housewife. Yet you seem to have achieved much more than I have. You seem to know everything that I have in mind, and probably much more, too. How is that possible?"

The Vyadhan said, "I believe in God. God created everything and everybody. As the life force, He functions through you and me and everything. We are all His gadgets. He is the main current. He has given me two elderly parents to care for. He made me a butcher and gave me this duty too. So I do my duty, knowing all the while that it is really God doing it through me. I take care of my parents and do my butcher's work. That is all I know. I am not doing anything for my sake; I am doing everything for the sake of others. I do it all as Karma Yoga, as service, so my mind is always calm and clean. There are no disturbances in my mind. You scholarly people might say I am a Yogi. All I know is that the truth is always clearly reflected in my mind."

If you do your duty with non-attachment as a service to others, your mind will become calm and clean, and you will realize the Truth.

22

Selfless Service (*Nishkama Karma*)

Introduction

Selfless service or action without desire for its fruits is Karma Yoga. It involves dedication of work as an offering unto the Lord. All beings are manifestations of God. So service to human beings and other creatures is service to God. Living in the world and doing selfless service with Divine consciousness is far superior to a life in a cave in seclusion.

Work in itself is neither selfish nor selfless. It is neutral. It is the motive behind it that makes it selfish or unselfish.

Motives

Some build temples and rest houses for pilgrims with the idea of getting their sins washed off. Some do some sacrifices for getting children. Some dig tanks and wells and construct schools with a view to getting their names remembered even after their death. Some give charity with the motive of being born as rich persons in the next birth. These are not selfless service. Actions are judged only by the motives. It is the selfish motive that binds you. So work unselfishly with dispassion, and without any expectations like reward, name, or fame. Forget your "self;" become nothing. Let your body and mind is used as an instrument by God for service.

Object of Service

Why should you serve the poor and needy and suffering beings? Service is a form of worship of God. It gives you joy. It purifies your heart and prepares you for attaining the knowledge of the Self. By serving the world, you really serve yourself. The Self in you is the same Self in all other beings. "The Lord dwells in the hearts of all beings," says Bhagavad Gita (18.61). By serving other beings you are serving God in you.

The goal of life is God-realization or Self-realization. Purity of mind and heart is indispensable for God-realization. "Blessed are those pure in heart, for they shall see God," says Jesus Christ. Selfless service alone – not selfish work – purifies the heart. Pure heart reflects the Divine Light within.

The nature of pure-hearted person is exalted and indescribable. He is dear to God. He enjoys unbounded peace and joy. The Bhagavad Gita says:

> "He who, abandoning all desires, moves about without longing, without the sense of mine and without egoism, attains peace." (2.71)

Thank God for giving you an opportunity to purify yourself by service. Be grateful to the person who gives you a chance to serve. Here is a story of *Three Questions* by Leo Tolstoy.

There was once a king who felt that if he always knew just when to undertake everything, and who were the right and wrong people to deal with, and above all, if he always knew the most important thing to do, he would never fail in anything.

The king proclaimed throughout his realm that he would bestow a large reward on anyone who would teach him how to know the right moment for every deed, how to know who were the most important people, and how not to make mistakes in deciding which pursuits were of the greatest importance.

Many wise people came before the king, but they were all in disagreement about the answers to his questions. Since there was so much disagreement, the king accepted none of their advice and gave no one a reward.

Finally the king decided to consult a hermit who was famous for his wisdom. The hermit never left the forest where he lived, and he received only the simple people. The king disguised himself as one of the common folk. He rode to a spot a little distance from the hermit's hut, dismounted, and left his horse and knights there to wait.

The king found the hermit digging a garden in front of his hut. When he saw the visitor, the hermit greeted him and returned to his digging. He was thin and frail, and each time he thrust his spade into the ground, he breathed heavily.

The king approached him and said, I have come to you, wise one, to ask you for answers to three questions: "How can I know which is the time I should attend to, so I do not regret later that it slipped past me? Who are the most important people, who should be given the greatest attention? What are the most important pursuits which should be undertaken first?"

The hermit gave no answer, but took up his spade and started digging again. "You have exhausted yourself," said the king, "Let me do that for you for a while." The hermit handed him the spade and sat down. After digging for a time, the king stopped and repeated his questions.

The hermit did not answer but rose, held out his hand for the spade, and said, "Now you rest and I will work." But the king went on digging.

Hour after hour passed. The sun began to set, and the king finally put the spade on the ground and said, "I came to you for answers to my questions. If you can not give me, tell me and I will return home."

The hermit simply said, "Someone is running this way. Let's find out who it is."

As the king looked up. He saw a bearded man running out of the woods. The man was holding his stomach, and blood rushed from between his fingers. He ran up to them and then fainted on the ground.

The king and the hermit found a large wound in the man's stomach. The king washed the wound and bandaged it with his own scarf and the hermit's towel, but the blood continues to flow. Again and again the king removed the bandage, washed it, and rebandaged the wound. When the bleeding finally stopped, the man regained consciousness and asked for water, the king gave him a drink.

The sun had completely set by now, and the air was quite cool. Aided by the hermit, the king carried the wounded man into the hut and laid him on the cot. The king, himself, was so tired from all this labour that he lay down on the floor and fell fast asleep. When he woke in the morning, he found the bearded man gazing at him.

"Forgive me," pleaded the man in a weak voice.

"I do not know you and have nothing to forgive you for," replied the king.

"No. You do not know me, but I know you. I am your enemy and had sworn to take vengeance on you for killing my brother and seizing my property. I knew you had come here, and I was waiting to ambush you. After some time I came out of hiding to find you, but your knights found me. They recognized me and wounded me. I escaped, but I should certainly have died if you had not cared for my wound. I set out to kill you, and you have saved my life. Now I will serve you as your most faithful servant and instruct my sons to do the same. Please forgive me." The king was happy to be reconciled with his enemy, and he forgave him and promised to return the property that had been taken from him.

Then the king went out to find the hermit ask the questions one more time. The hermit was in the garden sowing seeds in the beds that had been dug the preceding day.

"Once more, wise hermit, I ask you to answer my questions."

"But you have already been answered," the hermit replied.

"How have I been answered," demanded the king.

"If you had not taken pity on my weakness yesterday and dug these beds rather than going back, that fellow would have ambushed you. Therefore, the most important time was when you were digging the beds. I was the most important person, and the most important pursuit was doing good to me.

"Later, when the man ran to us, the most important time was when you took care of him. If you had not bound his wound, he would have died without making peace with you. Therefore, he was the most important person, and what you did for him was the most important deed.

"This is the answer to your questions. There is only one important time—the present. It is important because it is the only time we have dominion over ourselves.

"The most important person is the person is the one you are with at the moment.

"The most important pursuit is to do good to that person, because it is for that purpose alone that you were sent into this life."

Work through Love

Work incessantly, but do not do slave's work. Work as a master. Work through freedom. Work through Love. Love never comes until there is freedom. There is no true love in a slave. Working as slaves results in selfishness and attachment. Only when there is no selfish feeling, you are in a state of non-attachment.

Do you ask anything of your children in return for what you have given them? It is your duty to serve them and there ends the matter. In whatever you do for others, assume the same attitude, expecting nothing in return. Then your work will bring you no attachment.

You pay your karmic debts only by performing selfless actions. Without paying your karmic debts to the people among whom you live, you cannot attain freedom.

The Listening Mind

To know what help others really require, you must listen to them with a still mind, without judgment. The more deeply you listen, the more you attune yourself to the roots of suffering and the means to help alleviate it. It is through listening that wisdom, skill and opportunity find form in an act that truly helps. But more than all these, the very act of listening can dissolve distance between you and others as well.

Challenges to Service

Your personal identity—father and son/daughter, doctor and patient, server and served—often becomes an obstacle to the expression of our caring instincts; it limits the full measure of what you have to offer to another. But when you break through and meet in spirit above your separateness, you experience profound moments of companionship. These, in turn, enable you to reach deeper levels of loving-kindness. True compassion arises out of unity.

We feel cut off from one another, when we reach out to help or be helped and do not meet. Such moments are more painful. Despite the yearning of the heart, so often when we seek to care for one another, we feel far apart. Albert Einstein speaks about this challenge to service:

"A human being is a part of the whole called by us universe, a part limited in time and space. He experiences himself, his thoughts and feelings as something separated from the rest, a kind of optical delusion of his consciousness. This delusion is a kind of prison for us , restricting us to our personal desires and to affection for a few persons nearest to us. Our task must be to free ourselves from this prison by widening our circle of compassion to embrace all living creatures and the whole of nature in its beauty."

Service—a Great Teacher

Service is a great teacher. It shows your own limitations—your angularities, narrow self-images, reservations, etc. It also shows you your strengths as well, and you discover how those strengths contribute to genuinely helpful service. Each time you drop your masks and meet heart-to-heart, you reach out and understand others' needs. Each time you quiet your mind, your listening becomes sharp, clear and deep. Each time you are able to remain open to suffering, you sense a love in you. The dawn of pure love removes your sense of separateness and you start experiencing sense of unity. Then the mind and the heart work in harmony and barriers between us dissolve.

Selfless Devotional Service

Above all, service reveals you a larger vision of life. It is not an end in itself. It is a part of your spiritual journey. Service is a vehicle through which you understand the unity, the Oneness. The ultimate Reality is one only, called differently as Brahman, God, True Being, Supreme Spirit, Cosmic Self, etc. The entire universe and all the beings in it are just manifestations of that Reality.

When this awareness is dawn, compassion becomes an automatic response, and you find Divine Love infusing your service to others. This is the essence of selfless Devotional service. Service becomes an offering first to those you are with, but eventually to God in whom we are all united in love. Hanuman, the great devotee of Lord Rama is a great example of Devotional service. Every act he performed was a worship of Rama. Mother Teresa of twentieth century, bending down to hold a dying leper, saw there only "Christ in a distressing disguise." She gave herself to Christ, and through Him to her neighbor. In losing herself she found herself by virtue of divine transformation whereby we die in order to live. To Mother Teresa, the poorest of the poor and the destitutes were all children of God. Her love for them reflected her love of God.

Even the smallest acts of caring—taking a blind person to the place where he lives, making a sick friend's bed, welcoming a stranger, comforting a frightened child—can be a means of affirming the unity of life in love.

Placing service in a spiritual perspective in no way diminishes what you have to offer others through training, experience, special skills or sense of humor. Your particular talents and unique qualities are likely to manifest even more prominently when you are aware of your divine nature.

Thus you help yourself by helping others. Your service serves as a vehicle for your spiritual progress. As your practice continues, gradually your sense of unity becomes more and more real and ultimately you experience oneness with God. Then everything thereafter looks different. All is really One. You are in the world but not of the world. You are a part of what is formless though you are in form. You exist beyond polarities of positive and negative, dark and light, good and evil, pleasure and pain. In this vision of your Divinity selfless service becomes your inherent nature.

Grades of Service

Spiritual knowledge is the only thing that can destroy human miseries forever; any other knowledge removes wants only for a time. It is only with the knowledge of Self that the root cause of want is destroyed for ever; so helping a person spiritually is the highest service that can be rendered to him. He who gives spiritual knowledge to people is the greatest benefactor of humanity.

Next to spiritual service comes intellectual service. The gift of knowledge is far superior than that of food and clothes. Ignorance is death; knowledge is life. Life is of no value if it is a life in the darkness of ignorance and misery.

Next in order comes helping people physically. Therefore, in considering the question of helping others, we must not think that physical help is the only help that can be given. It is not only the last but the least, because it cannot give any permanent satisfaction. The misery of hunger of a starving person can be removed by giving him food, but hunger returns after a few hours. His misery can cease forever only when he goes beyond all physical wants.

The miseries of the world will continue to exist until their nature changes. Physical needs will always arise and miseries will always be felt, and no amount of physical help will cure them completely. The only lasting solution is to give people spiritual wisdom.

Helping Others to Spiritual Freedom

"The way to help others to attain spiritual freedom," says Meher Baba,[1] "is far different from the ways of rendering other kinds of help. To the hungry, food is provided, and they have only to eat it. To the naked, clothes are provided, and they have only to wear them. To the homeless, houses are provided, and they have but to dwell in them. But to those who are in the agonies of spiritual bondage, there is no ready-made means that can give them relief. Spiritual freedom has to be won by oneself, through watchful and unfailing war against the false self. You have to help others not only in launching upon the thrilling enterprise of attaining victory over oneself, but also in every step they take toward that attainment. There is no other way of sharing their burden."

You can help others to gain spiritual freedom and to come out of the illusion of duality only if you yourself do not lose this idea of unity while working for others. You have to win people to the life of truth; they cannot be coerced into spirituality. It is not enough that you should have friendliness and goodwill in your hearts. To succeed in your work, you have to bring home to others the conviction that you are helping them to redeem themselves from bondage and suffering and to realize the highest to which they belong.

Requirements of Spiritual Service

Meher Baba says that a spiritual worker should have an understanding of the following four points for rendering spiritual service:

1. Descending to the Lower Level. It may often be necessary for you apparently to descend to the lower level of those you are trying to help. Although your purpose is to raise people to the higher level of consciousness, they may fail to profit by what you say unless you talk in terms they understand. You have to adapt it to their capacity and experience. However, it is important to remember that while doing this you should not lose your own level of understanding. You have to change your technique as they arrive at deeper understanding.

2. *All-sided Progress.* Do not divide life into departments and then attempt to deal with them separately. Departmental thinking is an obstacle to integral vision. Thus, if you divide life into politics, education, morality, material advancement, science, art, religion and culture, and consider only one of these aspects, solutions to the problems of life cannot be found. But if you succeed in awakening spiritual inspiration and understanding, they will be active in all aspects of life. As a spiritual worker you have to aim at an inclusive and creative attitude to the individual and social problems of life.

3. *Wisdom from within.* As a spiritual worker you have also to remember that the spiritual wisdom that you desire to convey to others is latently present in them, and that you have only to be instrumental in awakening it. Spiritual progress does not come from without, but unfolds from within.

1. **Motivating to think.** As spiritual wisdom is latent in all, you should not be anxious to provide ready-made answers and solutions to problems. Motivate the people to think by posing questions to clarify the nature of the problem faced by people. Put them in a searching and questioning attitude, so that they begin to tackle their own problems. The questions that you may help them to formulate for themselves should neither be theoretical nor unnecessarily complicated. If they are simple, straightforward and fundamental, the questions will answer themselves, and people will find their own solutions.

Selfless Action–A Perfect Action

An act becomes perfect when you do it with all joy, without expecting anything in return. All other acts, however wonderful they may look, are still imperfect, because they will affect your mind. If you have a personal motive or if you expect a reward, you build up a tension even before you start. There is expectation and anxiety. There is fear of losing something. Instead, if the mind is kept free from any expectation whatsoever, and your action is done just for the sake of action, for the sake of others, then that action is a perfect one.

If the results of an action bring benefit to all people concerned, without bringing harm to anybody, then it is a perfect action. But if it brings harm even to one individual, or if it builds up a tension in your own mind, it is not a perfect action.

Sometimes even giving can cause harm to someone. If you give ten dollars to somebody who is standing at the door of a bar, you can not call it help. If a mother feeds her child all the candy it wants to eat, she is not really helping the child. So an act is judged by both the motive and effect.

Suppose you walk into a room and see someone cutting another person's arm with a sharp knife. It might look like a terrible act. But if you find out that it is a doctor lancing an abscess in order to save the arm, then even though it may look terrible, you realize it is a perfect act. On the other hand, if the same knife were being used by a scoundrel to hurt someone, it would not be a perfect act. So a little investigation is sometimes needed to understand the true nature of actions.

If you are not sure if you should do something, ask yourself whether you are doing it for selfish reasons or for the benefit of others. If it is for selfish reasons, you may go often wrong. But if it is for the benefit of others, you will never go wrong.

Often you are still selfish in a subtle way even though you think you are not attached to the fruits. If you insist others should be happy because of what you are doing, then you are still attached. You will build up anxiety that makes you unfit to serve. Instead, it is better just to think, "Well, I have done my duty to my satisfaction; I am not the destiny maker." If a person has done certain things and is destined to be unhappy for some time, you cannot make him happy however much you try. The satisfaction of having tried within your limit should be enough for you.

To be truly free, you must act without any expectation, renouncing both the good and the bad fruits of your actions. You might wonder, "Why can't I do something to gain some merit? Should not good results be sought?"

Whether acts are good or bad, they will bind you. The cause of birth and death is Karma, the result of your acts, whether good or bad. If you say, "How about the good acts?" it is like a parrot saying, "Take away this dirty steel cage and give me a golden one." It may look pretty, but it is still a cage. You are born as a result of meritorious deeds also. But of course it is not that easy to renounce both good and bad at first. So in the beginning at least, we are advised to overcome bad actions by doing things for the sake of merit and virtue. But ultimately, we must learn to act without expecting anything in return. That is Karma Yoga. We do everything for the sake of God or humanity. Whatever we do is done perfectly, as service to God, because we have no anxieties about future results. By seeking benefits in the future, we cannot live well in the present. It does not mean not to plan ahead; a little expectation can be good for your motivation. But do not expect some personal benefit; you will be easily disappointed and frustrated.

The joy of doing a work well is the best reward. Nobody can take that satisfaction away from you. If you wait to be satisfied by results, you are certainly going to be dissatisfied. If you ever feel disturbed or get excited with anticipation, know that you are not Karma Yogi.

The Karma Yogi acts without attachment to the fruits of his actions. He dedicates his service to God. As there is no personal motivation, he is free from all results. The Bhagavad Gita says, "Perfection in action is Yoga." Only selfless service can be perfect. When you do such service, you then you experience Yoga and attain supreme peace and joy.

Service after Realization

Realization does not mean termination of service. In fact the realized sages are more fit for selfless service than anybody else. Selfless service becomes an inherent nature of the realized sages. Sri Ramakrishna Paramahamsa gives a beautiful parable about this. Once a few people went to visit a garden, having been told that beautiful big fruit trees were in it. But the garden was completely surrounded by high walls, and they could not even see what was inside. With great effort one person managed to climb the wall and looked inside. He saw such delicious fruits that he immediately jumped in. Another person climbed up and immediately jumped in the same way. Finally, a third person climbed up, but when he saw it, he said, "My God, how can I jump in now? There are so many hungry people below who do not know what is here or how to climb up." So he sat on the wall and said, "Hey, there are a lot of fruits, come up. If you try hard you can come up like I have." He lent a hand pulling people in .

Such people are spiritual teachers. They guide others in doing spiritual practices for attaining Self-realization.

Reference

1. Meher Baba (1894-!969) was born in Poona, India in a family of Persian descent. He was a spiritual master who declared himself the avatar of God. He demonstrated the essential oneness of all life through the acts of love and service. He drew followers from many faiths and social classes.

23

Work as Worship

Work

Whatever you do is work—either physical or mental. Physically, you may be sitting quietly, but still mentally you may be doing a lot. So when are you not working? You work constantly, even unconsciously. Everything is work. Is work different from worship? And what is worship?

It is all in the mind. You think this is worship, and that is work. That is all. When you cook something for God, it becomes *prasad* (blessed food). When you cook something for yourself, it is not *prasad*, but cooking is the same. When you go round and round the temple, you are circumambulating, worshipping God. When you go round and round a cinema theater, you do not feel that way, but the walking is the same. The great saint Sankaracharya once said, "My puja (worship) should be a continuous puja. Whenever I walk, I feel that I am circumambulating Your shrine. Whenever I talk to someone, I am repeating Your mantra. Every word is a mantra; every word is a prayer." Swami Sivananda used to say, "You should have the magic wand that turns everything you touch to Gold." With right attitude everything becomes worship.

Worship

Work becomes worship when you understand it and do it with joy as a service to everybody. Otherwise, it becomes a burden. God needs work; that is why He created you, not for you to simply sit before an altar and say, "God, You are wonderful; all glory to You." He will say, "Nonsense, stop that and go and do My job."

God is omnipresent. Whatever you do to others, you are doing to God. So there is no difference between work and worship. You are working and worshipping at the same time. Even when you bathe, the scriptures say that you are washing the God within. When you eat, the food is going to the God within. If you think that way, then you are constantly worshipping and serving God.

There were many great saints who never even went inside a temple. For example, Thiruneelakandakuyavanar of Tamil Nadu (Southern India) was a potter. All he knew was how to make pots. He backed pots and pans for sale to provide him a living, and he set aside a few in the name of God, which he gave away free. He also backed alms-bowls for free distribution to the devotees of the Lord. This was the form in which he did service to fellowmen, and thus attained salvation.

Thirukkuurrippuththondar was a washer man in Kanchipuram (Southern India). He was endowed with a mind full of perfect love. He trod the path of righteous living. He washed with great eagerness the dirty clothes of devotees of the Lord. One day in a severe cold season, the Lord came up to him with the intention of conferring Grace to him. He assumed the guise of a great *Thapasvi* (saint) clothed in a very dirty garment. Seeing the approaching saint Thirukkuppuththondar went forward, received him with reverence. He prostrated at his feet. Then with joined palms, he said, "Please give me your waist cloth for washing. The *Thapasvi* graciously replied, "Though this dhoti is very dirty, I will not let it go on account of shivering cold. If, however, you could give it back before the sunset, take it with you for washing it. If you do not give it back, you would do great harm to this body."

The washer man received the cloth promising to deliver it before the sunset. He took it along with other clothes to the washing ghat. He washed the dirt out of the cloth, steamed it very well and was about to beat it again when rain began to pour down. He stood stunned, saying to himself, "Now, what shall I do?" He stood in the solitude with the hope that the rain might stop. The rain did not stop. And when night set in, he fainted and fell down crying, "Ah! I have failed in this small service to the great *Thapasvi* of shivering body. I have become the cause of the evil of making his body shiver in the cold." He decided to smite his head on the stone slab (used for beating the dirty clothes) and die. On his striking his head against it, appeared the hand of Lord Siva and caught hold of the head. The rain ceased and changed into a shower of flowers. The Lord appeared before the servitor and granted him immortality.

Nesar was a weaver by profession and a servitor of Lord Siva. He lived in Kambili, a town in Bellary District of Andhra Pradesh (Southern India). He dedicated the activities of his body, mind and profession to the servitor of the Lord. He wove dhotis and faultless loin cloths and gave them to the devotees of the Lord as an act of service to them and everyday worshipped their feet. Gaining merit by this act of service, he reached the haven of the feet of the Lord.

There was a barber saint in South India. Whenever he saw poor or sick people, he gave them a free shave. That was his service, and he attained realization just by that.

It is not what you do that is important, it is how you do it with what attitude. Do not think that only by sitting in front of the altar or by doing some chanting you are doing something spiritual. It is not even possible to sit and worship the whole day in front of an altar. Rituals are not that important, they are only there to mind you. May be that is how you begin, but it should not stop there. There should come a time when that spirit permeates your entire life.

Whatever you do should be done joyfully as a service to God. Then you do not even have to come and sit in front of the altar and do anything. You will always be happy doing things outside and feel that that is your spiritual practice. If you make a distinction between your spiritual practice and your work, then you have not grown up yet.

The *Bhagavad Gita* says, "Whatever you do, whatever you eat, whatever you offer in sacrifice, whatever you give, whatever austerity you practice, do it as an offering unto Me." (9. 27). Everything is doing. You *do* worship; you *do* meditation; you *do* asanas; you *do* walk; you *do* talk. Every action should be selfless; then you are a Karma Yogi. You are not even supposed to worship for yourself. You are not supposed to meditate for yourself. Even if you meditate for yourself, it is a selfish action.

Everything should be based on selflessness. Why should you meditate? To clean and calm the mind and make it strong so you can serve well. Why should you even eat? To have enough strength and vitality to serve. Then even your meditation and your eating become Karma Yoga. If you are living for the sake of everybody, serving God and His creation every minute with every breath, you are worshipping constantly. Work becomes worship and every act is a part of that worship.

24

Self-surrender

Meaning

Self-surrender means offering our body, mind, will and soul at the feet of God without any sense of ego. It is complete dedication of ourselves to the Supreme Spirit. Then, as Tukaram, a saint of India, sings, the self (ego) within us is dead and God is enthroned in its stead, and there is no longer any "me," "my" or "mine." It involves complete detachment to the objects of the world and our desires and prejudices.

Self-surrender is a state in which the thought of God runs in the mind in a ceaseless and continuous stream. It involves a total transformation in our attitude toward ourselves, toward the world and toward God. Is there anything that we can claim as "ours?" No. There is only one thing; that is God. Everything else – human beings, other living beings, objects of the world, the entire universe – all is God's manifestation. So it is foolish to think that we are separate entities and that possessions belong to us.

Perfect self-surrender is the culmination of spiritual life. It is the final step in the path of devotion. The devotee makes God the center of his life. As a river merges into the ocean, the devotee merges his small will into the Supreme Power that is the doer of all things. By taking refuge in God, by opening himself to the Divine Will, he sees that there are not millions of wills in the universe, not millions of separate minds, but only one Will, only one Mind. Like the leaves of a big tree, we are all parts of that One Force. God is not separate from us; the Will of God is really the will of our own higher Self. When we recognize this Force and align our lives with It, then our lives can begin to become integrated, focused and free.

The Divine Will manifests in the form of inner intuition. It is the inner voice that is often drowned out by other voices in the mind. But we have to learn how to hear it and how to obey it with grace of the spiritual Master, Guru. When we get the awareness that we are not the doers, we become a real instrument of God and God acts through us. "When you are acting in obedience to the command, in accordance with God's Will, the very power of God takes care of everything completely. It is both the path and the torch that reveals the path," says Gurumayi Chidvilasaananda, a living woman saint of India.

The devotee has no longer any sense of doership. He experiences inaction in action. He is not bound by the actions performed by his body and mind. He lives in the spirit of the following ancient prayer: "Whatever I do with my body, speech, mind, intellect and senses led by the *gunas* of Nature I hereby surrender completely to the Supreme Lord."

Self-surrender becomes perfect only after God-realization.

The Purpose of Self-surrender

We undergo suffering, because we are ignorant of our true being. The ignorance resides in our ego, our belief that we are separate beings. The ego veils our eyes, as it were, and causes us to dwell in ignorance. We are the Atman, the Spirit within ourselves. When we forget that we are the Atman, and identify ourselves with the body, mind and senses, then the sense of ego arises Then we lie on the sense-plane and become subject to the Law of Karma and rebirth. To fulfill our desires, we are driven to do all sorts of actions. And our actions, in their turn, involve us in the bondage of Karma. We get attached to what is pleasant, and dislike what is unpleasant. Out of this attachment and aversion grows a clinging to life. The ego clings to its ego-life, its sense of individuality.

Therefore, to find the real life, the life of our true nature, we have to transcend the ego. We shall never regain our inner peace and happiness, until we realize Brahman, in which we are rooted. The ego is the only barrier to this Knowledge of Brahman. Sri Ramakrishna used to say that when the ego dies all troubles cease. How can we kill the ego? We have to surrender ourselves to God completely and wholeheartedly. We must love God with all our hearts, all our souls and all our minds, and become absorbed in Him and forget ourselves in the consciousness of God.

Two Approaches

Have you ever seen the mother monkey jumping around with the baby monkey? The baby monkey catches the stomach of the mother and holds it with the forepaws and the legs. It holds her entire body, hanging underneath. The mother monkey does not even worry about the baby. She just jumps from branch to branch. It is the baby's duty to cling to the mother. Whenever the baby wants to go somewhere, all it has to do is to take hold of the mother, and then the mother jumps. When the mother jumps from branch to branch, which has the fear of falling down? The baby. The baby is depending upon the mother, no doubt, but it still depends on its own strength. Similarly, some devotees hold on to God. They say, "God, I won't leave you. I am holding on tight."

There is another animal that also depends on its mother for its movements – the kitten. Whenever the kitten wants to move, all it has to do is meow. The mother comes, picks it up by the back of the neck, and jumps here and there. When the mother jumps with the baby, who has the fear of dropping the baby? The mother. Both the baby monkey and the kitten depend upon their mothers for their movement. But in the first case, the anxiety is in the heart of the baby monkey, whereas with the cat, the responsibility rests with the mother. The kitten is totally free. Some devotees are of this type. Their surrender is absolute.

So there are two different views on surrendering to God. One group says, "You must be like a little monkey and hold on, and God will take you." The other group says, "Even to hold on, where would I get strength if God did not give it to me? So why should I worry? I am God's child." It is very difficult to have that kind of surrender to God, because the ego holds on to its supremacy. It will not give up that easily. There will be a big fight. You have to prove your capacity.

If you totally surrender yourself into the hands of God, you will feel, "God, I didn't plan to come here. You have sent me here. You have a purpose. I don't know what that purpose is. If I could ask you for anything, it would be this: Le me always remember that you are working through me. You are solely responsible for the actions. I am nothing. You are everything. Please let me not forget this."

Free will

You might ask, "Then what is free will?" Free will means you are free to take responsibility into your hands or to give it into the hands of God. If you take the responsibility into your hands, after going through all the problems, difficulties and turmoil, you will finally say, "I am tired, God, I can't handle this anymore. Let me take the back seat. You drive."

That happens when your ego has been completely cleared. Then, even though it might appear to others that you are doing something, you will know that you are not doing it. You are being made to do it. God's power will make you think, make you act. Your job is to simply allow it to happen. Then your life will be super peaceful.

Separateness

One who wants to retain his separateness as an individual cannot make a real self-surrender; his so-called surrender with that reservation does not destroy his ego-sense.

Once a young man came to Ramana Maharishi[1] in a disordered state of mind. He believed he had had a vision of God in which he was promised great things if he surrendered himself; he said he has done so, but that God failed to carry out His promise; and he demanded of the Maharishi, "Show me God and I shall chop off His head, or let Him chop off my head." Maharishi asked someone to read from a Tamil commentary on his own writings, and then made this remark: "If the surrender is real, then who is there remaining to question God's doings?" The young man's eyes were opened; he acknowledged his own mistake and left pacified. Self-surrender must be without any reservations and conditions; there is no room in it for any bargaining.

You achieve perfect surrender only when you give everything – body, mind, senses, ego and soul – without holding back anything. Your surrender should not be for any selfish motive, nor should you make a show of surrender. It should be genuine, real surrender. The Lord accepts the responsibility for the redemption of one who takes total refuge in Him.

Tests

God wants proof that you are totally surrendering yourself to Him. Tests will come. If you fail the tests, then your surrender is not complete. If you surrender is complete, no matter what tests come, you will pass them. Once you pass the tests, you do not have to worry about anything that happens in your life, because you are not responsible for your actions. Whatever comes, comes from God. Whatever goes is taken away by God.

It is not that easy in the beginning, because the ego will not allow you to surrender this way. Until you become the master of the ego and give yourself into the hands of God, the ego will create doubts in you. That is why Lord Krishna says in the *Bhagavad Gita*, "Flee unto Me for shelter with all thy being, O Bharata,

Total Surrender

One attains this highest spiritual stage only after prolonged struggle and intense spiritual practice. All forms of spiritual practice make the mind pure and fit for this total self-surrender.

Total self-surrender can come only when our "wings" are dead-tired like those of the bird in Sri Ramakrishna's parable:

A bird was sitting on the mast of a ship. It does not know that the ship was moving. When it suddenly realized that, it started flying towards the east, west, north and south, but found only limitless sea everywhere. Finally, when it wings were dead-tired, it came back and sat on the mast allowing itself to be carried by the ship.

In the same way, only a person, who has put forth maximum self-effort in the form of intense spiritual practices with great perseverance, can know what true self-surrender is. It is not enough to say simply, "All is Thine; thy Will be done." Self-surrender is an attitude of mind. One acquires it through the awareness that one's soul is a part of the Cosmic Spirit and that one's body and mind are instruments of that Spirit.

Surrender to the Source

According to Ramana Maharishi, self-surrender is surrendering to the Source of oneself. One's source is *within* oneself. To that source the surrender should be made; i.e., one should seek that source and by the force of that search merge into It. If the ego becomes merged into its source, the Self, then there is no ego, no sense of individuality, no individual soul; that is, the seeker becomes one with the source. That being the case where is surrendering? Who is to surrender and to whom?

Surrender—not a Gift

So self-surrender is not a gift of oneself to God. "The offering of oneself to God is similar to the offering, to a Ganesh-figure made of jaggery, of a portion of jaggery taken from the figure itself; for there is no individual self apart from God," says Ramana Maharishi. What is really meant by the term self-surrender is just the recognition by the devotee that he himself has no separate existence.

No Loss

There is no loss in self-surrender. You get from the Lord everything. The whole wealth of the Lord belongs to you. You become one with the Lord. That is why Lord Krishna, in the *Bhagavad Gita,* exhorts us,

"Fix thy mind on Me; be devoted to Me; sacrifice unto Me;

bow down to Me; having thus united thy whole self with Me, taking Me as the Supreme Goal, thou shall verily come unto Me." (9.34)

One Consciousness only

Upanishads, *Bhagavad Gita* and other scriptures say: there is only one Consciousness or Self everywhere in this world, and we are part of it. When through the grace of the Guru we begin to sense the all-pervasiveness of that great force, we realize that surrender to God's Will is not really a matter of choice. Whether we accept it or not, God's Will is already done. God will go on being the doer. Without His Will, not even a leaf moves.

> "The Lord dwells in the hearts of all beings, O Arjuna, causing all beings, by His illusive power, to revolve, as if mounted on a machine." (*Gita*, 18.61)

All creatures, according to their inherent nature, are activated by the supreme Being. Our past, present and future rest with the Lord. Let us play our part as best as we can as His instrument. Lord guides our destiny.

As we practice self-surrender to God, our ego is transmuted. The individual consciousness expands and finds a place for everybody within it. We develop equanimity or balance of mind in pairs of opposites like pleasure and pain, praise and blame, profit and loss, etc. We gain freedom from anxiety and tension, and thus attain peace with God's Grace.

Reference

1. A great Sage who lived in Tiruvanamalai in Southern India during twentieth century and attained Super-consciousness through Jnana Yoga.

25

Karma Yoga in Daily LIfe

Introduction

Karma Yoga involves selfless service, i.e., service without expectation of any personal benefit not even a word of thanks or appreciation. Such selfless service is possible as and when opportunities arise for serving others – needy neighbors, the sick, the destitutes, the poor – or when such opportunities are provided by social or spiritual organizations.

Such opportunities may not always available. That is, it may not always be possible to maintain the continuity of service. Moreover everyone has his own preoccupations, personal duties, family responsibilities and studying or working for one's own business or working for government or a private business firm. Hence it may not be possible to do selfless service everyday. Then what does happen to the practice of Yoga? Yoga needs sustained continuous practice. There will be no real progress, if Yoga is practiced occasionally as and when time is available for it, and working with attachments most of the time. This means you are a *bhogi* (enjoyer of karmic fruits) most of the time, but Yogi occasionally for a few hours. Is there a way out? Yes. Certainly indeed.

You have to make your entire life a practice of Yoga. How? By changing your attitude. Do not consider service to others alone as Karma Yoga. Treat all your physical and mental acts as Karma Yoga. From getting up in the morning until you go to bed in the night, you are doing actions and actions. Make all of them as your Karma Yoga. How is it done?

It is purely a matter of attitude. Know and realize that you are not the doer. Your body and mind alone are acting. Your real Self is a mere witness, silent observer. With this awareness if you do not identify with the action performed by your body and mind, you are not bound by those actions. Being an embodied soul, if you find it difficult to separate your Self from your actions, then there is another alternate. Consider yourself as an instrument in the hands of God. God is working through you. You are not the doer. Then all your work is divined. Your entire life is transformed into Karma Yoga with devotion.

"Selfless action" or "action without the sense of doership" sounds well in words, but when you try to put it into actual practice, you will encounter several difficulties. Egoism, old tendencies, desires and likes and dislikes may be lurking in the mind. They will disturb your peace. For example, while you are engaged in your daily activities, you may forget to consciously be aware of the non-acting real Self, and hence the sense of ego may rise to the surface; similarly when you do some service to another person, if he simply accepts your service without thanking you, you may get annoyed and feel, "What sort of a person is he? He does not have even the elementary courtesy of thanking a person who helps him." When you expect something—even thanks – in return, your service is not a selfless service. When such difficulties arise, you should make self-introspection. Reexamine or analyze the situation. "Am I the doer of actions? No, I am the actionless Self. So whatever be the action I do, I should not feel 'I am the doer.' I went to serve him, but got annoyed when he did not thank me. Why should I expect him to thank me? That is not right. Next time, I will do the service, but I won't look for thanks." That way you shape your mind well. By such analysis you can soon curtail the tendencies that disturb your peace. If you ignore the disturbances and simply try to continue your service, the problems will come back again and again.

Making mistakes is not really bad. We may fall down, but we should get up and walk. An intelligent person will learn something from a mistake, but a fool makes the same mistake again and again. Our failures should be stepping-stones to our success. All the great people, the sages and saints, have also fallen many times before they achieved their goals.

Sometimes the best test is what you call menial work. You often hear how great sages tested themselves in that way. To see if he had become proud after becoming a big Guru, Sri Ramakrishna went to the slum areas and washed the toilets with his hair. Jesus washed the feet of his followers. Great people have done this. So go, take the dirtiest, nastiest job. Remember you are not doing the job for the sake of yourself. It is easy to simply sit in a corner and meditate. But there is another form of meditation that is done in action. During Karma Yoga you meditate on what you are doing. You watch your feelings and mind. It is a program of mental training.

So if you are really interested in serving, you do not need to pick and choose what you want to do. Service is service wherever and whatever it is. Why you should think one is superior and the other is inferior? Would you say, "I will take care of my eyes, but not my feet?" Okay, you may take care of your eyes and wear nice glasses, but if you want to see something beautiful, the legs should take you there. If you do not take care of the legs, you can not even go there.

For a spiritual seeker, everything is beautiful. It does not matter what you do, where you do. From the shrine to the toilet, from the garden to the kitchen, whether you use a pen, or an axe, everything is equally dignified and all are a worthy field for your service.

Proper Attitude

Either do your service for others with the thought: "It is our home, our city, our world," or do it as the Lord's service: "All for Jesus, all for Allah or all for Krishna." It may be difficult to be always doing something for others. You may not respect and love everybody that much. May be you would wash the clothes of a person you love, but if you see some other person's clothing also mixed in, and if you do not like that person, you will say, "Oh, should I wash *all* these things?" You differentiate because you do not love everybody equally. So when you cannot do it for humanity, do it in the name of the Lord: "I am living in His home. Every foot of ground on which I step belongs to Him. Every tool I use belongs to Him. The kitchen, the garden, the office, the altar – all belong to Him. All are His children. Through everyone and everything, I am serving Him."

When you feel that way, you will work with even more zeal than otherwise. Because you are doing everything for God, you will have more interest than the person who works just for his own benefit will. There is a joy in doing something as an offering to God.

Only through service you can overcome your ego and petty limitations. That is the only way to kill your little self and to win God's blessings. If you do everything in the name of God, nothing will affect you. Do not use the will to carry unnecessary burdens. Instead, use your will to realize His Will. Then you become a beautiful instrument in the hands of God.

A man was carrying his child in one arm and a package in the other when the child said, "Dad, let me hold the package so that you will be carrying less." The dad laughed and gave the package to the child. Ultimately, everything is being carried by God, but childish or egoistic people still like to carry things themselves. The ego says, " I have to do it for myself." Fine, do it, and when you do it, you will become responsible for it.

That is what we call Karma. You do something by yourself, for your sake, and then you have to face the result. If you do something instead for God's sake, for the benefit of humanity in His name, without the least personal expectation, it becomes Karma Yoga. The benefit might come, but you do not expect it. There is no personal motivation, and you are free from the results, either pleasure or pain, virtue or demerit.

The World will take care of you

If you keep giving, the world will take care of you. If a cow gives milk, will not the cowherd take care of her? If she does not give milk, what would he do? Simply dispose of her. If a tree brings forth a lot of fruit, we take good care of it. We pour more water, nourish it, put a fence around it. But if it is not bearing fruit, we chop it down.

Some times when we first offer ourselves to God, we may run into problems. We may encounter suffering and losses. It is easy to be devoted to God when we are always gaining from God. If our business thrives, it is easy to love Him. But when we offer ourselves totally to God, and the next day we lose $ 10,000 in business, we then ask, "What kind of God is this?" The proof of our devotion is that we still love Him regardless of what happens. He may test us in the beginning.

But once God knows fully well that you are really offering your service and not expecting anything in return, once that is proved, then abundance will be with you. A person who is totally free from wanting will be wanted by God. He or she will be taken care of by God through friends and other people. You may not get proper care immediately, but it will come. God is never selfish. If you lead a selfless life, you are in God. When you have God, certainly everything else will be added unto you.

So do not think that by giving yourself completely you are losing yourself. When a drop gives itself completely to the sea, would you say that the drop loses itself? May be the drop loses its name "drop." It drops out as a drop, but it drops in to become the sea. So drop into that Cosmic Consciousness, and become one with the ocean of Divine bliss.

Treating Family People

When you practice Karma Yoga, someone in your family might say, "Hey, you are constantly doing for others. Don't you know that you have a spouse and children? They are missing your service." It is not that you should ignore them. But do not continually spend all your time, money and energy in serving one or two people alone. The husband might demand all the wife's service. She can simply say, "Sir, there are various things you deserve and need. I will certainly do them for you. But the rest of the time other people may need my service. Let me do some service to other people also. That is God's work." Your spouse should understand. Your life must be well divided this way.

A family is given to you by God. It is not really yours, but you have a responsibility toward it. If God has given you a few people under your care, you are their servant and caretaker. The mother is the servant of the baby and the husband is the trustee of both. Family members should not demand more than their due. Do the service to the family members without attachment. Dedicate that service to God. Serving them is also serving God. All are manifestations of God.

Karma Yoga on a Job

One may ask, "when I do thing for others, that is Karma Yoga, but when I work for an employer and get a salary, can I think of that also as Karma Yoga?" Yes. What are you going to do with your salary? Why do you want to live in a house? Why do you want to eat? Why do you even want to live? To serve others. Is it not so? How can you serve without eating? You have to fill up the tank so the car will move. You have to keep it tuned and washed. You have to have a garage for it. So, too, you have to have a garage and fuel for this body, and how can you do that without money? With money you equip yourself with enough energy to give energy back.

Even your eating and sleeping become Karma Yoga if you do them selflessly, thinking, "I am only keeping myself fit to serve others. If I am not going to serve others, I do not need to eat, I do not need to sleep, I do not need to have a house, I do not even need to live."

If you serve others and your salary is not enough to take care of your day-to-day expenses, you can even demand more. With that money, you are not just enjoying yourself. You are not simply satisfying your senses. You are just taking care of yourself and others who are under your care. That is also part of your duty.

You can say that you are getting something in return for your work. Even the so-called return goes back to others. So the entire life becomes Karma Yoga. You live for the sake of others, serving

God and His creation every minute with every breath. Your very work becomes worship. Your every act is worship of the Lord manifested as this world. You should understand your daily activities in this light.

Application of these Principles in Life

If you really apply these principles in your life, people will respect you. Employers say that they want to hire more Yogis. Selfless service melts even the hardest heart. Everyone has a soft corner somewhere. You find that place through your sincerity and love. Even the most dangerous and hateful person can be absorbed by love.

You may be operating a business and earn some profit. This is all right in Yoga, but your profit should not be your motive. Your motive should be the benefit of the community. The seller should put himself in the position of the buyer. The buyer should put himself in the position of the seller. Always recognize the need of the other person. Do not exploit. The confidence and goodwill of the customer is worth more than the money.

Businessman should do fair business. People who work in different industries and factories should work for the sake of everyone. Professional people should not just sell their knowledge, they should serve others well.

So do your work sincerely. Do it in a meditative way. Repeat your mantra mentally while you work. Love and salute your tools. Nothing is inert, everything has a kind of feeling. When you handle things, feel as if you are touching God. Feel that the work you are doing is the worship of God, that you are working for His sake, and that He is receiving the benefit. Then your work will become Karma Yoga.

Whatever is your position in a business, help that business grow. Whether you are a secretary, engineer, or manager, think of the welfare of the business and its customers. Consider how it can grow and best perform its service. Be scrupulously honest. Do not use the office facilities for your own personal purposes. If every Friday you use the telephone for your weekend appointments, you are not a good employee. In a way you are even stealing from the business. Always think of the benefit others should get.

If you are getting fifty dollars from your employer, your conscience should tell you that you are doing at least seventy-five dollars worth of work. Do not just look at the time and say, "I only have to work for eight hours." Even for those eight hours, are you really working? You should know. May be you can cheat him, but you cannot cheat the Cosmic Law. There is a big Divine computer that computes everything in your mind. Temporarily, you may be able to exploit that person and escape. He might not ask, "How much work have you done?" He will just keep sending you checks and everything will seem fine. But one day, all of a sudden, something may go wrong in your house or you may hurt your ankle. The doctor will feel both your purse and pulse, and all the money you cheated will go to somebody else.

There are five types of dealing, of giving and taking in life. If you take one hundred and if you give nothing, you are a thief. If you take one hundred and give fifty, you are a debtor. If you take one hundred and give one hundred you are a righteous person. But if you take nothing and give one hundred, then you are a saint or yogi. You should always examine your dealings and see to what category you belong.

Put others first. Only then will you really find peace and joy. The people whom we call great saints and prophets are the ones who gave themselves completely. We never worship a millionaire who had a lot of money and died without being of any use to anybody. If you want to live forever, if you want to be immortal, let every minute of your life be useful to the world at large. See that you bring peace and joy to everybody and no harm to anybody. That is the only way; there is no shortcut.

Common Problems

Sometimes, you may face problems in your work situation. May be where you are working now does not have the best atmosphere. In due course you can find more suitable work to fit your taste and temperament. But until then you can still work where you are and be a yogi. Until you find better work, do not leave your present one. Perhaps working in such a place could give you more mental strength., because following your principles while working in such an atmosphere is not easy. However, if your conscience makes it very clear that you cannot stay; no matter what your economic situation, you should not sell your conscience for money. You may have to say, "I am sorry, I do not want this job. Money is not really important to me, I can not do it." You may be without job for sometime; it does not matter. Your principles are important. Many people have even given their lives to maintain their principles. Can't you lose a few dollars? Which is more important – the money you get from the job or your mental peace? Money alone can not bring everything. Many wealthy people are living in misery. However poor you are your mental peace is more important. Shun as poison anything that will interfere with your peace of mind.

If you resent your work or your employer, it is better not to stay. The work, then, will not have any charm to you. You can not love the work if you can not love the employer. If you feel resentment analyze the cause. If you have a proper reason and can not get over it, do not continue there, because your negative vibration is carried with your work. If you type a letter with resentment, the letter itself will carry that resentment. Try to change your attitude, but if you really have good reason for resentment, then change your job.

Try to have a good and respectful relationship with your employer. Do not always think that the employer is out to exploit you. Without the employer, you would not even be working. It is his money and energy that started the place of work that provides jobs. You give energy, but for that energy, he gives you money to provide for your needs. Try to have some compassion and understanding. If he makes a mistake help him to correct it by passive means if you can, but never through hatred. That is Yoga in business.

Purposes of Actions

Actions are performed for three different reasons. Normally, the gross physical person will perform actions out of competition. He wants to compete to get more. That is where rivalry comes in, whether it is an individual or community or even a country. You have something, I must have a little more. When I have something, you will feel, "Oh, I must have a little more." It is this attitude that prompts competition.

This is just gross, physical, totally earth-bound. We should rise above that and begin to work in a cooperative way. Instead of "me," let us say "us." Let us work together. Another way is not even worry about yourself. Do not even think of sharing, but just give everything. This is dedication.

You might ask, "How I could survive?" If you keep giving, the world that receives everything from you will take care of you, because they will not want to lose your service. If they do not, then what are you doing here? If we can not be useful to people, we should say goodbye and go. Let our place be occupied by somebody else. That should be our attitude. So our actions should be, if not totally dedicated, at least cooperative, never competitive. It is mainly the competition that is creating all the calamities in the world. If we only we knew how to care and share, there would be plenty for everyone. Jalaluddin Rumi, an Islamic mystic, says, inside the great Mystery that is, we do not really own anything.

What is this competition we feel then,

Before we go, one at a time, through the same gate?

Remember that God is a first class businessman. What you give you get. If you give only ten per cent, you get only ten per cent of God. If you give twenty-five per cent, you get twenty-five per cent of God. Suppose you give one hundred per cent, what will you get? One hundred per cent of God. And your one hundred per cent is worth nothing; may be one hundred fifty pounds of flesh and bones, with some rotten stuff here and there. Yet with all this rubbish, it does not matter. God accepts your surrendering. You are not of much use to God, but he is a fair businessman: "He has given his hundred per cent to Me. What am I to do? I have to give My hundred per cent to him. Otherwise I am unfair." So He gives Himself to you totally. And when God comes to you, all that belongs to God becomes yours. The entire universe is yours. That is the secret of dedication.

The Experience of a disciple of Swami Satchidananda

Paul Condylis, a disciple of Sri Swami Satchidananda, narrates his experience as under:

> "I work very long hours, sometimes eighteen to twenty-four hours a day, seven days a week, under tremendous pressure. I hold a very responsible position supervising a major project and the many people involved in it; and I am daily, hourly, pressed by problems with the budgeting of hundreds of thousands of dollars and crucial timetables and deadlines. In a field known for its sensitive, emotional and volatile personalities, I serve as a producer-director for a company that does multimedia shows for business corporations. The show may be a simple presentation for a small meeting or a major production with film, slides, stage sets, and even live actors and musicians to demonstrate a product or service to a company's sales people or clients. Sometimes these projects can cost astronomical amounts of money, and they usually have insufficient time allotted for their production.
>
> "This causes much anguish, frustration, show of temper and unreasonable demands, which frequently cause participants to wonder why they should submit to such conditions: "Is it necessary to work in such terrible situations just for the sake of supporting my family?"
>
> "However, for myself, an additional ingredient makes the whole experience bearable – considering my work as a testing ground for my cherished beliefs. The principles of Yoga are tested at every turn in my work. Although there are times when I am disappointed in myself for not responding to problems and pressures in the way I would consider best, I am very grateful and pleased when I find myself responding with joy, patience and love to difficult situations.
>
> "In the midst of my righteous indignation over some incident, it is good for me to remember how effortlessly Swamiji can stand

over a broken septic tank as it leaks with a repugnant odor, approaching the task of repairing the tank and handling the ugly sewage with the same calmness and quiet attention that he shows in pleasant circumstances.

"This humbles me. If Swamiji can have such clear perception while standing over a septic tank, can I not do the same in the midst of my daily work? What is my job if not an opportunity to express charity, generosity, joy, peacefulness, selfless service, tolerance, patience, enthusiasm and love when it is hardest to do so. For what great accomplishment can it be to express those qualities when conditions are easiest?

"Sometimes I make it easier on myself when I remember who is really doing the work. If I think it is me, only me, it does not always go well. If I remember that God within is doing it all, then it is better, much better." (*Integral Yoga Magazine*, (X.2), Yogaville: Satchidananda Ashram, pp. 12-13).

26

Death

Introduction

The idea of death is something repulsive and dismal to the average person. He shuns to think about it. As he is ever seeking after sensual pleasure, he refuses to consider seriously the inevitability of death. What does death mean? Death does not mean total annihilation as ordinarily assumed; it simply means *change*, change of our physical conditions. The physical body is transformed into its elements, but the life continues. The current Western tendency is to dissociate death from life. The vision of death in Hinduism and Buddhism stands out in contrast to this modern view. In these earliest religions death is considered as an integral part of human life; it is not only an event of life, but also an ever present ingredient in the life process itself. The *Vedas* of Hinduism reveal a realistic and affirmative view of the world and a willing acceptance of the fate of death.

In Hinduism

The sages of *Upanishads*, which constitute the final and "knowledge" part of the *Vedas*, have discovered the real nature of human beings and the world. There exists an eternal changeless Self concealed beneath the constantly changing forms of existence that characterize both human beings and the whole universe. While the body is mortal, bound by death and subject to pleasure and pain, the true Self is "free from evil, old age, death, grief, hunger and thirst." The body is merely a support for the deathless soul.

The person who realizes the Self gains immortality, i.e., freedom from the wheel of births and deaths. A person who is ignorant of his real nature identifies himself with the body, mind and senses, and undergoes pleasure and pain. He is subject to the wheel of births and deaths. Death is a "way-station" between one life and the next one.

Approach of death. The *Brahadaranyaka Upanishad* describes the approach of death. The approach of death is heralded by the weakening of the body, mind and senses through old age or disease. The body groans as a heavily loaded cart creaks under its burden. The senses cease to operate. The principle of intelligence absorbs all the powers of the senses, and descends into the heart. The heart becomes lighted up and by that light, the pure intelligence (the subtle body) departs either through eye or through the head or through other apertures of the body, accompanied by the vital breaths. It enters into a new existence. The dying person's knowledge, past work (Karma), experiences and dispositions take hold of it. (4.3.35–36; 4.4.1–2).

Next, the *Brahadaranyaka Upanishad* describes the transition to another body:

> "Just as a caterpillar, on reaching the tip of a blade of grass, in moving to the next blade, draws itself together toward itself, so does the self, having cast off this body, and dispelled ignorance, in taking the next step, draws itself together (for making the transition to another body). And as a goldsmith, taking a piece of gold, turns it into another, newer and more beautiful form, even so this self, after casting off this body and dispelled its ignorance takes another, newer and more beautiful form like that of the ancestors, or of the heavenly musicians or of the gods or of other beings. (4.4.3–4)
>
> "That Self is Brahman." It constitutes everything that exists. It consists of all that is perceived and all that is inferred. What does a dying person become in the next life? The *Brahadaryaka Upanishad* answers this question:

> "According as one acts, according as one behaves, so does he

> become. The doer of good becomes good; the doer of evil becomes evil. One becomes virtuous by virtuous action, bad by bad action. . . . A person consists of desires. As is his desire so is his will; as his will, so is the deed he does, whatever deed he does, that he attains." (4.4.5)

A human being is a bundle of desires, and desire is the root of empirical existence.

When does Death end? With the death of the body, all the faculties of the mind, memories of past experiences and all the fruits of past actions unite with the subtle body. It is this subtle body that serves as the vehicle for transporting a person's dispositions and the fruits of unexhausted deeds (Karma) from one life to the next. When one becomes free from desires, then the inner Self is released from the bonds of rebirth and death and goes to Brahman by becoming Brahman. Note what the *Brahadaryaka Upanishad* declares:

> "When all the desires are cast away, then does the mortal become immortal and attains Brahman in this very body." (4.4.7)

The person who is free from desires realizes Brahman even here. What the blind needs is to receive sight. Sight is not change of place or transporting into another world. So also one need not wait for the death of the body to become free. Freedom is the cessation of ignorance. He in whom desire is stilled becomes free and suffers no rebirth. He, who identifies himself with the body under the influence of the desires and past work, is embodied and mortal. When he becomes disembodied he becomes immortal, as he is no longer committed to embodiment.

The *Bhagavad Gita* symbolizes the spirit of Hinduism. It introduces for the first time the Path of Devotion (*Bhakti Yoga*) and integrates the Path of Action (*Karma Yoga*), the Path of Knowledge (*Jnana Yoga*) and the Path of Devotion as a means of liberation. It affirms, "None can ever remain for even a moment without performing action; for, everyone is made to act helplessly indeed by the forces (*gunas*) of Nature." (3.5). But the actions themselves do not determine their outcome. Rather it is the attitude and motive that is crucial. Actions performed for selfish purposes with attachment to their fruits lead to the bondage of Karma. On the other hand, Selfless actions or actions performed without any personal desire and without expectation of reward do not bind the doer to Karma. Death is conquered and immortality is attained by performing actions as a form of worship of the Lord without attachment. (3.19)

Death is not something to be grieved. The *Bhagavad Gita* declares: "The wise grieve neither for the living nor for the dead." (2.11). Those who are endowed with the knowledge of the Self are wise. They grieve neither for the living nor for the dead, because they know very well that the Self is immortal and unborn. They also know that there is no such thing as death, that it is merely a separation of the subtle body from the physical. The five elements of which the body is composed return to their source. Just as the Self passed unchanged from childhood to youth and from youth to old age, so also does it pass unchanged from one body to another. So the wise men do not grieve for the dead. (2.13). What is death after all? The *Bhagavad Gita* says, "Just as a person casts off worn-out clothes and puts on new ones, so also the embodied soul casts off the worn-out body enters a new one." (2.22). "Certain is death for the born and certain is birth for the dead." (2.27). This is the inexorable Law of Nature. So one should not grieve over the inevitable event. "The Self, the indweller in the body of everyone, is always indestructible. . . ." (2.30). The body of any creature may be destroyed but the Self dwelling within it cannot be killed. Therefore, one should not grieve for anyone.

What determines the next Birth? What is the state one attains after death? The *Bhagavad Gita* gives a specific answer to this question:

> "Whosoever, leaving the body, goes forth remembering Me (Lord) alone at the time of death, he attains My Being, there is no doubt about this." (8.5)

"Whosoever at the end leaves the body, thinking of any being, to the being only does he go, because of his constant thoughts of that being." (8.6)

"At the time of death, with unshaken mind, endowed with devotion and by the power of Yoga, fixing the whole life-breath in the middle of the two eyebrows, the Yogi reaches that Supreme Lord." (8.10)

"Having closed all the gates, confined the mind in the heart and fixed the life-breath in the head, engaged in the practice of concentration, uttering the monosyllable OM—the Brahman—and remembering Me, he who departs thus, leaving the body, attains to the Supreme Goal." (8.12–13)

"I (Lord) am easily attainable by that ever-steadfast Yogi who constantly and daily remembers Me, not thinking of anything else." (8.14)

The last thoughts of a dying person determine his next birth. The most prominent thought of one's life occupies the mind at the time of death.

If you constantly think of God during your lifetime, you will remember the thought of God alone even at the time of death, and you will attain God-realization. If you think of your pet dog at the time of death, you will be born as a dog.

Everyone has a definite outlook on life, definite character, temperament, taste, disposition and attitude. This is all due to his past experiences that have left their indelible impressions in his subconscious mind. The ordinary person always thinks of his body and its physical needs. He seeks happiness from perishable objects of senses. Desires are endless. He cannot gratify them in one lifetime. At the time of death the most prominent cherished desire comes to his mind. That desire will become very prominent in his next birth.

A Yogi, on the other hand, constantly meditates on the Self or on God throughout his life, so he will think of God at the time of his death and will go to God. Remembering the Lord throughout one's life is the easiest way of attaining Him.

In Buddhism

In Buddhism, there are several approaches to understanding of death. Death is the key that unlocks the seeming mystery of life. It is part of the process of life.

Contemplation of Death. It is the contemplation of death that softens the hardest of hearts, binds one to another with cords of love and compassion, and destroys the barriers of caste, creed and race among the people. The contemplation of death destroys the infatuation of sense-pleasure and vanity; it gives balance, strength and steadiness to the erratic human mind. Hence Buddha commended to his disciples the practice of mindfulness regarding death.

The contemplation of death yields several benefits. The disciple who practices this is always vigilant, takes no delight in any form of existence, gives up hankering after life, and censures evil doings. The contemplation of death thus purifies the mind and removes the fear of death.

Karma. What is the cause of death? The cause of death is not old age, disease or accident as ordinarily thought. It is the Karma (*Kamma* in Pali) that determines the time and mode of death of a person. It sees to it that each person gets in life what he deserves as per the result of his own past actions. Each person weaves his own web of fate. He is the architect of his own destiny.

Law of Aggregates. Another approach to the understanding of death is through the Law of Aggregates (*Sankharas*). "All things in this world," says Buddha, "are aggregates or combinations." The human body is only a name for a combination of changing energies, and the mind is a name for succession of thoughts. The psycho-physical combination called "man" is not an entity except by way of conventional speech. When we say, "a car moves or a man walks," it is correct only figuratively. Actually, in the ultimate sense there is only a movement or walking. Hence it has been said in the Buddhist scripture *Visuddhi Magga*:

> "There is no doer but deed. There is no experiencer but experience.

Constituent parts alone roll on. This is the true and correct view." This analysis reveals that there is no person but only a process. Accordingly there is no person who dies, but there is only a process of dying; moving is a process, walking is a process, so dying is a process. It is indeed a revelation. With the dawn of this realization, will disappear all worries and fears regarding death. In our ignorance we are used to believe that there is some subtle "ego" or "soul" behind all our actions and thoughts. We fail to realize that the ego-feeling within us is nothing more than the simple changing "stream of consciousness" as described by the American psychologist William James. If one can train himself to reflect on these lines, he is gradually gives up the habit of identifying himself with his bodily and mental processes; he then gradually replaces that habit by a frequent contemplation of *anatta* (this does not belong to me). When one thus ceases to hug the ego-delusion, there is complete detachment of the mind from such allurements. Then shall one be able to face the phenomenon of death with fortitude and calm.

The Law of Change. In addition to the Law of Karma and the Law of Aggregates, the third great law, the Law of Change, can also assist us to form a correct view of death. Nothing in this world is stable. Everything is changing. The change may be perceptible or imperceptible. Growth and decay are due to the Law of Change. It is the process of change that causes color to fade, iron to rust, and wood to rot. The tendency to change is inherent in all things. The elements of the world – air, water, earth and fire – are subject to the Law of Change. So the human body that is formed of the same elements must necessarily be subject to the Law of Change. In fact, science has shown that the cells in the body are going on changing constantly. For one who is familiar with the Law of Change, death will appear as something to be expected.

The Law of Conditionality. We can study death also from the angle of Law of Conditionality, which is related to the Law of Change. Everything is not only made up of several things, but also conditioned by several factors. Conditioned by ignorance, activities arise; conditioned by sensation, craving arises; and so on. In the same way, depending upon past actions, present birth arises. The actions of the past are mental energies. They are potent enough to create the conditions for the being to be reborn in an appropriate place.

What does Travel. What is that travels from one existence to another? The karmic energies travel or do their resultant forces travel? Or does consciousness itself travel? No. None of these travel, but the karmic energy of actions performed is a tremendous force or power that makes its influence felt. To effect this influence, distance is no far. No physical contact is necessary for the mind to influence matter. Sir William Crooke, in his Edinburgh lectures on mental science has said, "It has been proved by experiment that by an act of will the mind can cause objects such as metal levers to move."

In other sphere of existence, we are employing a figure of speech when we say that Karma travels or that energy travels. Nothing travels from one life to another. It is just a process of one life to another. It is just a process of one condition influencing another. The karmic energies of outstanding human activities are so powerful that they condition the formation of an embryo in another place and give it consciousness. The embryo inherits the impressions of the past experiences of the dying person.

We have thus studied death from several angles. From whatever angle we look at death, it is an integral part of the process of life. Death is like the break up of an electric bulb. The light is extinguished but not the current, and when a fresh bulb is fixed the light reappears. Similarly there is a continuity of life current; the death of the present body does not extinguish the current of karmic energy that will manifest itself in an appropriate fresh body. Thus the dying person is drawn to an environment, good or bad, that he has created for himself by his thought, word and deed, for on these depend the nature of one's future life. Every death is part of the endless series of births and deaths through which one passes. Why should one fear the one death?

The Law of Becoming. There is yet another law known as the Law of becoming, which is a corollary to the Law of Change. Not only is everything changing, but also the nature of that change is a process of becoming something else.

Biology says that the human body undergoes a continual change, all the cells composing the body being replaced every seven years. According to Buddhism, changes in the body are taking place every moment. At no two consecutive moments is the body the same. The body is thus dying and re-living every moment of our existence.

The *Visuddhi Magga*, a scripture of Buddhism, says, "Just as a chariot wheel, when it is rolling, touches the ground at one point only of the circumference of its tire, so too the life of living beings lasts only for a single conscious moment. When that consciousness ceases, the being is said to have ceased." Thus we see that at every moment of our lives we are dying and being reborn. This being so why should be dread just one particular moment of death, the moment that marks the end of this existence?

The process of becoming continues into the series of future existence, because there is a continuity of consciousness. Life is a process of grasping and becoming, and death is just a change in that process. What does cause grasping? Where there is thirst to live, there is grasping. It is this thirst, this desire, this will-to-live that causes grasping. The karmic energy resulting from this thirst is ever in search of fresh conditions for its continued existence. At the moment of the death of the body, that pending desire-energy, that residuum of Karma seeks a fresh habitation where it can sustain itself. Thus proceeds the continuous flux of life.

Dying Moment. The physical condition of a dying person is so weak that his mind lacks the power to choose its own thoughts. Hence, the memory of some powerfully impressive event of the dying person's life will force itself upon the threshold of his mind. This terminal thought can be one of three forms:

1. It can be the thought of some powerfully impressive act done, that now surfaces the mind.
2. The powerfully impressive act of the past may come to the memory by way of a symbol of that act. For instance, if he

had stolen money from a safe, he may see the safe.

3. The powerfully impressive act of the past may come to the memory by way of a sign or indication of the place where he is destined to be reborn by reason of such act.

This last thought-form is most important since it fashions the nature of his next life. In general the type of action that one habitually performed or his strongest cherished desire becomes the last active thought. When any of the foregoing three types of Karma is not present, one of the accumulated reserves of the endless past is drawn out.

After Death. What does happen after death? No sooner has the death-consciousness in the dying person passes away than rebirth consciousness arises. At the moment of rebirth through the contact with the outer world, the sub-conscious state becomes conscious mind. From rebirth onwards activity again comes into play propelled by desire. Thus proceeds the onward course of the life-flux.

To one who understands this life process, there is no more reason to grieve at death than at life. Both life and death are part of the same process. To him birth is death and death is birth. An appreciation of the Law of Conditionality will reveal to him the importance of living his life well. When he has lived his life well, death is the birth of greater opportunities to live a still better life.

The Parable of Mustard Seed. The doctrine of the inevitability of death is beautifully brought out in one of the famous Buddhist stories, the "Parable of the Mustard Seeds." A woman's only child died. Her grief was so great she clung to the dead body, not allowing it to be cremated. Holding the dead child firmly to her body, she went from house to house inquiring for some medicine that would bring back life to her child. She was directed to Buddha. He asked her to get a pinch of mustard seeds, but it should be only from a house where no death had taken place. She went from house to house. She could not find a house where no death had taken place. She heard the word "death" echoing from every house. She realized the inevitability of death. She buried the dead child and went back to Buddha with peace of mind and became his devotee.

The essence of the Buddhist teaching about death is expressed beautifully in a sermon by the famous Zen Master Dogen of the thirteenth century:

> To find release you must begin to regard life and death as identical to *Nirvana* (Liberation), neither loathing the former nor coveting the latter. It is fallacious to think that you simply move from birth to death. Birth, from the Buddhist point of view, is a temporary point between the preceding and succeeding; hence it can be called "birthlessness." The same holds for death and deathlessness. In life there is nothing more than life, in death nothing more than death; we are being born and dying at every moment.

27

Transmigration

Introduction

The doctrine of transmigration is inseparably connected with that of Karma (For details, *see* Chapter 10. The Doctrine of Karma, *above*). Transmigration or metempsychosis means the process by which a soul, after the death of the body, leaves the body and enters into another body (i.e., reborn) whether animal, human or celestial. It takes place repeatedly in a countless series of births and deaths, until the soul attains liberation, freedom from bondage. The soul's course in the wheel of births and deaths (*samsara*) is determined by its actions in every life.

The embodied soul (*jiva*), due to its ignorance, identifies itself with the body, mind and senses, and thus it is engulfed by desire. Desire produces action (karma) and karma leads to bondage and rebirth. This has been going on from beginningless time. In the course of its journey through *samsara*, the soul gains experience and knowledge through purification and spiritual practices, and ultimately attains freedom from bondage or liberation (*moksa*). (*See* Chapter 37. Bondage of Karma and 39. Freedom from Karma and Rebirth, *below*).

The theory of transmigration presupposes the existence of the soul as an entity that lives even when the gross material body is dead. Buddhism accepts transmigration but does not believe in the existence of soul. It conceives that consciousness along with the impressions of the accumulated actions passes into a new body. The materialistic thinkers do not accept the theory of transmigration.

The modern scientists and agnostics who accept the theory of heredity do not believe in the theory of transmigration. But we shall find that the theory of transmigration is much more rational than that of heredity.

Hinduism

The notion of transmigration and reincarnation is a pivotal aspect of the general socio-religious belief system in India. In the Hindu religious tradition and culture, the concept of transmigration is an inseparable part of the doctrine of Karma or the Law of Action and Reaction. Human souls are bound by this irresistible law. Their future reincarnation does not depend upon their free choice, but it is determined by the nature of their thoughts and actions of their previous lives. As one life is not enough to gain experience in all the stages of evolution, successive rebirths become necessary to progress and fulfill the ultimate purpose of earthly life. Prof. Huxley says, "None but hasty thinkers will reject it on the ground of inherent absurdity. Like the doctrine of evolution itself that of transmigration has its roots in the world of reality." The doctrine of transmigration has played a dominant role in shaping the ethics and ideologies of the people of India. Thus India and the cultures influenced by her are dominated by the notion of *samsara,* the wheel of births and deaths.

In the Upanishads. The weary round of *samsara* was not part of *Vedic* ritualism. The notion seems to have evolved in the post-*Vedic* Aranyaka literature and developed more fully in the *Upanishads*. The fact that the idea was taken for granted in Jainism and Buddhism suggests that by the sixth century B.C. it was already widespread in India.

The *Upanishadic* sages were influenced by *non-Vedic* ascetic teachers, *munis* and *sramanas*, and they attempted to harmonize *sramanic* ideas and *Vedic* tradition. The *Upanishads* teach the moral doctrine of karma and the notion of transmigration, the idea of unity of Atman and Brahman, and the highest ideal of Self-realization through spiritual practices. They also deal with the mystic experiences of the ancient sages.

The theory of rebirth goes along with the moral Law of Karma, which states that one has to reap the fruits – good or bad – according to the nature of one's deeds; as you sow so you must reap. The *Katha Upanishad* states:

> "Some souls enter the womb for embodiment; others go into inorganic objects according to their deeds and according to their thoughts." (2.2.7)

In the *Brahadaranyaka Upanishad*, it is stated that after death the different elements of the body return to their source, and the soul goes into the space. Karma remains. One becomes good by good action, and bad by bad action. (3.2.13). There is considerable moral element in the *Upanishadic* doctrine of Karma The doer of good becomes good. The doer of evil becomes evil. One becomes virtuous by virtuous action, bad by bad action. The nature of actions depends upon his desires. The *Brahadaranyaka Upanishad* affirms,

> "A person consists of desires. As his desire so is his will; as his will so his deed, and whatever he does that he attains." (4.4.5)

The *Brahadaranyaka Upanishad* compares the idea of transmigration of self with a goldsmith's work:

> As a goldsmith, taking a piece of gold, turns it into another, newer and more beautiful shape, so does this self, after having thrown away this body and dispelled its ignorance, make unto himself another newer and more beautiful shape, whether it be like that of the Fathers, or of the Gandharvas, or of the gods, or of Brahma or of other beings." (4.4.4)

A person is bound in the chain of birth and death by his own selfish actions. Every little thought or action has its effect on his destiny. The sages of *Upanishads* believed that the thoughts and deeds of one earthly life might bear fruit in the next life. The *Chandogya Upanishad* states:

> "Those whose conduct has been good, will quickly attain a good birth, ... But those whose conduct has been evil, will quickly attain an evil birth, the birth of a dog, or a hog, or a *candala.*" (5.10.7)

Those, who know the reality of Karma and rebirth, and attain God-realization are freed from Karma, and attain liberation. The *Svetasvatara Upanishad* declares:

> "When God is known, all fetters fall off, the sufferings are destroyed, and birth and death cease. By meditating on Him, there is the third state; on the dissolution of the body, universal Lordship; being alone, his desire is fulfilled." (1.11).

This verse describes the different sides and stages of liberation. Negatively it is freedom from birth and death; positively it is oneness with *Isvara*, so long as there is the manifested world and oneness with *Brahman* when the manifested world ceases to exist. A distinction is also made between meditation, which leads to lordship, and *jnana* or wisdom, which leads to liberation. So long as the cosmic process continues, the Personal God presides over it and freed individual becomes a co-worker with him. When the cosmic process terminates, the Personal God lapses into the Absolute and so does the freed individual. The *Mundaka Upanishad* also states:

> "The knot of the heart is cut, all doubts are dispelled, and all his deeds (and their effects) terminate, when He is seen – the higher and the lower. (2.2.9)

When a person sees the Real, which comprehends himself, he asserts the non-reality of all that is opposed to it. The evil in him through his past bad acts falls away. With this change in his nature he attains liberation.

The descriptions in the *Brahadaranyaka Upanishad*, (6.2.15f) (also *Kausitaki Upanishad*, 1.2f, and *Mundaka Upanishad*, 1.2.11) exhibit a somewhat mythological character. Those who achieved perfection and have realized their true Self go, after death, along the way of sun; they enter the abode of Brahman never to return again. Those who have not achieved the ultimate goal of Self-realization but have lived a life of sinless piety and devotion go along the path of the moon to the world of moon where they become rain and subsequently food; gods feed upon them, and when they pass away from them, they start on their journey to be reborn as human beings. Thus they rotate.

What does Transmigrate?

What is it that transmigrates? The *Upanishads* call it *jive* or *purusa*.

Jainism. In Jainism the living entity is called *jiva* or soul and it is doomed to unending rebirths as long as it is covered by *karma* which is considered as a kind of fine matter. The generation of new *karma* must be stopped and the accumulated *karma* already present must be removed if liberation is to be attained. The force that leads the soul to rebirth is known as the *karmanasarira*, i. e., the body of *karmas*. It is a mixture of soul and matter. It is the very seed of rebirth and regulates one's destiny.

Buddhism. According to the Buddhism, the human personality is a combination of five aggregates, viz., *rupa, vedana, samjna, samskara* and *vijnana*. This combination is formed according to the actions of the past life. At death, *vijnana* (consciousness) with the resultant *karmas* remains and takes new birth.

Theosophy. According to the Theosophy, when the physical body dies, the astral body flies away to another state. The astral body is made up of matter of very fine texture as compared with the visible body, and has a great tensile strength. It is composed of electrical and magnetic matter. The astral body retains all the memories of the life lived by the dead person and his passions and desires, and thus reflexively and automatically can repeat what he knew, said, thought and saw. It has a life period of its own and exists in the world of desire (*kama loka*). The astral person in *kama loka* is a mere shell, devoid of soul and mind, without conscience and also unable to act unless vivified by outside forces. He may stay in *kama loka,* passing the period in great suffering, or in a dreamy sort of sleep, according to his particular desire while on earth.

Here in *kama loka* come into operation the *skandhas*, the aggregates that make man. During his stay in *kama loka*, the real being has to struggle to divest himself from the lower *skandhas*; as sheds them, the being falls into a state of unconsciousness which precedes the change into the next stage called *devachan* (the place of the gods). From this the real being, the triad of soul, intellect and mind emerges into the state of *devachan* where the soul enjoys felicity. The self in *devachan* is devoid of moral body. It exists in that state "for years of infinite number proportionate" to the unexhausted psychic impulses originated in earth life.

Devachan, then, is an interlude between birth in the world. The Law of Karma which forces us to enter into the world being ceaseless in operation and also universal in scope, acts also on the being in *devachan*, for only by the force or operation of Karma are we taken out of *devachan*. "The whole period allotted by the soul's forces," says William Q. Judge, "being ended in *devachan*, the magnetic threads that bind it to earth begin to assert their power. The Self wakes from the dream, it is borne swiftly off to a new body and then, just before birth, it sees for a moment all the causes that led it to *devachan* and back to life it is about to begin, and knowing it to be all just, to be the result of its own past life, it repines not but takes up the cross again."[1]

Tibet. The application of the doctrine of rebirth in Tibet is shaped by one particular form of Buddhism. Competent sages identify incarnations of a high order by determining into which newborn baby a recently diseased personage has passed. The succession of Dalai Lamas and Panchen Lamas is assured by this method.

Reference

1 *The Ocean of Theosophy*, Pasadena, CA.: Theosophical University Press, 1973, p. 131.

28

Heaven and Hell

Introduction

The concepts of heaven and hell are symbolic expressions found in various religious traditions. They are polar components of a religious vision: a state of bliss and a state of suffering respectively. Heaven is considered to be a realm "above," the earth and hell is a realm "below" the earth. Heaven is often symbolized by light or brightness as a realm of bliss, whereas hell is characterized as dark, a realm of anguish and suffering.

Heaven and hell are not specific places, but are states of mind. Though subjectively they mean a great deal to the individual soul, they are both illusions. In these states of mind, desires become much more intense, as they no longer require expression through the gross medium. The fulfillment of desires does not dependent upon having the objects of desire. It comes merely through thinking of the objects desired.

Heaven and hell are both states of bondage. Their duration is determined by the nature and intensity of the accumulated impressions. The quality of expressions the soul passes through after the death of the gross body is determined by the kind of its life on earth in the physical body.

Consciousness in the states of heaven and hell is in a position to make a leisurely and effective survey of the animated record of earthly life. Through intensification of experiences, it can observe their nature with better facility and results. All the experiences of the earthly life are now available for vivid reflection. Thus the states of heaven and hell become instrumental in the assimilation of experiences acquired in the earthly existence; and the soul can start its next earthly life with all the advantages of digested experience.

In Hinduism

The *Rig Veda* portrays heaven as the realm of the fathers, who proceed there after death in order to be with the gods. *Yama*, the god of dead, was the first human to die. He overseas the heavenly realm. Those who perform rituals, sacrifices, and offerings to the gods go to heaven after death. They enjoy the pleasures they have known on earth.

The *Brahmanas,* composed primarily for the ritual performance of the priests, describe heaven as an abode of joy and goodness.

The *Upanishads* give a cyclical world-view. The notions of transmigration and reincarnation imply a series of lives, deaths and rebirths in cyclical continuity. Heaven and Hell are not ultimate destinations, but are intermediate states intermitted with a series of earthly existences in a cycle of births and deaths. One's past accumulated karmas determine the nature of soul's passage from only earthly existence to another through heaven or hell. There are several levels of heaven or hell with varying degrees of relative bliss or suffering.

In the traditional Hindu cosmology, three realms (*lokas*)—heaven, the earth and a netherworld—are supplemented by fourteen additional realms, seven heavens above the earth and seven hells below the earth. Those who perform good deeds and cherish good thoughts go to heaven to enjoy the celestial pleasures. But they will stay there so long as their good deeds and thoughts entitle them to do so. There is a limit to good thoughts and deeds, and therefore there is a limit to the period of their stay in heaven. The *Bhagavad Gita* says:

> "The knowers of the three *Vedas*, purified of all sins, worshipping Me by sacrifices, pray for the way to heaven; they reach the holy world of the Lord of the gods and enjoy in the heaven the

divine pleasures of the gods. They having enjoyed the vast heaven, enter the world of mortals when their merits are exhausted; thus abiding by the injunctions of the *Vedas* and desiring objects of desires, they attain to the state of going and returning." (9.20–21)

Many spiritual aspirants climb up to a certain height on the ladder of Yoga and are swept away by the temptations of the higher planes – heaven and the plane of celestial beings. They lose their power of discrimination and the right understanding, and are overcome by the enjoyment of heavenly pleasures. When all their accumulated merits are exhausted, they descend to this world again. They thus come and go.

The dispassionate Yogi, on the other hand, who is endowed with strong discrimination and burning aspiration for liberation, can resist these temptations. He alone can attain the highest goal of liberation.

Just as good doers go to heaven, evil doers go to hell to experience suffering for their evil karma and stay there so long as their bad thoughts and crimes entitle them to do so. No soul is eternally damned. There is no eternal heaven or hell according to the religions of India. The word eternal denotes that which is beginningless and endless. According to the rational theory of Vedanta, heaven and hell cannot by their nature be eternal, for all things that are subject to the laws of time, space and causation are impermanent and perishable. Worldly pleasures are limited by time; they do not continue for ever. Celestial pleasures are similar to the pleasures of the world. Even though they may last for a long time, they must eventually come to an end. Those desires that cannot be fulfilled anywhere except in this world will bring us back to this place of existence.

Journey to Heaven or Hell

It is the results of our actions that entitle us to heaven or condemn us to hell. The Yoga scriptures do not deal with the ideas of heaven and hell. But many secular texts like *Puranas* and related texts give a detailed picture of both realms. The period just proceeding the moment of dying is crucial. This is when the messengers of the king of dead (*Yama*) arrive. Those who have surrendered themselves and all their desires, thoughts, feelings, attachments and aversions and everything else to God, however, are visited by the messengers of the Divine Being.

With the exception of these blessed ones, every dying person must obey the command of the messengers of the king of dead. He must leave the body behind. If he tries to cling to the body out of fear, attachment and desire, nature joins the forces with the dead's messengers and evicts him. Then accompanied by the messengers, he reaches a broad river inhabited by all kinds of creatures – crocodiles, fish, dolphins, sharks and even cows. The river has several crossing points, and the messengers drop him at one. They remain on the bank and he has to cross the river on his own.

The river is deep, and when he swims across it he has to confront the creatures that dwell there. Anything may happen. He may get caught in the current or be chased by a crocodile; he may begin to drown and then suddenly pushed back to the surface by a friendly fish. He may notice his friends or his enemies swimming or drowning near him. If he is lucky, the messengers may drop him at a crossing where there are special cows that are expert swimmers. They offer their tail as a rope and pull him safely across the river.

Whether his crossing has been easy or difficult, he meets the messengers again on the other shore, and they take him to the city of the king of dead, where he meets the king's accountant.

The Yogis interpret this scenario symbolically. The messengers of the king represent the forces of time. These forces are punctual. Their coming denotes that it is time to leave the body.

Desire, worry, insecurity, fear, disease and old age set the stage for the messengers. When the death comes these feelings intensify. Those who do not willingly face death with calmness die miserably.

Most of us have strong attachment to our bodies, our families, our friends and our passions, and this attachment impels us to cling to life. This creates a deep sense of fear of death, and the fear of losing our relationships and possessions intensifies. Death itself is not painful, but it is the fear that torments our mind.

When the time of death comes, the life-force (*prana*) withdraws from the body, brains and the conscious mind. This is the moment of death. The mind and senses follow the *prana*. They exit the body by the gate through which the *prana* leaves.

When the *prana* leaves, the body becomes lifeless, and the afterlife journey begins. We arrive at the river of the mind. Its name is *Vaitarani* which means "that which can be crossed only by skillful swimmers." This river is the repository of our karmas, and we cannot escape the contents of our unconscious mind during this inner journey. Problems and worries that we have faced during our lifetime ensnare us even more intensively now, because now we have no family and friends and intellect to help us to manage them. Moreover, while we were living on the earth, events and experiences took place in sequence. But the unconscious mind does not follow any law of orderliness. Desire, greed, attachment, hatred, anger, jealousy, repulsion, kindness, cruelty, compassion, pride, guilt and a host of other emotions assail us simultaneously. We sink, float, get caught in the current, confront a crocodile, or get a push from a friendly dolphin in a random and chaotic fashion. The messengers of the ruler of dead are neutral; they operate in perfect conformity with the Law of Karma. They drop us at the exact point of the river where we belong. One section of the river is the repository of our active virtuous deeds; that is where special cows reside. If we have earned enough merit to be deposited there, these intelligent and expert swimmers pull us across the river. (The Sanskrit word for "cow" is *go*, which is also the word for "senses" and "rays of light"). These cows are charity, selfless service, self-restraint and spiritual practices that purify the heart. They come to our rescue if we had risen above sense cravings and ignorance.

On the other hand, if we had accumulated complicated and mixed *samskaras* (impressions), we will confront difficulties in crossing the river.

Next we arrive at the city of the ruler of dead. This is

Samyamanipuri, the city of inner controller – conscience. Here we meet the king's accountant, Chitra Gupta. *Chitra* means "picture" or "reflection of various forms;" *Gupta* means "hidden or mysterious." Thus Chitra Gupta is the voice of our conscience residing within and witnessing our thoughts, words and deeds. Nothing escapes Chitra Gupta. He assigns us either to heaven or hell according to our karmas. But if we have managed to kill our conscience while we were alive and to live comfortably with self-deception, the sub-impressions of this self-deception will prompt us to argue with our conscience. If that happens, the accountant takes us to the court of the ruler of dead, *Yamaraja*, the representative of the pure Self (Divinity) within us. In his dazzling light, truth alone can stand. Our self-deception vanishes and we are bound to go to our rightful place.

It is our karmas that determine our journey to heaven or hell. If we knew what our karmas were, we could predict our destination. The problem is that we cannot remember the infinite number of our accumulated karmas.

The flow of *prana* is regulated by the forces of our karma. We can make some predictions about our destination of the departed soul, the scriptures say, by observing the flow of *prana* and the precise time it leaves the body.

The Destination of the departed Soul. The *Bhagavad Gita* states the time at which if the Yogis leave their bodies, they will not be born again, and also when, if they die, they will be reborn. Yogis who have attained the knowledge of Self go to *Brahman*, if they die during the six months of the northern path of the sun (the northern solstice). (8. 24). This period is from the middle of January to the middle of July. It is regarded as the better period for dying. It is the northern path or the path of light, by which the Yogis go to *Brahman*.

There are vivid descriptions in the *Chandogya Upanishad*, (4.15.5), the *Kaushitaki Upanishad* (2.14) and the *Brahma Sutras*:

> "On the road beginning with light the departed soul proceeds, on account of that being widely known."

> "Having reached the path of the gods, it comes to the world of *Agni* (fire), to the world of *Vayu* (air), to the world of *Varuna* (rain), to the world of *Indra* (the king of gods), to the world of *Prajapati* (the creator) and to the world of *Brahman."*
> "They go to the light, from light to day, from day to the waxing half of the moon, from the waxing half of the moon to the six months when the sun goes to the north, from those months to the year, from the year to the sun."
> "From the moon to the lightning; there, a person that is not a human being leads it to *Brahman*."

Time is used here in the sense of a path or the stage on the path. "Fire" and "Light" are Deities who preside over time. The northern path of illumination leads to liberation. The life-breaths of those liberated sages who have attained the knowledge of Self do not depart. They are absorbed in the Self. They attain immediate liberation.

Each step may mean a "plane" or a "state of consciousness" or "degree of purity or illumination." The more the purity , the more the Divine Light. There is illumination or knowledge when one passes along the path. Hence it is called the path of light.

In the *Mahabharata* war, when Bhisma was mortally wounded, he was lying on a bed of arrows till the onset of the northern solstice and then departed to the abode of the Lord.

The next verse (8.25) of the *Bhagavad Gita* describes the path of darkness:

> "Attaining to the lunar light by smoke, night time, the dark fortnight or the six months of the southern path of the sun (the southern solstice), the Yogi returns."

This is the path of darkness or the path of the ancestors, which leads to rebirth. Those who perform sacrifices to the gods and do other charitable works with the expectation of rewards, go to the world of moon through this path, and return to the earth when the merits of their deeds are exhausted.

Smoke, night-time, the dark fortnight, the six months of the southern solstice: these show the degree of ignorance, attachment and passion. There are dark-colored objects and smoke throughout the course. There is no illumination when one passes along this path. Hence it is called the path of darkness or smoke.

> "The bright and dark paths of the world are verily thought to be eternal; by the one (the bright path) one goes not to return, and the other (the dark path) he returns." (*Gita*, 8.26)

The bright path is the path to God. It is taken by devotees and Yogis. The dark path is the path to the manes. It is taken by those who perform sacrifices or charitable acts with the expectation of rewards.

The Yogic interpretation of the above is that the six month period from the middle of January to the middle of July corresponds to the dominance of solar energy in our body, and this is indicated by the flow of breath through the right nostril; the next six month period corresponds to the dominance of lunar energy, indicated by the flow of the breath through the left nostril. Accomplished Yogis who can leave their bodies at will often do so during twilight when the breath is flowing equally in both nostrils; then they transcend heaven and hell.

In Buddhism

Like the Hindu tradition Buddhism also holds the cyclical view of individual existence. The world of time, space and causation is transitory and constantly in flux. Heaven and hell are intermediate states between one earthly existence and another. The cycle of births and deaths is caused by desires and attachments. One's karmas determine the type of rebirths. The enlightened ones (*arhats*) are free from the cycle of rebirths.

The realm of *kamaloka* (the world of desires) includes various hells and lower heavens. Each hell involves different forms of suffering by which the consequences of bad karmas are exhausted. The heavens of the *kamaloka* are inhabited by the kings and gods.

The heavens of *rupaloka* (the world of form) and *arupaloka* (the formless world)—often referred to as the world of consciousness—are accessible only to those accomplished in the practice of the discipline of meditation and spiritual pursuits.

Bodhisattvas manifest themselves in various forms in any of the realms, in which there are suffering beings, to share their merit with all that are in need of enlightenment.

In Chinese Tradition

The aspiration to achieve harmony in society has characterized all of Chinese religion and philosophy. The worship of Heaven (*T'ien*) was regarded as essential for the maintenance of harmony between Heaven and earth.

In the Confucian tradition the underlying conviction was if harmony is achieved in human affairs—relationships of ruler-subject, father-son, husband-wife, elder brother-younger brother, and friend and friend – harmony with Heaven will be assured. The Will of Heaven is the primary reality and the ultimate basis of Confucian thought. Whatever happening that is not the direct responsibility of human beings is attributed to the Will of Heaven. Taoist cosmology includes levels of heavens above and hells below the earth.

In Japanese Tradition

There are, in the indigenous traditions of Japan, concepts analogous to those of heaven and hell in other religions. *Ame*, a realm analogous to heaven, is the dwelling place of the gods, and notable persons are thought to proceed there after death. It is a bounteous realm. Its beauty is beyond anything known on earth.

In Judaism

The heaven is the dwelling place of Yahweh. It is regarded as the destiny of the righteous. Hell is a place of punishment. The period of punishment depends upon the degree of seriousness of one's transgression. The concepts of heaven and hell imply eternal existence and the continuance of the same condition without end.

Multiple heavens are mentioned in Jewish apocryphal literature and in the teachings of the rabbinical tradition.

Traditional Judaism views the final destiny of humans in terms of three doctrines of recompense, immortality and resurrection. Resurrection has been understood as a climactic event reanimating the dead, and including the final judgment of bliss or damnation.

In Christianity

Heaven is envisioned in early Christianity as the fulfilling state of bliss. In Roman Catholic Christianity hell is deemed to be a state of unending punishment for the unrepentant that die without the grace of God. This state is characterized by the suffering of fire and other tortures.

Eastern Orthodox Christianity shares the teaching that hell is a destiny of eternal fire and punishment awaiting the cursed and unredeemed following the Last Judgment, and that heaven is the ultimate destiny of the redeemed. In sharing this teaching it has placed focal emphasis on the resurrection of Jesus as assuring the resurrection of the faithful.

Literal and spatial interpretations of heaven and hell have been found untenable by some Protestant thinkers. It is contended that it is contradictory to posit hell as eternal punishment, while affirming God as one who is loving and merciful and wills all to be saved and forever seeks the lost.

In Islam

In the *Koran* and the traditions of Islam are manifold descriptions of heaven and hell. Perfect justice will be disclosed at the Last Judgment following resurrection. God's Judgment will be pronounced on the basis of an expansive record of each person's deeds. It will be followed by the entrance of the believers into heaven and the relegation of the infidels to hell. Each person will proceed across the bridge of al-Aaraf following the judgment. This will be felicitous crossing for the true Muslim, but a travesty for the infidel, who will fall from the bridge into the pits of hell. Sufferings in hell will be unending.

In the *Koran* the conditions of heaven and hell are described vividly. Heaven abounds in deep river of cool, crystal water, lush fruits and vegetation, boundless fertility and beautiful mansions with gracious attendants.

Hell contains rotten metal, boiling liquids and blazing fire. A Muslim's happiness or misery after life depends upon how well he has observed God's laws:

> "There is no such thing as heaven and hell. Heaven and hell," asserts Igbal, "are states, not localities." Their descriptions in the *Koran* are visual representations of an inner fact. Hell is the painful realization of one's failure as a person. Heaven, by contrast, is the joy of triumph over the forces of disintegration. (Mohammed Igbal, *The Reconstruction of Religious Thought in Islam*, Lahore: Shaik Muhammad Ashraf, Book sellers, 1954, pp. 116 – 121).

29

The Doctrine of Reincarnation

Introduction

The doctrine of reincarnation means re-entry of a soul into earthly life after the end of its previous existence. When a living being dies, it is the body alone that dies. The life force or soul within the body does not die. With its storehouse of the impressions (*samskaras*) of the past thoughts and actions, subtle intense desires (*vasanas*) and dispositions and tendencies it leaves the body and at a later time re-enters another body to redeem its past karmas. This re-entry is called reincarnation or simply rebirth. A soul passes through innumerable reincarnations before it attains liberation. It is a cycle or wheel of rebirths. Before taking each reincarnation, the soul may pass through different subtle higher worlds or planes depending upon the nature of its past-accumulated karmas.

The Wheel of Rebirth

In Sanskrit the wheel of rebirth is called *samsara*. In the Buddhist art, sculpture and architecture, the wheel is widely used to symbolize karma and rebirth. The Cambridge philosopher F.M. Cornford writes:

> "Caught in the wheel of Time, the soul, preserving its individual identity, passes through all shapes of life. .Its substance is divine and immutable, and it is the same substance, as all other souls in the world, but, on the other hand, each soul is an atomic individual, which persists throughout its cycle of reincarnation."[1]

The wheel of rebirth is also found in Greece and Italy. Speaking of transmigration, A. C. Pearson of Cambridge says that "the prevalence of this mystical belief and its religious potency are illustrated with remarkable clearance in certain inscriptions on golden tablets found in South Italy near Rome, and in Crete, which are attributed to the fourth and fifth centuries BC.. . . . ." W. R. Inge, Dean of Saint Paul's in London, writes, "Even in the most Judaic of the epistles, attributed to St. James, we find the Orphic phrase 'the wheel of birth'."

Reincarnation and Karma

The doctrine of rebirth is a corollary to the Law of Karma, the universal Law of Cause and Effect. For each action there is an equal reaction. Every action—in the form of thought, word or deed—brings its reaction to the doer. Everyone has to reap the repercussions of his actions sooner or latter. "Whatsoever a man soweth, that shall he also reap." Everyone performs innumerable actions during his lifetime. All of them cannot bring their reactions in this life itself. Therefore his soul has to take another embodiment in order to experience the results of the remaining actions. In the course of that life he again accumulates new karmas and has to take another birth, and in this way each soul has to pass through a series of successive reincarnations. So long as karmas—7good or bad—remain unexhausted, it cannot avoid reincarnation and attain final liberation. Both good and bad karmas bind the soul to the wheel of births and deaths.

Fallacy of One-birth Theory and Predestination

Judaism, Christianity, Islam and Zoroastrianism uphold the one-birth theory. The followers of these faiths seem to have closed their eyes to the absurdity and unreasonableness of such a theory; they believe that human souls are created out of nothing at the time of birth of their bodies and that the ultimate fate of righteous is eternal happiness and that of the evildoers is eternal damnation. Calvin defines predestination as "the eternal degree of God by which He has determined in Himself what He would have every individual of mankind to become, for they are not all created with a similar destiny; but eternal life is foreordained for some and eternal damnation for others."[2] How could this be? Calvin himself confessed, "It is an awful decree." No opportunity is afforded to the predestined sinner to purify himself. Why should a person be held responsible throughout eternity for the deeds, which he was predestined to perform by the will of the Lord? The theory of predestination instead of giving an answer to this question makes God partial and unjust. Why could He not make all souls equally good and happy? If God created one human to enjoy and another to suffer throughout eternity, then how partial and unjust must He be?

The doctrine of reincarnation provides a satisfactory solution to this problem. The soul is immortal It is a life force. It existed before the birth of the body and it will continue to exist after the death of the body. Therefore it is an entity by itself. The Law of Conservation of Energy holds well not only in the physical world but also in the spiritual world. Therefore just as no atom can be created or destroyed, so also no soul-entity can be created or destroyed. Its pays its karmic debts through its successive reincarnations; it learns from past experiences and evolves spiritually. Even a sinner can become a saint. Thus the one-birth or one-life theory is absurd, and the concept of reincarnation of souls is tenable.

An individual can hardly attain perfection in one life. He has to develop his heart, intellect and hand. He has to mould his character in a perfect manner. He has to cultivate various virtues such as compassion, love, tolerance, forgiveness, equal vision, truthfulness, etc. He has to learn many lessons and experiences in this great world school. The scale and variety of experiences is enormous. The range of powers latent in us is vast. Infinite knowledge lies before us. We have no time to reach up to our high aspirations, while limitless passions and desires, selfish motives and ambitions war with us and among themselves, pursuing us even to the door of death. All these have to be conquered, used and subdued. One life is not enough for all this.

A human life is around seventy years, and out of that a large part is spent in sleep and another part in childhood. Thus in one life it is impossible to attain even a fraction of what Nature evidently has in view. Therefore a series of incarnation is needed to complete the process.

Justification for prevailing Inequalities

Neither the one-birth theory nor the theory of hereditary transmission can provide a satisfactory answer to the question of inequalities and diversities existing in the world. Why is one born healthy and another crippled and diseased? Why does one live long and another die at young age? Why are the children of the same parents have a marked dissimilar personality traits? Why do twins develop into dissimilar characters and possess opposite qualities? Can heredity explain such cases? No. who made such differences? They cannot be accidents? There is no such thing as accident. Every event of the universe is bound by the Law of Cause and Effect. There must be some cause of these inequalities. Are they due to God's will? Can all-merciful God be so unjust as to make one honest and saintly, another an idiot; one rich, another poor and so forth? No. The doctrine of karma and reincarnation alone can explain rationally such inequalities and differences. One's richness or poverty, beauty or deformity, saintly character or cruel tendency is the effect of his past good or evil actions, and he has to be born again to reap the fruits of such actions. The inequalities of life are the result of differences in people's past actions.

The Purpose of Reincarnation

Plants, insects, fishes, reptiles, birds, animals, man and all living beings have evolved from minute germs of life. Man did not come into existence all of a sudden. The germ of life had passed through various stages of physical form before it could become a man. Man is thus the epitome of the whole creation.

Man's self consists of two natures: animal and spiritual. Animal nature includes all the animal propensities, desire for sense enjoyments, procreation, love of self, fear of death and struggle for existence. The energy of this lower nature is spent chiefly in the struggle for material existence.

Spiritual nature expresses itself in various ways on a higher plane. Truthfulness, dispassion, control of the senses, self sacrifice, mercy and kindness to all creatures, desire to help the distressed, forgiveness, faith in God and devotion are the expressions of the higher spiritual nature. These higher qualities have not evolved out of lower ones. Vedanta philosophy of India says, "That which exists in the end existed also in the beginning." Modern scientists like J. Arthur Thomson have found out the same truth. The animal nature, spiritual nature, faculties of mind, intellect, spirit—all these exist potentially in the germ of life. Each germ of life, according to Vedanta, possesses infinite potentialities. The powers that remain latent have the natural tendency to manifest perfectly and to become actual. By seeing the tiny seed of a gigantic Banyan tree, one who has never seen that tree cannot imagine what powers lie dormant in it. The manifestation of latent powers is the basis of the evolution of one species into another. This idea has been expressed in a few words in the *Yoga Sutras* by Patanjali who lived long before the Christian era, "The evolution[3]of one species into another is caused by the in-filling (flow) of Nature" (4.2). The Nature is filled not from without but from within. Nothing is super-added to the individual soul from outside. The germ of life or the individual soul possesses infinite possibilities. When it has gone through all the stages of evolution, perfect knowledge is acquired.

Saint Manickavasagar (eighth century) of Tamil Nadu, Southern India, in his great devotional scripture *Thiruvasagam* sings, "*Pullagip pudaagip puzhuvaagi . . . . Ellaap pirappum pirandhu illaiththen.*" Its English version is: "I had gone through the births of the grass, the shrub, the worm and the tree, varied beasts, the birds and snakes, the stones the human, the devil and the ganas, powerful demons, ascetics and the celestials – and became exhausted. Oh my Lord, This is true of me. I saw your golden feet and attained liberation."

The end and aim of evolution is the attainment of perfection. Physical evolution of animal life reached its perfection in human form. No other higher form evolved out of human body. Human form is the end of physical evolution. The end of intellectual, moral and spiritual evolution will be reached when intellectual, moral and spiritual perfection is attained.

Intellectual perfection means perfect understanding of the true nature of things and never mistaking the unreal for the real and non-eternal for eternal or *vice versa.* Moral perfection consists in the destruction of selfishness. Spiritual perfection means Self-realization.

The human birth is very precious because only in a human form moral perfection and Self-realization are possible. Even the gods have to take human birth on this earth to strive for attaining Godhead.

When the animal nature is predominant the moral and spiritual nature remains dormant. When moral and spiritual nature is predominant, the animal nature remains latent. As the higher nature becomes powerful, the lower nature is eclipsed, and its energy is transformed into that of the higher nature, and ultimately it disappears altogether. There are many stages in the higher nature as well as in the lower. Each of these stages binds the individual soul so long as it stays there. When it passes through all the stages of the spiritual nature and reaches the ultimate point of perfection, it realizes its true nature of immortality and divinity. As this growth cannot be expected in one life, reincarnation becomes necessary. If anyone does not succeed in reaching perfection in this life, he can try again in his next incarnation, not starting from the beginning but from the last stage he arrived. Thus we find that reincarnation is the logical sequence of evolution, and it means a continuous evolution of an individual soul until it attains Self-realization or perfection.

The sole purpose of reincarnation of an individual soul is to destroy the accumulated karmas and to overcome all the obstacles to Self-realization through spiritual practices and service to humanity without any attachment. The pace of this progress depends upon the self-effort of each soul. If it makes progress in each incarnation consciously then it is expediting its spiritual liberation. Otherwise, liberation might take thousands of years and need thousands of rebirths.

Evidences of Validity of the Theory of Rebirth

While the theory of reincarnation is still not proved scientifically, there are nevertheless numerous evidences of its validity. Everyone has at one time or another met new people or visited new places with the strange feeling of past familiarity. Something deep within the unconscious memory seems to strike a familiar chord. Lord Buddha told his wife of her kindness to him in the previous birth. The poet Shelly, while walking in a countryside he had never visited before, remarked to a companion of his strange feeling of having been there before. "Over that hill," he said, "is an old windmill." They continued their stroll with expectation. Upon reaching the summit of the hill, the windmill came into the view, and Shelly was overwhelmed by emotion.

Who does teach the duckling to swim or a child to suckle and smile? They must have had past lives. It is the memory that leads one to perform the same acts repeatedly. Saints tell us that the memory of past lives appears just after birth, but soon fades away.

There are many instances of children with uncommon powers and genius. Sankaracharya, the great commentator of the Vedanta philosophy, finished his commentary when he was twelve-year-old. Mozart, the great musician, wrote a sonata when he was four-year-old and an opera in his eighth year. Zerah Colburn, under eight years of age, could solve the most difficult mathematical problems instantly. In one instance, he took the number 8 and raised it to the sixteenth power and instantly mentioned the result, which contained 15 figures. Without looking at the book, how could a seven-year old boy recite the *Bhagavad Gita* from beginning to end? The doctrine of reincarnation alone can explain rationally such extraordinary cases of child prodigies. By repeatedly accumulating knowledge in a particular field in many births, in some future birth one attains perfection in it. The impressions of past thoughts and actions recorded in the subconscious mind are carried forward from birth to birth and it is those impressions that determine one's present character, skills and dispositions. Whatever the soul has mastered in previous lives manifests in the present.

Non-remembrance of Past Incarnations

It may then be asked, "if we existed before our birth, why do we not remember it? Our memory is short. We do not remember always past doings. Can anyone remember the wonderful epoch of his or her infancy? So no wonder that we do not remember our past incarnations. What would be the flight of a person who stumbled across the memory of the wicked deeds of his past life? He knows that those deeds would surely react on him and would bring misery and suffering shortly. Such a person would be so restless and unhappy that he would not be able to do any work properly; he would constantly think in what form misery would come to him. He would not be able to eat or sleep. Therefore it is a great blessing that we do not recollect our past lives and past deeds. However a very few are able to remember their past incarnations.

If you have the knowledge of the Raja Yoga technique of *Samyama* (combination of concentration, meditation and samadhi at a time) you can remember your past lives. Patanjali states in his *Yoga Sutras,*

> "By perceiving the impressions, one acquires the knowledge of past life." (3.18)

All experiences that you have had in various births remain dormant in the form of impressions (*samskaras*) in the subconscious mind. They remain in a very subtle form, just as sound remains in a subtle form in C.D. cassette. These subtle impressions assume the form of waves and you get the memory of past experiences. Therefore if a yogi can do *samyama* on the impressions of past experiences, he can attain the knowledge of all the details of his past lives. This power can also be directed toward other minds for acquiring the knowledge of their past lives. There have been many instances in India of Yogis who knew not only their own past lives but also correctly those of others. For example, on that night when Buddha attained enlightenment he went through several stages of awakening. In the first he recollected his previous lives. He tells us:

I remembered many, many former existences I had passed through,.a hundred thousand, in various world-periods. I know everything about these various births . . .with exact characteristic features and circumstances.[4]

Vedanta says, do not waste your valuable time in thinking of your past lives always, look forward and try first to attain to the highest level of spiritual development; then if you want to know your past lives you will recollect them all, like Buddha who remembered several hundreds of his previous births. When the all-knowing Divine Self manifests in you, time and space will vanish and past and future will become the eternal present. Then you will say as Sri Krishna said to Arjuna in the *Bhagavad Gita,*

> "Both you and I have passed through many lives, you do not recollect any, but I know them all." (4.5)

Though all do not recollect their past lives, from time to time some remember their past lives and their cases are reported all over the world and investigated and found correct.

Remembrances of Past Lives

There are many case histories of individuals who had remembered former lives. Most of them have been investigated and reported in newspapers and magazines. These bear valid evidence to the doctrine of reincarnation of souls.

The monumental book on *Reincarnation: The Phoenix Fire Mystery* edited by Joseph Head and S.L. Craston (New York: Crown Publishers, 1977) carries remembrance stories of Anne of U.S.A, a woman patient of Dr. Arthur Guirdham, Edward Ryall of England, Eduardo Esplugus-Cabrera of Havana, Robert of Belgium, Alexandrina Samona of Sicily, Thomas Greene Bethune (a slave boy of Georgia farmer), a New England Child, a man of Irish author Shaw Desmond's acquaintance, General Homer Lea (1876–1912) (the American cripple), W. Martin of Liverpool, David spangler, and Blanche of London (pp. 395-416)

Sogyal Rinpoche, in his *The Tibetan Book of Living and Dying,* New York: Harper Collins Publishers, 1994, describes the fascinating stories of

1. Arthur Flowerdew of Norfolk, England, who from the age of twelve experienced inexplicable but vivid mental pictures of experiences of his past life.
2. A little girl, Kamaljit Kour, the daughter of a Sikh family in the Punjab in India, who vividly remembered the details of her past life and the people with whom she lived then. (pp. 84 – 85).

In his book *What Becomes to the soul After Death*, Sri Swami Sivananda (1887-1963), founder of the Divine Life Society in Rishikesh, at the foot of Himalayas, India, presents the case histories of children who have accurately recalled their past life. Such cases have been investigated by eminent men and found correct. When a soul is reborn within a short period after death, the memory of its past life is still fresh, and so it is able to recall all its details.

In 1936 a very interesting case was thoroughly investigated and reported by the governmental authorities of India. A girl, Shanti Devi of Delhi, could accurately describe her previous life (at Muttra, five hundred miles from Delhi), which ended about a year before her second birthday. She gave the name of her husband and child and described her home and life history. The investigation commission brought her to her former relatives, who verified all her statements. (Gustaf Stromberg, *The Soul of the Universe*, New York: David Mc Kay, 1940)

The case of a young housewife of South Wales, who remembered her six previous lives and other such cases were related in a BBC—TV documentary and a Book *More Lives Than One* published by Souvenir Press (*Washington Post*, Nov. 13, 1976). Both the TV series and the book were based on twenty years of work by Arnall Bloxham, a hypnotherapist in Cardiff, Wales. He had tape-recorded trance sessions in which more than 400 people "regressed" to previous lives.

The National Institute of Mental Health Sciences in Bangalore, India has investigated 16 cases. One of them was a five year old girl who recalled that she was a night-soil carrier in her previous life. Another was a 38-year old Maharashtrian lady who spoke fluent Bengali of the nineteenth century—a language that she could not possibly have picked up in her native town. The Institute minutely checked each case of reincarnation and found the details given by them were correct.

One of the most remarkable studies made on reincarnation is Gina Cerminara's book *Many Mansions* (The New American Library), which deals with the extraordinary work of Edgar Cayce (1877-1945), who became famous for his life-readings based on clairvoyance. Cayce first discovered his mystical powers in 1923 and by the time he died in 1945, he had given about 2,500 life-readings. His spontaneous mystic ability was the result of the accumulated tendencies of previous incarnations. Cayce gave his readings when he was under trance-like sleep. His readings have been consistent and "accurate" and when a reading of the same person was given some months later, they never contradicted each other. Most readings contained some background information about past eras of history, such as Egypt and Atlantis. According to Dr. Cerminara, the Cayce readings agreed in many respects with the facts of recorded history, no matter how obscure.

In addition to the historical confirmations of past life data, there were innumerable confirmations in Cayce's reading of present life material. Even in reading adult minds Cayce could get in touch with the unconscious levels of those minds. The unconscious mind, according to him, retained the memory of every experience through which the individual had passed, not only from the time of birth, but also before birth, in all its previous experiences. This confirms what is stated in the ancient Yoga texts and the Vedanta texts of India.

Prof. Frederick Lenz of New School for Social Research, New York city has studied one hundred and twenty-seven cases of past-life remembrances: ninety-five in United States, thirteen in Canada and nineteen in Great Britain. Based on the evidence of his research he concludes that reincarnation does exist. He presents his study in his *Life Times: True Accounts of Reincarnation*, Indianapolis, N.Y.: The Bobbs-Merrill Company, 1979.

Dr. Ian Stevenson (1918 –), Professor of Psychiatry and Director of the Division of Personality Studies at the University of Virginia is the world's leading authority on the subject of life after death. He has been doing reincarnation research for the past several decades and studied hundreds of cases of remembrances of past life. Stevenson became interested in reincarnation because of a growing feeling of dissatisfaction that the doctrine of heredity and environmental influences often did not account for personality as we see it.

His book *Twenty Cases Suggestive of Reincarnation* published in 1966 (revised edition in 1974) by the University Press of Virginia is a classic in the field. The twenty cases presented in this Volume provide a representative sample of several hundred cases he investigated at first hand. Later his new book under the title *Cases of the Reincarnation Type* was published in a series of volumes. His another book called *Xenoglossy* was published in four volumes. The word "xenoglossy" refers to the ability to speak an identified language not learned by the speaker in any normal way. His conclusion is: "There is an impressive body of evidence and it is getting stronger all the time. I think a rational man can believe in reincarnation on the basis of evidence." Copies of four volumes of *Xenoglossy* are available from the Division of Personality Studies, University of Virginia.

Prof. Stevenson's other publications on Reincarnation research are:

- *Reincarnation and Biology* in two volumes, Westport, Ct.: Praegaer Publishers, 1996 (Vol. I, 1200 pages; Vol. II, 1100 pages)
  Based on 30 years of research on people who claim to remember past lives, this work encompasses the full spectrum of theory and case study. Specific information from children's memories has been collected and verified.
  Where Reincarnation and Biology Intersect, Westport, Ct.:

Praegaer Publishers, 1996.
This book summarizes Stevenson's findings presented in full in the above two-volume work.
Writing as a specialist in psychiatry and as a world-renowned scientific investigator of reported paranormal events, Stevenson asks us to suspend our Western tendencies to disbelieve in "reincarnation" and consider the reality of the burgeoning record of cases now available.
Children Who Remember Previous Lives (Out of print) Revised edition will be available in the summer of 2000.

As of September, 1999 the files on reincarnation cases in the University of Virginia Division of Parapsychology contained a total of about 2,500 cases of persons claiming such memories that were investigated by Dr. Stevenson or his associates. These cases were from the United States, Thailand, Burma, India, Sri Lanka, Lebanon, Great Britain and other countries.

Even birthmark evidences confirmed the validity of the cases investigated. Among the memories given by the children, in those cases covering the circumstances of a violent death in their previous life, they described, being shot in particular parts of their body, and these remembered wounds correspond in location to the scar-like birthmarks on the body of the child. Dr. Stevenson has been able, after identifying and locating the previous family, to find the medical records covering the death of the previous personality and has confirmed that the location of the wounds did indeed correspond with the child's memories as well as with the location of the birthmarks.

What does reincarnate?

At the time of death of the physical body, the soul with subtle body goes out. The subtle body is invisible. It is made up of five senses of action, five senses of perception, mind, intellect, five *pranas* (life forces) and egoism. It carries with it all the impressions of past actions and experiences and the subtle tendencies of the soul. It either reincarnates or goes to higher planes and then reincarnates on this earth. This depends upon the nature and strength of one's life-long tendency and disposition.

Journey through Higher Worlds

The *Tibetan Book of the Dead* is one of the most ancient texts on the subject of reincarnation. It was written thousands of years ago by advanced Yogis who claim to have recalled the passage of their souls between death and rebirth. It outlines both the nature and type of experiences a soul will have after death.

According to the *Book of the Dead*, after death a soul will pass through several distinct nonphysical worlds before returning to earth to be reborn. The soul will spend varying periods of time in each of these higher planes, depending on its spiritual development. The Tibetans believe that souls that are in higher stages of their human incarnations will tend to reincarnate so quickly, because these souls no longer desire earthly experiences so intensely as do souls that are in either their prehuman or early human incarnations.

Souls that are in their early incarnations are not so conscious of the process of reincarnation as are more mature souls. These young souls are like children in first or second grade that go to a school but are not cognizant of how the school operates. Souls in their intermediate human incarnations are more keenly aware of their passage through the nonphysical worlds; they are like older students who are consciously striving to learn and develop. Souls in the last stage of their human incarnations are like teachers; they help other souls in their development.

After death of the body, the soul may linger in its old environment on earth for several days, visiting familiar places where it has lived during its former life. After the soul has lingered on earth for a time, it will feel a pull to go beyond this world. Then it begins its journey through the higher worlds. The first world it enters into is a vital world filled with chaos. The *Book of the Dead* describes that many unpleasant-looking beings, which live in this world, try to torment the soul. After staying in this vital world, the soul will go to a mental world that is composed of abstract ideas and qualities. Thereafter it enters into a number of psychic worlds filled with pleasing colors, fragrances and beautiful beings that will help the soul on its journey. Finally the soul will rest in its own world and reflect upon the experiences it has had in its most recent lifetime. After it has rested for some time in its own world, it will return to the earth to be reborn.

Out of 127 cases investigated by Prof. Frederick Lunz, fifteen persons claimed to have recalled the passage of their souls through the nonphysical worlds. It is interesting to note that although none of them was aware of the *Book of the Dead*, their descriptions of both the order and nature of experiences were strikingly similar to the descriptions of the death and rebirth process found in the *Tibetan Book of the Dead.* (For details, refer his *Lifetimes: True Accounts of Reincarnation*, Indianapolis, NY.: The Bobbs-Merrill Company, 1979).

Reincarnation in Other Worlds

The soul that has taken a human body cannot and does not reincarnate in other worlds. It can go through other planes: the physical, vital, mental and psychic worlds. As soon the soul leaves the body, it goes through these planes to its own world, but it does not reincarnate there. It reincarnates only in the physical world on earth. Here alone the soul has to manifest its divinity.

References

1 F.M. Cornford, *From Religion to Philosophy*, London: Edward Arnold, 1914, pp. 161, 229).

2 Paul Tillich, *History of Christian Thought*, New York: Simon & Sherster, 1968, p. 268.

3 The doctrine of evolution was known in India long before the Christian era. Kapila (about seventh century BC) explained this theory in his Samkhya Philosophy. Sir Monier Williams says, "The Hindus were. . . . Evolutionists many centuries before the doctrine of evolution had been accepted by the scientists of our time and before

any word like evolution existed in any of the languages of the world." (*Hinduism and Brahminism*, p. 12).

4 Quoted in H.W. Schumann, *The Historical Buddha*, London: Arkana, 1989, pp. 54–55.

30

Reincarnation in World Religions

Introduction

The belief in reincarnation is as old as the human culture itself. People have this belief right from ancient times to the present day. The belief in reincarnation is found even among ancient tribal people all over the world. It was also believed by the thinkers and philosophers of ancient civilizations in India, Egypt, Greece, Rome, Babylonia and Arabia. However, the logical explanation of the doctrine is found nowhere except in the teachings and writings of the ancient sages and philosophers of India.

Primitive Tribes

The belief in reincarnation is found among many tribes of primitive people all over the world:

- In Central Australia among the Arunta
- In West Africa among the Ewe, Edo, Igbo and Yoruba
- In Southern Africa among the Bantu speakers and Zulu
- In South Pacific Islands among the New Zealand Maoris, the Tamanians, Tahitians, Fijians, Solomon Islanders, Marquesans, tribes of New Caledonia and the Melanesians
- In East Indian islands among the Balinese, the Bakongs and Dyaks of Boreneo, the Papuans of New Guinea, and the Poso Alfures of Celebes
- In North Pacific islands among the Okinawans and others

Australians. The Australian Aborigines have firm belief in reincarnation of the spirits of human beings. This belief is based upon the presupposition that the soul is separable from the body and that it possesses the capacity to travel from body to body.[1]

Africans. In Africa rebirth is not only viewed positively, but failure to be reborn and thereby not gaining another opportunity to improve is regarded as an evil. The African groups who believe in many rebirths are numerous.[2]

Tribes of Americas. American Indians believed in rebirth. Prof. Brinton states that this doctrine was one of the American Indians' deeply rooted and widespread convictions especially among the tribes of eastern United States.[3] There were some who claimed to have full knowledge of a previous birth.

The idea of reincarnation was known to the Iroquois, Algonquins and Creeks in the east; the Dakotas, Hurons and Winnebagos in the north; the Kiowas of the Plains; and the Hopi and Mohaves of Arizona; the Ahls of Vancouver Island; the Montagnais of Quebec and Labrador; and five northern tribes: the Tlingits, Haidas, Tsimsyans, Aleuts and Athapa. The Mayans and Quiches of Central America, the Powhattans and Tiacalans of Mexico and the tribes of South America also believed in rebirth.

Eskimos. Vilhjalmur Stefansson, a naturalist and explorer describes in *Red book* the doctrines of the Eskimos. He lived with the Eskimos in northern Canada for ten years and discovered among his Eskimo friends beliefs that resembled the reincarnation theories associated with India. He suggests that many so-called primitives may be descendants of once highly civilized races.

Ancient Europeans. Beliefs in reincarnation have been found among the Finns, Lapps, Danes, Norse, Icelandic peoples, Early Saxons, Celts of Great Britain, Old Prussians, Early Teutonics, Lithuvanians, Letts and Lombards of Italy.

The northern European Caucasians are known to ethnologists as the Old Teutons. They hold the doctrine of transmigration as evidenced by the Scandinavian prose records.

In *Viking Civilization* (New York: W.W. Norton, 1930) Axel Olrik states that it was believed that one newly deceased was reborn in his descendants, and the latter were accordingly given the name of the deceased. (p. 23).

The Germans who followed Ariovistus did not fear death because of their hope of rebirth.

Celtic. Evans-Wentz in his *The Fairy-Faith in Celtic Countries* (Oxford University Press, 1911) describes in detail the Celtic doctrine of reincarnation, and also provided evidence that even to the present day the idea is alive among some of these peoples. Chapters 7 and 12). The territory of the ancient Celts included, in addition to Great Britain and Ireland, Northern Italy, France, Belgium, western Switzerland and western Germany. Celtic beliefs in reincarnation were pre-Roman. In his *Atlantis: The Antediluvian World*[4] Ignatius Donnelly writes that the Old World recognized Ireland as possessing a very ancient civilization. In Sanskrit books it is referred as *Hiranya*, the "Island of the Sun." The Greeks called Ireland the "Sacred Isle." The people of Ireland believed in reincarnation of souls long before the time of Pythagoras.

In Hinduism

The doctrine of karma and the theory of reincarnation are the two pillars of the Hindu philosophy. The cultural background dates back to Indus Valley civilization discovered by archaeological excavations.

Vedas. Historically the *Vedas* are the earliest scriptures of Hinduism. The eminent philosopher and scholar Dr. S. Radhakrishnan, in the introduction to his translation of the principal *Upanishads,*[5] observes that though there is no reference to rebirth in the *Rig Veda*, its elements are found. The passage of the soul from the body, its dwelling in other forms of existence, its return to human form, the determination of future existence by the principle of karma are all mentioned. "The immortal soul will be reborn in a new body due to its meritorious deeds." (I.164.30). There is retribution for good and evil deeds in a life after death. Good people go to heaven (I.154.5), and others to the world presided over by Yama (the king of death) (X.14.2).

The Upanishads. The *Upanishads* form the final part of the

Vedas. They are rich in philosophical thoughts. The doctrine of reincarnation receives articulate expression in the *Upanishads*. The soul has chances of acquiring merit and advancing to life eternal. Until its union with the eternal Reality is attained, there will be some form of life or other, which will give scope to the individual soul to acquire enlightenment and attain eternal life.

As stated in chapter 27. Transmigration, above, the *Upanishads* give detailed descriptions of the manner in which a person dies and is reborn (*Brahadaranyaka Upanishad,* 4.3.37–38). The transition is illustrated by certain examples. As grasshopper, when it has come to the end of a blade of grass, finds another place of support, and then draws itself towards it, similarly this soul, after reaching the end of the body, finds another place of support and then draws itself towards it. As a goldsmith gives a piece of gold another, newer and more beautiful shape, similarly does this soul, after having thrown off this body, takes another, newer and more beautiful form, whether it be of the manes, or demigods or gods or of any other beings. (*Brahadaranyaka Upanishad*, 4.4.2–4).

These passages bring out several aspects of the theory of rebirth. The soul finds out its future body before it leaves the present one. The soul is creative in the sense that it creates a body. At every change of body, the soul takes a newer form. The state of each existence is conditioned and determined by its knowledge and karma in the previous existence. From the *Brahadaranyaka Upanishad*, it appears that accompanied by all the organs the departing soul enters into perception and becomes possessed of knowledge and consciousness. The results of learning and conduct cling to the soul.

The ignorant, the unenlightened go after death to sunless demoniac regions. (*Isa Upanishad*, 3; *Brahadaranyaka Upanishad,* 4.4.11). The *Chandogya Upanishad* speaks of two paths open to mortals, the bright and dark, the path of the gods and the path of the fathers. Those who practice penance and faith enter the path of light, and they never return to the cycle of human existence. Those who are only ethical, performing works useful to the public, travel by the path of smoke, dwell in the world of ancestors till the time comes for them to come down to earth, then they are born again according to their past karma. (5.10.1–6). Those who have done good deeds will attain a good birth; but those who have done evil deeds will attain an evil birth. (5.10.7)

Rebirth is the lot of a human being until he obtains true knowledge. By virtuous acts he furthers his evolution. The reward of goodness is to grow in goodness. The reward of growing in purity of heart is to gain a clearer vision of Reality. Knowledge of Reality leads to liberation.

It is suggested that the soul before undergoing rebirth experiences reward or punishment for its deeds in heaven or hell. The original Vedic belief of reward in heaven or punishment in hell gets mixed up with the doctrine of rebirth.

The soul is said to be a very minute entity residing in the cavity of the heart and resembling in every respect, except size, the visible human.

Bhagavad Gita. This celebrated scripture contains the essence of the *Upanishads.* The theme of reincarnation pervades much of this scripture. Its second Chapter is largely devoted to rebirth. The interest in reincarnation of various American and European Transcendentalists in the nineteenth century can be traced to the study of the *Bhagavad Gita.*

Bhagavad Gita asserts that the Self (Atman) is eternal (2.11–25). It is part of the universal Self, the eternal Reality. When the body dies, the soul does not die, but merely leaves the body and takes a new body. The soul is subject to the cycle of births and deaths so long as actions are performed with attachment to their fruits. However it is freed from this bondage when actions are performed dispassionately without any desire for their fruits. *Gita* makes it clear that one cannot avoid performing actions out of fear they would produce reaction, because:

> "Verily none can ever remain for even a moment without performing action, for everyone is made to act helplessly indeed by the forces (*gunas*) of Nature." (3.5)

Again,

> "Not by non-performance of actions does a person reach actionlessness, nor by mere renunciation does he attain to perfection." (3.4)

It is the desire for the fruits of action that causes reaction. If there is no attachment to action or its fruits, then it is no action at all. Therefore perform actions without attachment; you will attain purity of heart and finally liberation. (3.19)

A liberated person is not bound or tainted by karma though he continues to live and work. He lives only to exhaust the *prarabdha* (active) karma. After he has exhausted it, his body falls away and he attains absolute freedom or immortality.

Manu Smriti. This scripture of righteousness, among other things, deals with the doctrine of karma and rebirth. It declares:

> "With whatever disposition of mind a person performs any act, he reaps its result in a future body endowed with the same quality." (12.81)
>
> "Those endowed with goodness (*sattva*) reach the state of gods, and those endowed with activity (*rajas*) the state of humans, and those endowed with darkness (*tamas*) ever sink to the condition of beasts; that is the threefold course of transmigration." (12.40)

The Samkhya System. The Samkhya is considered to be the oldest of all philosophical systems. It is attributed to the sage Kapila. It admits two ultimate realities: conscious *Purusa* (Self) and unconscious *Prakrti* (primordial Nature).

Purusa is ever pure and ever free, but it is subject to pain and pleasure, when it forgets its true nature and identifies itself with *Prakrti*. Once it realizes its true nature through spiritual practice, it attains freedom from suffering.

The gross body dies with physical death, but the subtle body, which contains within itself the intellect, the mind and senses, continues to exist and reincarnates. In the subtle body are stored all the impressions of all our experiences and karma, and in accordance with the Law of Karma, the impressions determine the circumstances of our future birth.

Yoga Philosophy. In India Yoga has been practiced since ages by Yogis and sages for attaining liberation. But it was not formally systematized until it was codified by the sage Patanjali of India, in his *Yoga Sutras*, a few centuries before Christ.

The Yoga system studies all aspects of human personality, and teaches us how to control the modifications of the mind through the observance of ethical discipline, practice of meditation, dispassion and surrender to God.

According to the *Yoga Sutras*, the root cause of human sufferings, karmic involvement and the endless cycle of births and deaths is ignorance (*avidya*). (2.4). Ignorance means taking the non-eternal as the eternal, the impure as the pure, and the not-self (body, mind, senses, intellect and ego) as the Self. (2.5). It is the source of egoism, attachment, aversion and clinging to life. It is the impressions (*samskaras*) of these five afflictions that give rise to bondage of karma and suffering. (2.12).

Patanjali has prescribed an eight-stage Yoga popularly known as Raja Yoga for the destruction of these afflictions. The eight stages of Yoga are: restraints (*Yama*), observances (*Niyamas*), postures (*Asana*), breathing exercises (*Pranayama*), withdrawal of senses, concentration, meditation and samadhi (super-consciousness).

When a Yogi attains the highest form of samadhi, the five afflictions and bondage of karma are destroyed and he attains liberation. (For full details, refer, Swami Satchidananda, *Raja Yoga: Yoga of Meditation,* ed. by O. R. Krishnaswami)

The Carvaka System. The word *carvaka* means "materialist." The *Carvaka* system believes in pure materialism. Its origin can be traced as back as the *Veda* period. The *Carvaka* is mentioned in *Epics* and the *Dialogues of Buddha.*

The *Carvaka*'s doctrine is called *lokayata*, as it holds that only this world (*loka*) exists and nothing beyond, nor any future life.

The highest end of life is enjoyment of pleasure in this life. Perception is the only valid source of knowledge. What is not directly perceived does not exist. Perception reveals only material world. There is no evidence to show the existence of a soul in man. When a man dies nothing is left of him to enjoy or suffer the consequences of his actions hereafter.

Lokayata admits of no God, dismisses the concepts of heaven and hell as down-right silly.

In all ages there are a few such materialists, who just believe in animalistic life of sensual pleasure.

Sri Ramana Maharishi (1879–1950). He was a great Jnana Yogi of the twentieth century. His views on Reincarnation are: Reincarnation exists only so long as there is ignorance, ignorance of identifying Self with the body.

If there is birth there must be not only one birth but also a series of successive births. But if you ask who has the birth and whether the birth and death are for you or for somebody distinct from you, then you realize the truth and the truth burns up all karmas and frees you from all births. The books describe how it would take countless lives to exhaust all *sanchita karma* (karmas accumulated from previous births). But all the accumulated karma is burnt up by one little spark of *jnana*, just as a mountain of gunpowder is blown up by a single spark of fire. It is the ego that is the cause of all the world and of the countless sciences whose researches are so great as to baffle description, and if the ego is dissolved by enquiry all this immediately crumbles and the Reality or Self alone remains.

Integral Yoga of Aurobindo. Aurobindo (1872–1950) was a great Yogi, nationalist, poet, critic, thinker and spiritual leader of India. The evolution of consciousness is the central framework of his thought._This spiritual evolution is seen as a series of ascends from material, physical existence up to "supramental" existence, in which we reach our perfection. Aurobindo conceived Integral Yoga as a means for speeding up the spiritual evolution. Integral Yoga seeks to incorporate the essence and process of the traditional Yogas, blending their methods into one system. It seeks an integral and total change of consciousness and nature, not for the individual alone but for all of humanity and the entire cosmos. It seeks a transformation of life and existence by and through the divine.

According to Aurobindo the true foundation of the theory of rebirth is the evolution of the soul. Reincarnation is an indispensable means for working out of the spiritual evolution. In this process of evolution, successive deaths and rebirths are only stations in the long path of the soul's spiritual journey. This journey ends when the soul attains supreme consciousness and reunites with the Godhead.

Jainism

The origin of Jainism in India lies far back in the prehistoric times. The long line of teachers who handed down the faith consists of twenty-four *Tirthankaras*, liberated saints. The last *Tirthankaras* was Mahavira Vardhamana (599 – 527 B.C.), a contemporary of Gautama Buddha.

According to Jainism everything in the world – fire, wind, plant, insects and leaves – have a spirit in them. Each of living things (*jivas*) consists of a body and soul. Souls are infinite in number, and are sharply differentiated according to their character. The unenlightened souls are subject to the cycle of births and deaths due to the bondage of karma. Actions prompted by passions or desire and attachment attract the invisible particles of karmic matter to the souls and bind them to the cycle of births and deaths.

The Jains propound that there is no creation of a new substance or destruction of the old; it is only an endless fusion of elements in different forms. Birth and death are seen as modifications of the soul. The soul is capable of existing independent of the body.

The ultimate goal of life is to attain absolute liberation of the soul from the body by removal of karma. The Jains hold that when a particular karma (action) produces its effect, it is purged from the soul. The process of purging could go on until all taint of matter is wiped out. But along with purging of past karma, the soul accumulates new karma, thus making for the endless chain of births and deaths.

What is the process that binds the soul to the body? The Jains attribute it to wrong belief, non-renunciation, carelessness, passions and vibrations set up in the soul through mind, body and speech. Perfect faith in the teachings of the Jain teachers, correct knowledge of the teachings, and the practice of non-injury to life, truthfulness, non-stealing, celibacy and non-attachment are the means for removing the bondage of karma. When the karmas are removed the soul attains its natural perfection.

Buddhism

Buddhism believes in the successive cycles of births and deaths. However it does not accept the doctrine of eternal Self. The human being like everything else is the offspring of an unbroken, ever-changing process of birth and death according to the doctrine of Conditioned Origination. This means, "If this exists then that comes to be." The entire universe perishes and is created afresh in every moment. Nothing remains the same from one moment to the next. The human being is continually changing, but is always determined by its previous actions.

When a being dies and is reborn, what transmigrates is its karma. Karma is nothing but a "series," a combination of sensation, thought, feeling, volition and material elements. It is not a unified and independently existing entity that moves from life to life. It is rather the life process itself, the blending of energy and form that coordinates an unending flow of life moments. It is a continual process of becoming. It is the residue of all past actions, thoughts and experiences. The term "rebirth" means, in Buddhism, only the psycho-physical process, which is cut off at death and continues immediately somewhere else like the image in the mirror or the echo of one's voice. It is the arising of rebirth consciousness, just as the image that is produced through the contact of face and mirror. It is the passing away of the present consciousness only that conditions a fresh one in another life. Life is a flame, and rebirth is the transmitting of the flame from one candle to another and nothing more. Flame is one and the same, as an observed continuity, but the candle is not the same.

Buddhist reincarnation is the endless transmission of such an impulse through an endless series of forms; nothing is transmitted but an impulse, dependent on the heaping up of the past. It is a person's character, and not the soul, that goes on. What provides the continuity between lives, says H. H. Dalai Lama, is not an entity, but the subtlest level of consciousness.

Tibetan Buddhism

Those who master the Law of Karma and achieve realization can choose to return in life after life to serve others. In Tibet a tradition of recognizing such incarnations (*tulkus*) began in the thirteenth century and continues to the present day. When a realized master dies, he may leave precise indications of where he will be reborn. One of his closest disciple or spiritual friends may have a vision or dream foretelling his imminent rebirth. In some cases his former disciples might approach a master known for having the ability to recognize *tulkus*, and this master might have a dream or vision that would enable him to direct the search for the *tulkus*. When a child is found, this master authenticates him. The purpose of this tradition is to ensure that the wisdom memory of the realized masters is not lost. In the course of training of the incarnated child the inherited wisdom awakens. His Holiness the Dalai Lama, for example, was able to understand at an early age without much difficulty to grasp.

It is common for small children who are reincarnations to remember objects and people from their previous lives. Some can also recite scriptures although they have not yet been taught them.

Zoroastrianism

This is older than Buddhism. It was founded by Zoroaster (628 BC – 551 BC) in Persia. Its dogma is that there is transmigration of souls. The souls of good men, after their death, go to sun paradise and enjoy delights; the souls of bad people fall into hell and undergo torture. The imperfectly good migrate from one body to another until, by the efficacy of good thoughts and actions, they are finally emancipated from matter.

Under Islamic rule, many of the Zoroastrians fled from Iran in the seventh century to India. Their modern successors are the Parsees, living chiefly in Bombay, India.

Egypt

Herodotus, Plato and other writers spoke of reincarnation as the general belief of the Egyptians during the Persian period (about 500 B. C). Dr. Margaret Murray, a distinguished Egyptologist, in her *The Splendor That was Egypt* (New York: Philosophical Library, 1949) points to evidences of reincarnation belief far anterior to the Persian invasion. In his volume *Oldest Books in the World* (London: Kegan Paul, Trench, Trubner, 1900) states that life on this earth to the ancient people of Egypt was only a part of many lives which had preceded and would follow it.

The most celebrated scripture of the Egyptians is the *Book of the Dead.* It describes the journey of the soul through the states following the death of the body. It would take rebirth again and again until finally purged of all desire for any further existence on this earth.

Judaism

The strictly orthodox Jews tend to reject reincarnation. Others, including some orthodox rabbis, accepted rebirth as an integral part of Judaism as does Sholem Asch in the opening of *The Nazarene*, New York: 1877, II. P. 526.

In the first century the Jewish historian Flavius Josephus speaks of reincarnation in his famous work *The Jewish War* (The Works of Flavius Josephus), Tr. By William Wiston, Philadelphia: J. Grigg, 1835, II, p. 316).

In *The Antiquities of the Jews*, Josephus repeats that the Pharisees (one of the three chief schools of Jewish philosophy) believe that souls have an immortal vigor and that the virtuous "shall have power to revive and live again" on earth.

In *Die Christliche Mystick* (Regensburg, 1840, III, p. 27) J. V. Gorres says that the Jewish Cabala was held in high esteem particularly by the Essenes (another school of Jewish Philosophy) and reincarnation is basic in Cabalistic thinking. Other scholars show that the Essenes came under the influence of Buddhist monks who crowed into the Middle East in the centuries preceding the Christian era. In addition, they had affinities with other reincarnationists, namely the Pythagoreans.

Another witness to this period is the Alexandrian philosopher Philo Judaeus. He penetrated into the esotericism of the oldest Judaic teachings and made correlation with the Platonic philosophy. In his *De Somniis* (I. 22) he said that, "the air is full of souls; those who are nearest to earth descending to be tied to mortal bodies, return to other bodies, desiring to live in them."

Rabbi Moses Gaster considers Judaic reincarnation belief in his article "Transmigration" in the *Encyclopaedia of Religion and Ethics* (James Hastings, ed., New York: Scribner's, 1955, Vol. 12, pp. 435–40). He says: "There cannot be any doubt that these views are extremely old (in Judaism). Simon Magus raises the claim of former existences, his soul passing through many bodies before it reaches that known as Simon. The Samaritan doctrine of the *taheb* teaches the same doctrine of a pre-existing soul which was given to Adam, but which, through successive incarnations in Seth, Noah and Abraham, reached Moses."

The Old Testament. One biblical reference suggesting reincarnation is found in Psalms, 90:3–6 at the beginning of a prayer of Moses: Thou turnest man to destruction (dust); and sayest, Return, ye children of men. For a thousand years in Thy sight are but as yesterday when it is past, and as a watch in the night. Plato and Vergil spoke of a thousand year cycle between incarnations. Could Moses have had something like this in mind when he uses the words quoted above?

The Samaritans believed Adam returned as Seth,, then as Noah, Abraham and Moses. The Cabalists (Jewish mystics) affirm that Adam was reincarnated as David. These traditions may have a bearing on interpreting the following verse from Jeremiah 1: 4–5, in which it is said that this prophet existed before birth: "Then the word of the Lord came unto me (Jeremiah) saying, Before I formed thee in the belly, I knew thee; and before thou camest forth out of the womb I sanctified thee, and I ordained thee a prophet unto the nations."

Reincarnation is an essential part of the Jewish Cabala, which is said to represent the hidden wisdom behind the Old Testament. In attempting to answer the intriguing question where the ancient Jews originally obtained these teachings, Isaac Myer writes:

> "The Cabala most likely, originally came from Aryan sources, through Central Asia, Persia, India and Mesopotamia. . . . Communications between the ancient nations of Asia was much more general than has been usually thought by the learned of our day."[6]

There was another strong influence exercised on Judaism. Moses was educated in Egypt and Midian, where there was much occult knowledge.

Early Christianity

Reincarnation was a universal teaching among the Christian Gnostics, the most learned of the Christians. In the ninth century B.C the Hebrew prophet Elijah is supposed to have lived. Four centuries later, Malachi recorded this prophecy in the closing lines of the Old Testament: "Behold I will send you Elijah the prophet before the coming of the great and dreadful day of the Lord." The first book of the New Testament, Matthew, refers to his prophecy on three occasions (16: 13–14; 17: 9–13; 11: 7; 11: 10–11, 14–15) and the remaining gospels speak of it seven times (Mark 8: 27–28, 9: 9–13; Luke 9: 7–9, 9:18–19; John 1: 19–23) .

The rebirth of saviors and prophets is clear enough in Christian teaching, but what about ordinary people? That it may be legitimate to look to a previous life for the source of individual goodness or badness seems clear from Saint Paul's comments on Jacob and Esau. He says that the Lord loved the one and hated the other before they were born. (Romans 9:10–13; Malachi 1: 2–3). A non-existent being could not be loved or hated.

Another illustration of what the East calls Law of Karma is the one in which Christ warns that those who live by the sword shall die by the sword (Matthew 26: 52). This could only be universally true if there is more than one life in which to experience the reaction, for many professional combat soldiers die quietly in their own beds.

St. John states in Revelation 3: 12, "Him that overcometh will I make a pillar in the temple of my God, and he shall go *no more* out." Possibly he had gone out into incarnation before, otherwise the words "no more" could have no place or meaning. Several Church Fathers like Justin Martyr (AD 100–*c.* 165), Clement of Alexandria (second century AD), Origen (third century) and Synesius (c.370 – 430) hold the doctrine of reincarnation of souls. The Christian Gnostics were all have belief in reincarnation. Jung was convinced that "the central ideas of Christianity are rooted in Gnostic philosophy . . . ." (*Psychology and Alchemy*, New York: Pantheon, 1953, p. 35). G. R. S. Mead who translated the important Gnostic scripture the *Pistis Sophia* (Knowledge or Wisdom) writes in the Introduction: "In this respect (reincarnation) the *Pistis Sophia* offers richer material for those interested in this ancient and widespread doctrine than can be found in any other old-world document in the West." (London: John M. Watkins, 1921, p. xiv).

All outward manifestations of Christian Gnosticism and Gnostic Manicheism were eventually suppressed by emperors and Popes alike; the death penalty was often inflicted for belief. Yet these movements long maintained an underground existence even in the West. In the Byzantine empire where the Eastern half of the Church prevailed, they withdrew to the boundaries of the empire, maintaining secret relations with kindred groups. Later in the medieval period Gnostic ideas have revived on a large-scale.

For fourteen centuries the dialogue on reincarnation was silenced in orthodox Christendom because in the year 553 the Fifth Ecumenical Council rejected the doctrine of pre-existence of the soul. Emperor Justinian, the head of the Eastern Empire, declared war against the followers of the Church Father Origen. In 553 Justinian issued his anathemas (curses) against Origen's teachings including the doctrine of reincarnation. The Fifth Ecumenical Council was called. Justinian refused Pope Vigilius's request for equal representation of bishops from East and West, and summarily convened the Council on his own terms. So Pope refused to attend. Of the 165 bishops attended the final meeting, 159 were from the Eastern Church. Hence the voting was very much in Justinian's hands. This improper Council's decision was influenced by him. Four of the fifteen anathemas were aimed at pre-existence of souls and their reincarnation, because this doctrine conflicted with the assumed powers of the priest class to "remit sins;" clearly the priest class would not let mere philosophical assertions come in the way of temporal power. As Reverend William Alva Gifford has written in *The Story of the Faith*, Justinian assumed the headship of the Church, directed ecclesiastical discipline, and even dictated theological doctrines. He also closed the University of Athens, the last stronghold of Neo-Platonism (p. 178).

The curse (553 AD) against reincarnation proved effective due to the indefatigable work of the Inquisitors. Reincarnation was dead to the masses of people in the West. But truth suppressed leads disconcertingly to a host of errors. The millions have not utilized their "one Life-time" to seek God, but to enjoy this world – so shortly to be forever lost! The truth is that man reincarnates until he has consciously regained his status as a son of God.

Later Christianity

The door that was shut by the anathemas against pre-existence and reincarnation in AD 553 was reopened prior to the Renaissance when Platonic philosophy was reborn.

"The pre-existence of the soul . . . . . is the principal foundation of the belief in metempsychosis," writes the Rev. William R. Algers in *A Critical History of the Doctrine of a Future Life* (New York: 1878, p. 476). From the seventeenth century onward, many ministers and religious writers taught pre-existence of the souls and their reincarnation. They include ministers and clergymen from Britain, Scotland, Germany, America, Italy, Belgium and Russia. (For details, refer Joseph Head and S.L. Cranston, eds., *Reincarnation: The Phoenix Fire Mystery*, New York: Crown Publications, 1977, pp. 176–186).

Islam

Islam was founded by the Prophet Muhammad (571 A.D. – 632) in the deserts of Arabia. Starved of material possessions, bereft of any intellectual direction, the Bedouins of the desert followed a religion of animistic polytheism that did not provide them with any spiritual anchor. In the sixth century A. D. life in Arabia's leading city Mecca was barbaric. It was this world that Muhammad set out to instruct and to reach.

The persecution of scholars by the medieval Church had gradually driven most students of science and philosophy out of Europe. Some found refuge in Persia, others in Arabia, the land of liberty in those days. They gave Arabs a knowledge of Greek philosophy, Gnosticism and Cabala. Alberuni, a Muslim scholar who accompanied Sultan Muhammad of Ghazni into India, acquired a knowledge of Hindu religious classics: a number of them were translated into Arabic. All these influences combined to make Islamic thinkers natural heirs to the philosophy of reincarnation.

In a series of articles on "Reincarnation – Islamic Conceptions" in *Theosophy in Pakistan* (Karachi), October – December, 1965, M. H. Abdi, a Muslim scholar expresses interesting thoughts on how rebirth gradually lost popularity in Islam:

> "The position adopted by the successive luminaries who followed the Prophet Muhammad was to affirm the belief in reincarnation but not to propagate it as a teaching for the masses. This attitude was due to psychological reasons. The emphasis in Islamic teachings has throughout been on the purity of action.
>
> "Another factor to remember is the defensive wars (described as holy wars) which the Muslims fought. . . . . gave a different shift to Islamic teachings. Philosophical, mystical and ethical teachings, which received impetus in the first phase, had subdued existence in the later phase. During this phase the republican character of the State was changed into monarchy and the supremacy no more belonged to the saints and philosophers. A subject like reincarnation demands a subtle mental attitude. It entails understanding of the higher planes of consciousness, the

Law of Cause and Effect and the working of the Laws of evolution. The monarchs had no interest in such subjects; like so many other teachings, reincarnation was confined to the study and attention of the outer and inner students of Sufism. However there is no danger for a Muslim being called a heretic if he believes and expresses himself in favor of reincarnation."

But it was not only through Sufism that the doctrine of rebirth was transmitted, but also through liberal theologians. G. F. Moore states, in his Ingersoll lecture on Metempsychosis, that "among Mohammedans the difficulty of reconciling the sufferings of innocent children . . . .with the goodness or even the justice of God led some of the liberal theologians to seek a solution to sins committed in a former existence. . . Reincarnation is fundamental to the doctrine of the Imam (Divine Reincarnate) as held by the Shiites(one of the two great religious divisions of Islam); It was developed in a characteristic form by the Ismailis."[7]

E.G. Browne confirms all this in his three-volume work, *The literary History of Persia* (London:1902), particularly the Chapters on the Ismailis and the other esoteric schools of Islam.

The following verses of the Koran, the scripture of Islam, clearly indicate reincarnation:

"And you were dead, and He brought you back to life. And He shall cause you to die, and shall bring you back to life, and in the end shall gather you unto Himself." (Sutra 2: 28)

The other verses which indicate reincarnation include:

Chapter 8—Sura Iraf—Meccan Verses: 6–6–13

Chapter 25—Sura Zakhraf—Meccan Verses: 5–10–6

Chapter 14—Sura Nahel Verses: 4–0–10

The Sufis. They are Islamic mystics. It was among the Sufis that the teaching of reincarnation was especially preserved. They believe in conscious evolution and the limitless perfection of man.

The Eastern school of Sufis was derived from certain ancient Zoroastrian mystics. These Sufis taught:

> "When the souls not yet come forth from the pit of the natural darkness of bodily matter, are nevertheless in a state of increasing improvement, then , in an ascending way, they migrate from body to body, each purer than the former one, until the time of climbing up to the steps of the wished-for perfection of mankind . . . .after which, purified of the defilement of the body, they join the world of sanctity. . . . (Shea and Troyer, trans., *The Dabistan*, London: 1843, III, pp. 149–50).

Mansur Al-Hallaj (Tenth century) held to all the cardinal teachings of reincarnation. Jalal U'L-Din Rumi (1207–73), the greatest of the Persian Sufi poet, sings in his Mathnawi:

> I died as mineral and became a plant,
> I died as plant and rose to animal,
> I died as animal and I was man.
> Why should I fear? When was I-less by dying?
> Yet once more I shall die as man, to soar with angels blest,
> But even from angel-hood I must pass on. . . .
> (R. A. Nicholson, *Rumi, Poet and Mystic*, London: Allen & Unwin, 1950).

The Sufis of Syria are known as the Druses of Mount Lebanon. They came to prominence in the eleventh century. They exist today mainly in Syria, Lebanon and Jordan. Reincarnation is one of their fundamental teachings.

References

1. Baldwin Spencer and F. J. Gillen, *Northern Tribes of Central Australia*, London: Macmillan, 1904
2. Edwin Smith, *Knowing the African*, London: Luthernworth, 1947; E. G. Parrinder, "Varities of belief in Reincarnation," *The Hibbert Journal*, April, 1957
3. Daniel Brinton, *Myths of the New World*
4. New York: Harper Brothers, revised edition, 1949, pp. 251, 254-55.

5. *The Principal Upanisads*, New York: Harper & Row, 1953, pp. 43–44.
6. Isaac Myer, *Qabbalah*, Philadelphia, 1888, p. 221.
7. G.F. Moore, *Metempsychosis*, Cambridge: Harvard University Press, 1914, pp. 52– 54.

31

Reincarnation in the Western Tradition

In the previous Chapter the doctrine of reincarnation in the world religions was surveyed. In this Chapter reincarnation in the Western Tradition is discussed.

Greek and Roman Heritage

It seems that the ancient Greeks derived the idea of reincarnation from India. There was a great deal of intellectual traffic between the early great civilizations.

According to Prof. Edward Zeller, the author of *History of Greek Philosophy* (London: Longmans, Green, 1880), the doctrine of rebirth seems to have passed from the theology of the Orphic mystics into philosophy. The Orphics believed that the soul is divine and immortal but due to the impurities of earthly life, it is subject to the wheel of rebirths. The Orphic belief seems to have been widely current in the Greek colonies in Southern Italy and Sicily.

Pherecydes of Syros (sixth century B.C.), one of the Seven Wise Men of Greeks, was the master of Pythagoras. The most important subject he dealt with was the doctrine of transmigration and the immortality of the soul.[1]

Pythagoras (*c.* 582–507 BC), Greek philosopher and mathematician, knew his former lives.[2] Reincarnation was one of the main teachings of Pythagoras. He traveled widely and some say he visited India. It seems that Pythagoras derived the heart of his philosophy from the wise men of the East.

The Greek Mystics. The doctrine of transmigration appears to have been one of the deepest doctrines of the Greek mystics. The Greek Mystical Schools are believed to be copies of the more ancient Indian and Egyptian mysticism. Herodotus, Greek Historian, stated that they were introduced into Greece by Orpheus.

Orphic sages declared that humans are composed of an invisible soul that was originally good and pure but that has become polluted by some kind of primordial sin or error. As a consequence of this ancient transgression, the originally pure soul has become imprisoned within a physical body that is believed to be impure by nature.

The ultimate aim of Orphism was to raise the soul of each devotee to increasingly purer levels of spiritual existence. The elevation of the soul was promoted by participation in the sacramental practices of the Orphic brotherhoods. By continually practicing meditation, prayer, and vegetarianism, the devotee eventually would gain immortality and thereby achieve release from any future reincarnations.

Complete and lasting freedom from bondage to the material order could be realized only after undergoing a series of births in a variety of physical forms that are determined by the merits of the previous lives.

The Greek Philosophers. Philosopher Heraclitus of Ephesus (*c.* 540–480 BC) and Greek Historian Herodotus (fifth century BC) also asserted the immortality and transmigration of souls. Philosopher Empedocles (490–430 BC), under the influence of the writings of the mystic-mathematician Pythagoras, asserted that nothing in the cosmos is either created or destroyed. All living things undergo changes as they are composed of the four basic elements (air, fire, water and earth). The souls of the impure are condemned to transmigrate through numerous types of incarnations. Escape from this dark destiny is achieved through lengthy purification process, the primary requirement of which is the avoidance of eating the flesh of animals whose souls once may have inhabited by human bodies.

Socrates (469–399 BC) was a great Greek philosopher and a master of the most famous Greek philosopher Plato. He was a great advocate of the immortality and reincarnation of the soul. His favorite doctrine that knowledge is simply recollection implies a previous life in which what has been learned is now recollected.

Plato (427?–347 BC) was the most famous philosopher of Greece. "Out of Plato come all things that are still written and debated among men of thought," wrote Emerson. Plato's ideas on reincarnation of souls have considerably influenced the Western literature and philosophy. He states: "the soul, as being immortal, and having been born again many times, and having seen all things that exist in this world or the world below, has knowledge of them all."[3]

In his *Phaedrus*, Plato compares the soul to a charioteer who drives a pair of winged horses, one being of noble breed and the second of opposite character. The noble horse is obedient to the rein, but the vicious horse sways and sinks the charioteer towards earth. This analogy is similar to the famous analogy of the *Katha Upanishad* of India (1.3.3–9). Plato lays stress on the unbroken continuity of the Self-evolving its character in a series of life-changes. One's destiny is not allotted to him but he chooses it for himself, which depends upon the disposition formed in the previous life.

Aristotle (384–322 BC) was a student of Plato. He accepted the preexistence and reincarnation of the soul in his *Eudemus* (On the Soul).

The Roman Renaissance

The classical Roman history was closely linked with that of her neighbor Greece. All the Greek Gods were eventually transformed into Roman deities. There was even a linkage through reincarnation.. The Calabrian poet Ennius (239?–169 BC) relates in his *Annals* that Homer appeared to him in a dream and said that their bodies have been animated by the same soul.

But by the end of the Roman Republic—signaled by the assassination of Julius Caesar in 44 BC)—faith in a future life reached its lowest ebb, and a vulgarized Epicureanism had become popular. Epicurus glorified death as annihilation and the end of all men's troubles.[4]

Another system that shared the dominance of minds in Rome was Stoicism. The Stoics held man to be a microcosm who reproduces in his being the constitution of the universe and that he periodically reincarnates. This view reflects the corresponding doctrine of the Vedanta philosophy of India.

In the first century BC, says Cumont, the teachings of Plato and Pythagoras gained new life in the Roman world. Epicureanism died away and stoicism, which had become materialistic, was replaced by Neo-Stoicism. The belief in soul's immortality and reincarnation of the Pythagoreans found a powerful advocate in Posidonius (135–51 BC), a thinker who exercised a powerful influence over his contemporaries and the succeeding generation.

Cicero (106–43 BC), Roman Orator and philosopher, was an advocate of Platonism. In his dialogue *On Old Age* Cicero speaks of his conviction on the immortality and reincarnation of the soul.

Roman General Julius Caesar (100–44 BC) found the Celts to be remarkably fearless in battle. He investigated the reason for this and wrote in his volumes on the wars with the Gauls: They (Celts) wish to inculcate, as one of their leading tenets that souls do not become extinct, but pass after death from one body to another, and so they disregard the fear of death. (*Gallic War*, Book VI, p. 14).

The Neo-platonists

Neo-platonic thought is the most matured metaphysical thought the European world has seen. Pagan Greek philosophy was Neo-platonist till it faded out in the sixth century A.D. Many of the greatest Christian thinkers of the period and later the great Islamic philosophers were deeply influenced by Neo-Platonism.

The famous Alexandrian School of Neo-Platonism was founded in Egypt by Ammonius Saccas in A.D. 193. Origen and Plotinus were among his immediate disciples. With the revival of the teachings of Plato, the doctrine of reincarnation again came into prominence. The Neo-platonists did not limit themselves to Plato. Known as "the lovers of Truth," they sought to reconcile all religions and philosophies under one system of truth.

Plotinus (AD 205–70), a philosophical genius and one of the world's greatest mystical writers, made the Neo-Platonism into one of the great religious philosophies. According to Plotinus, souls have a wide choice of place; they themselves determine the honor or discredit, since their place and part are in keeping with their quality. Man is not a made-thing, acting and acted upon according to a fixed nature. If it were so, he could be no different from animals. But man is singled out for condemnation when he does evil, and this with justice.

The last grand master of Neo-Platonism was Ploclus (410–85), a Greek philosopher. He goes into the vital question of what may be the need for repeated incarnations. Proclus treats the soul's descent into the world as a necessary part of its education or as a necessary cosmic service. This is similar to the views of the ancient Indian sages and philosophers.[5]

The Middle Ages (A.D. 500 to about 1500)

The reasonable ideas of the Gnostic sects were a serious threat to the orthodox religion, and they were suppressed by mass execution and torture in the thirteenth century. During the latter part of the Middle Ages the various Gnostic groups spread many parts of Europe and eventually contributed to the great ferment of religious ideas that brought in the Reformation. These European bearers of Gnostic teachings are known to history as the Cathars and the Albigenses. They taught the doctrine of rebirth; the departed soul is reborn again and again until the time comes for its final deliverance from earth. Zoe Oldenbourg, in her history of the crusade against the Albigenses, remarks that their doctrine of transmigration of souls was like that of the Hindus.[6]

The moral code of Albigenses involved the renunciation of property, truthfulness, vegetarianism, chastity and harmlessness. After the destruction of the wide-ranging Cathari movement, the philosophy of rebirth was preserved chiefly in esoteric form in Europe. The flame was hidden but did not die.

Renaissance and Reformation (14th to 17th century)

The light of Renaissance dawned gradually upon Europe. It was like an awakening from a deep sleep. With the revival of Platonism, the theory of transmigration of soul revived in European philosophy.[7] The Neo-platonic revival appeared first in the city of Florence and latter spread in France, England and Germany in the fifteenth century. Leading scientists, philosophers and poets including Edmund Spencer, William Shakespeare and John Milton came under the Platonic influence. In the seventeenth century Cambridge University became the center of Platonic movement.

The Age of Enlightenment (18th century)

The Age of Reason or Enlightenment was a period of transition in the West. The Enlightenment philosophers advocated a logical and scientific approach to religious and social issues. Among the leaders were Rousseau and Voltaire in France, David Hume and Alexander Pope in England, Kant, Lessing and Herder in Germany, and Benjamin Franklin and Thomas Paine in America. Many of these thinkers believed that there is a universal religion natural to all men and all times and places. They also believed in the immortality and reincarnation of the souls. The Grecian and Roman influence still predominated, but in the latter part of the century two fresh movements began to penetrate: one the philosophical and Cultural Revolution of Germany, and the other from India. This was the time when India's religious treasures were being discovered by the West and some of her scriptures appeared in translation.

Eastern and Transcendental Influences in the 19th Century

During the classical period of German literature reincarnation attracted such attention that the period may almost be styled the flourishing epoch of the doctrine.[8] This period had its origin in the transcendental philosophy of Immanuel Kant (1724 – 1804). Kant posited the existence of two selves in man: the empirical self and the transcendental self. The latter is a continuing self; by its virtue we belong to the world of Reality. Transcendentalism took root in New England (of America) through Unitarianism.

Among Kant's successors the influence of Indian thought became more and more pronounced. August Schlegel published the first German translation of the *Bhagavad Gita* and other Sanskrit works and paid high tribute to Sri Krishna. In *The Wonder that was India* (London: 1954, p. 487), "From Goethe (1749–1832) onwards most of the great German philosophers knew something of Indian philosophy. Schopenhauer . . . openly admitted his debt (to Indian philosophy)." The *Upanishads* of India were translated into German. Beethoven also came under the spell of India. He was fond of copying mystical sentences from Indian scriptures, and he permanently framed on his desk this *Upanishadic* quotation: "I am That which is, I am all That was, That is, and That shall be." The music of Richard Wagner was strongly influenced by Buddhist ideas on reincarnation. Goethe (1749–1832), German poet, had strong belief on reincarnation. He once said: "Surely I must have lived before the time of Emperor Hadrian, for everything Roman attracts me with impressible force."

British poet and mystic William Blake (1757–1827), British classical scholar Thomas Taylor (1758–1835), German poet Friedrich Schiller (1759–1805), German philosopher J. G. Fichte (1762–1814), German philosopher Hegel (1770–1831), British poet Wordsworth (1770–1850), Scottish Novelist Sir Walter Scott (1771–1832), French Social reformer Charles Fourier (1772–1837), German philosopher Schopenhauer (1788–1860), American philosopher Ralph Waldo Emerson(1803–1882), American Transcendalists Frederic H. Hedge (1805–1890), Charles C. Emerson (1808–1836) and Henry David Thoreau (1817–1862), Italian Liberator G. Mazzani (1805–1872), British poet Alfred Lord Tennyson (1809–1892), Russian Philosopher Leo Tolstoy (1828–1910) and other famous Western poets, writers and philosophers of the nineteenth century were all strong advocates of immortality and reincarnation of souls. (For details, *see* Joseph Head and S. Cranston, *Reincarnation: The Phoenix Fire Mystery*, New York: Crown Publishers, 1977, pp. 277–347).

The Theosophical Movement

The advent of Theosophical Society in 1875 has caused the

ennobling doctrine of reincarnation to become a household topic among all classes in the Western world thanks to the wide circulation of *Reincarnation: A Study of Forgotten Truth* by the Theosophist E.D. Walker published in 1888 and underwent numerous editions.

"Karma and reincarnation," wrote Madame H. P. Blavatsky, "are in reality the ABC of Theosophy. She in her first work *Isis Unveiled* (1877) discusses reincarnation at both the individual and cosmic levels.

The *Secret Doctrine* is a monumental book of Blavatsky published in 1888. As stated by George Russell, it is one of the most exciting and stimulating books written during the last hundred years. It is a book of world religions, disclosing an underlying unity among them.

Volume One of this book describes the reincarnation of our own universe. The second volume discusses the evolution of human form and the subsequent reincarnation of human beings.

Reincarnation of the soul is intimately connected with karma. The soul reincarnates again and again to undergo the effects of the actions of body and mind in the previous births. Ultimately through the process of experiences and purification it realizes its real nature and reunites with the Cosmic Spirit, just as a dewdrop becomes the sea.

William Q. Judge in his *The Ocean of Theosophy* gives an answer to the question: What is that reincarnates? It is not the body, not the astral body, nor is the desire. It is the inner Ego that reincarnates, taking body after body, storing up the impressions of life after life. This is the permanent individuality, which gives to everyone the feeling of "I."

Everything done in a former body has consequences, which in the new birth the Ego must enjoy or suffer, for, as St. Paul said: "Brethren, be not deceived. God is not mocked, for whatsoever a man soweth that shall he also reap."

Reincarnation does not mean that we go into animal forms after death, as is believed by some Eastern peoples. "Once a man always a man" is the saying of Masters. As H.P.B. has written: "Nature, propelled by Karma, never recedes, but strives ever forward in her work on the physical plane; that she may lodge a human soul in the body of a man, normally ten times lower than any animal, but she will not reverse the order of her kingdoms . . ."[9]

Judge has written of the rare exception to "Once a man always a man;" "but of course there is the exception of the case where men live bad lives persistently for ages." (*Path,* March, p. 383).

Blavatsky's *Key to Theosophy* (1889) also discusses reincarnation along with other topics. Once people learn Karma and Reincarnation, the greatest of all laws, and feel in themselves the true dignity of human nature, they will turn from evil and eschew it. Here then are the four links of the chain, which would bind humanity into one family: universal brotherhood, universal unity and causation, human solidarity, the Law of Karma and Reincarnation.(Los Angels: Theosophy Co.)

Why does the human spirit incarnate? Anna Kennedy Winner, in *The Basic Ideas of Occult Wisdom,*[10] answers this question. The human spirit seeks to acquire from life on earth the benefits, which only such a life can bestow. But the one-life theory advocated by the Christian Church is absurd. Life is a school for souls. Just as a child cannot learn anything in one day or one term, so also a soul cannot learn much in one life on earth. If we find different human beings at different levels of development, it is because of a difference in the level of evolution of consciousness. Like physical and biological form, consciousness is also a product of gradual evolutionary growth. The speed of each person's spiritual evolution varies according to the degree of effort exerted. So reincarnation is justifiable rationally. An individual human soul passes through hundreds of successive incarnations with alternating periods in subtle worlds and gradually develops from savagery to perfection.

One may wonder why so much stress is laid on the doctrines of karma and reincarnation in the publications of the Theosophical Society! It is not only because these doctrines provide a solid foundation for all human conduct, but also because they are the very keynotes of the higher evolution of mankind. It is only in the light of karma and reincarnation, evolution becomes a logical process and the circles of reason and of life become complete. Karma gives the eternal Law of Action and Justice, and reincarnation furnishes the boundless field for its display. People can understand these two principles, apply them in their lives and strive to achieve moral and spiritual perfection.

19th and 20th Century Scientists, Psychologists, Philosophers and Writers

Thomas H. Huxley (1825–1895), a great British scientist, writes in *Evolution and Ethics and Other Essays*, "Like the doctrine of evolution itself, that of transmigration has its roots in the world of Reality; and it may claim such support as the great argument from analogy is capable of supplying." (New York: Appleton, 1894, pp. 60–61).

Thomas Edison (1847–1931), American Inventor, was a lifelong member of the Theosophical Society. No wonder that he believed in reincarnation.

Luther Burbank (1849–1926), American Horticulturist, had close contact with many Hindu leaders and disciples of the Vedanta Philosophy of India. The bond between their philosophy of life and that of Burbank was so close that he was deeply interested in the claim that reincarnation was based on evolution and founded on the Law of Cause and Effect.

George Foot Moore (1851–1931), Professor of History of Religion-Harvard University, in his Ingersoll Lecture on Immortality, said: "A theory (metempsychosis) which has been embraced by so large a part of mankind of many races and religions and has commended itself to some of the most profound thinkers of all time, cannot be lightly dismissed. . . . If man's earthly existence be conceived as a probation, it must be admitted that in any one life men are put upon this probation under very unequal conditions of every kind, and that the theory of a series of embodiments in which the soul is tested under various conditions accord better with our opinions of justice in the order of things. Finally if an end of perfection is set for the soul, metempsychosis affords the opportunity for a progressive approach to that infinite attainment. . . ."

Carl G. Jung (1875–1961), Swiss psychologist, in his work *Archetypes and the Collective Unconscious* writes, "Rebirth is an affirmation that must be counted among the primordial affirmations of mankind. These primordial affirmations are based on what I call arch-types."[11]

Albert Schweitzer (1875–1965),French physician and clergyman, thought that the idea of reincarnation contains "a most comforting explanation of reality by means of which Indian thought surmounts difficulties which baffle the thinkers of Europe."

Gustaf Stromberg (1882–1931), Swedish-American astronomer and physicist, in his book *The Soul of the Universe*, asserts: "A soul is indestructible and immortal. It carries an indelible record of all its activities. . . ." (New York: David Mc Kay, 1940). In a later work, *The Searchers*, Dr. Stromberg speaks more affirmatively on reincarnation: "Our real selves, our souls, belong before our birth, during our organic life and after our death, to the non-physical world. . . . All the memories of our last and previous lives can be reviewed there in full details in an instant, since there are no atoms which in the physical world block and slow down all our mental activities." (New York: David Mc Kay, 1948, pp. ix, 198).

Julian Huxley (1887–1975), British biologist, initially did not accept the doctrine of reincarnation. But at a later date, in his contribution to a book of essays called *Where Are the Dead?* he no longer spoke of reincarnation as a superstitious belief, but offered a materialistic theory as to how it could work. "The wireless message only becomes a message when it comes in contact with a new, material structure—the receiver. So with our possible spirit-emanation. It . . . would never think or feel unless again embodied in some way." (Quoted in *The Middle Way* (London), August 1969, p. 71).

John Middleton Murray (1889–1957) writes in the *Aryan Path*, June 1938, "The doctrine of reincarnation . . . is an answer to the deep desire of the spiritually awakened soul for divine justice . . . and . . . for an opportunity of self-redemption and self-purification."

Aldous Huxley (1894–1963), well-known American author, in his *The Perennial Philosophy* examines both the Christian and Eastern propositions and comes to the conclusion that the Hindu or Buddhist logic, in the circumstances is self-consistent. He writes, "Orthodox Christian doctrine does not admit the possibility, either in the posthumous state or in some other embodiment, of any further growth towards the ultimate perfection of a total union with the Godhead. But in the Hindu and Buddhist versions of the perennial philosophy, the divine mercy is matched by the divine patience, both are infinite. For Oriental theologians there is no eternal damnation; there are only purgatories and then an indefinite series of second chances to go forward toward not only man's but the whole creation's final end—total reunion with the Ground of all beings. . . ." (New York: Harper & Row, Publishers, 1945, pp. 214–15)

Raynor C. Johnson (1901-), British physicist, has sought to integrate science and religion. In his widely read volume *The Imprisoned Splendor*, he writes about pre-existence, reincarnation and karma: "In any attempt to formulate a philosophy of life and endeavor to see meaning in our pilgrimage, these ancient beliefs cannot be lightly set aside. . . . The idea of reincarnation presents no logical difficulties, whatever be the emotional reaction to it. What the soul has done once by the process of incarnation in a physical body, it can presumably do again. . . ." (New York: Harper and Row, 1953, chapter 18).

Ian Stevenson (1918–) is a Canadian-born American Psychiatrist and Para-psychologist at the University of Virginia. He is regarded as the world's leading authority on the subject of reincarnation. He has done extensive research on reincarnation. He has studied hundreds of cases in which children or adults remember a past life. His book *Twenty Cases Suggestive of Reincarnation* published originally in 1966 (revised ed. 1974) has become a classic in the field. These twenty cases were a representative sample of about 200 cases investigated by him. Stevenson had traveled to Europe, the Near East, Asia, South America, Alaska and other parts of the United States to conduct on-the-spot investigation of reported cases. (For further details about his research and publications, *see* "Remembrances of Past lives" in Chapter 29. The Doctrine of Reincarnation, *above*).

William James (1842–1910), American psychologist, accepts the doctrine of karma. He states: "As I apprehend the Buddhist doctrine of karma, I agree in principle with that. All super naturalists admit that facts are under the judgment of higher laws. . . ."[12]

Sigmund Freud (1856–1939) was great Austrian psychiatrist. In his *The Self in Transformation*, Dr. Herbert Fingarett draws on Freud's later ideas and reveals how they could support the concepts of karma and rebirth. Fingarett is not concerned with "proving" reincarnation and karma, but rather in assessing their self-transforming capacity. In doing this he finds significant parallels between the insights achieved by Freud and those of the ancient psychologists of the East.

Carl G. Jung (1875–1961) was a famous Swiss Psychiatrist and Psychologist. In his autobiography *Memories, Dreams, Reflections*, Jung relates that he had listened attentively to the Indian teaching of reincarnation and searched the world of his own experience for authentic signs to justify this idea. In his final years, he had a series of dreams, which seemed to illustrate the process of reincarnation in a deceased person of his acquaintance. Thereafter he viewed the problem of rebirth in another light. (New York: Pantheon, 1963, p. 319).

Erik H. Erikson (!902 -), American psychoanalyst, is a leading figure in the field of Psychoanalysis. In *Gandhi's Truth* which won the Pulitzer Prize and the National Book Award, he narrates the Hindu view of rebirth and concludes with his conviction: "Nobody in his right mind can visualize his own existence without assuming that he has always lived and will live hereafter." (New York: Norton, 1969, pp. 35–36).

Gina Cerminara, American psychologist, has worked hard to widen the Western conception of immortality, particularly through her books on the Edgar Cayce readings. Her *Many Mansions* has revoked widespread serious interest in reincarnation and Cayce and has been translated into various languages. She described in an interview in *The American Theosophist* (February 1977) that her background was theosophical. She found the readings of Cayce resonated with her theosophical education. In *Many Mansions* she writes: "Psychiatrists concur in the view that the major life attitudes of the psyche arise from the unconscious. The reincarnation principle merely expands the scope of the unconscious to include the dynamics of past-life experience." (New York: William Sloane, 1957, p. 3).

In the *World Within* she writes that at a certain stage of evolution a knowledge of reincarnation is indispensable for full comprehension of oneself and of life in general. (New York: William Sloane, 1957, pp. 199-200).

Herbert Fingarette (1921 -) is an American philosopher and psychologist. His book *The Self in Transformation* is considered a major contribution to psychoanalytic thought. In the Chapter "Karma and the Inner World," he says, "I am not psychologizing reincarnation. I want to present it as a reality, not as a metaphor. . . . The Law of Karma is not the edict of an all-powerful Disciplinarian. . . . It purports to be a factual description: . . . things do eventually 'balanced out' in the normal realm; each moral action produces eventually its quite specific moral reaction. And our constant strivings are constantly producing new 'karma' as well as bringing past karma to fruition; the weary round of births and deaths perpetuated."

John Ellis Mc Taggart (!866–1925) was considered the most distinguished metaphysician since Hegel. His monumental work *The Nature of Existence* gives his grounds for justifying his belief in the immortality and pre-existence of souls. (Cambridge University Press, 1927).

Christmas Humphreys (1901–), British author and Buddhist philosopher, has written a wide variety of books on Buddhism and founded the Buddhist Society in London—the oldest and the most active center in the West. In his best selling *Buddhism,* karma and reincarnation are given special treatment as ideas of indispensable value to humanity in its progress. His small volume *Karma and Rebirth*, published by John Murray in 1943, attempts to reconsider the subject in the light of available scriptures of Hinduism and

Buddhism. No one knows the nature of karma just as no one knows the nature of electricity, but like our knowledge of electricity, we know just a little how it works. The rest is a matter of research and experience. "Life becomes what it does." This is the essence of the Law.

Other Philosophers. Friedrich Nietzshe (1844–1900), Bernard Bosanquet (1848–1923), James Ward (1843–1925), G. Lowes Dickinson (1862–932), John Mc Taggar (1866–1925), W. Macneile Dixon, Hustan Smith and C.J. Ducasse have played a great role in interesting students, professional colleagues and readers in immortality and reincarnation of souls.

Twentieth Century. The literature on reincarnation in the twentieth century has grown to great proportions. Many famous Western scientists, psychologists, philosophers, poets, writers and others were all advocates of the immortality and reincarnation of souls. They include:

- Charles Kelsey Gaines (1854–1944),American Educator
- George Bernard Shaw (1856 –1950), Irish Novelist and Critic
- Arthur Conan Doylc (1859–1930), British Novelist
- James M. Barrie (1860–1937), Scottish Novelist
- Ernest Thomson Seton (1860–1946), American Nature writer
- Maurice Maeterlinck (1862–1949), Belgian Poet
- Wincenty Lutoslawski (1863–), Polish Educator
- David Lloyd George (1863–1945), British Statesman
- Henry Ford (1863–1947), American Industrialist
- Rudyard Kipling (1865–1936), British Writer
- George w. Russell (1867–1935), Irish Writer
- Romain Rolland (1866–1950), French Author of *New Prophets of India*
- Jack London (1876–1916), American Novelist
- Hermann Hesse (1877–1962), German-Swiss Author
- Edgar Cayce (1877–1945), American Healer
- Somerset Maugham (1874–1965), British Novelist
- T. S. Eliot (1888–1965), British Poet

And many other authors were strong believers in the doctrine of immortality and reincarnation of souls. Some of them came under the influence of the Vedanta Philosophy and the *Upanishads* and *Bhagavad Gita* of India, and some others were influenced by Buddhism or theosophical Movement. (For details, *see* Joseph Head and S.L. Cranston, *ibid.* pp. 347–95).

A Gallup poll taken in 1982 showed that nearly one in four Americans believed in reincarnation. A poll in the London *Sunday Telegraph*, April 15, 1979 indicated that 28 per cent of British people believed in reincarnation.

Vedanta and Yoga Centers

Swami Vivekananda (1863–1902) was the greatest disciple of Sri Ramakrishna, the nineteenth century Godman of India. He visited United States in 1893 and participated in the first Parliament of Religions held in Chicago in September, 1893. Swami Vivekananda's first short speech captivated the audience. He proclaimed the universality of religious truths and unity of the goal of all religions. The effect of his mighty words was tremendous. He became a man of mark. The newspapers proclaimed him a Prophet and Seer. Accepting the offer of a lecture bureau for a tour of the United States he delivered lectures in the various centers of learning, and wrote a book on Karma Yoga, the first of its kind.

Several philosophers, psychologists, clergymen, etc. became his ardent followers. His lecture tour opened a new avenue for beginning systematic work in America. It was mainly through him that American People began to know about the greatness of Indian culture and spirituality.

Later Swami Vivekananda toured England and Europe to carry to the English and European people the message of Vedanta. He invited his brother-monks Swami Saradananda and Swami Abedananda for the work in New York and London respetively. Swami Abedananda delivered lectures on Reincarnation in various places.

Soon Vedanta Societies were organized in New York, San Francisco and other major Centers.

Since then there has been a continuous flow of Vedanta teachers to the West. Many spiritual and Yoga Masters have also come from India and Tibet to the West and established Yoga Centers and Buddhist Centers in various places. They are fueling the fire of interest in reincarnation in the West.

To conclude, the doctrine of reincarnation has made great inroads into the contemporary Western thought by Indian religious traditions along with theosophy, transpersonal psychology and academic study of Eastern religions and comparative philosophy.

References

1. Mead, *Orpheus*, London: John Watkins, 1965, p. 21.
2. Lamblichus, *Life of Pythagoras*, tr., Thomas Taylor, London: Watkins, 1965, p. 31.
3. *Dialogues of Plato*, New York: Random House, 1937, I.pp. 360– 61.
4. Franz Cumont, *After life in Roman Paganism,* Yale University Press, 1922; (Reprint New York: Dover, 1959).
5. E.R. Dodds, tr., *Proclus's Elements of Theology*, Oxford University Press, 1963.
6. A History of the Albigensian Crusade, New York: Pantheon, 1961, p. 35.
7. See G.F. Moore, Metampsychosis, Cambridge, Massachusetts: Harvard university Press, 1914, p. 56.
8. See Alfred Bertholet, Transmigration of Souls, London: Harper, 1909, p. 103.
9. Quoted in *The Heart Doctrine* by W. G. Judge, Los Angels and Bombay: The Theosophy Co., 1951, p. 127.
10. Wheaton, Ill.: The Theosophical Publishing House, 1982.
11. See Carl G. Jung in *The Meaning of Death*, New York: McGraw-Hill Book Co., 1959, pp. 3-15.
12. *The varieties of Religious Experience*, New York: Longmans, Green, p. 522

32

Resurrection

Meaning

Resurrection means the revival of the body or rather of the person as a whole, after a period of death. This concept is found in Zoroastrianism, Judaism, Christianity and Islam. There are two views: monistic and dualistic. Monistic view implies that human as a whole disappears in death and is then revived to a new existence. According to dualistic view, the body dies but the soul or spirit lives on and is later united with the body into a renewed being.

Zoroastrianism

The earliest documents of this religion do not mention the resurrection of the body but rather the soul's ascent to paradise. But in the later parts of the *Avesta* there is one reference to resurrection: "When the dead rise, the Living Incorruptible One will come and life will be transfigured." (*Yashts*, 19.11).

In the cosmological treatise, the *Bundahishn* (ninth century AD), resurrection is mentioned in chapter 34. At the arrival of the third and last savior, Saoshyant, the dead will be roused, first the primeval man, then the first human pair and finally all mankind. Then the great gathering will take place at which everyone's good and evil deeds are revealed. The sinners will be punished and the righteous will enter the bliss of paradise. A stream of molten metal will spread over the earth, and all men will have to pass through it; the evil will be burned and purified, the righteous will experience it like lukewarm milk. At the end, all will be saved, and creation will be renewed.

Judaism

From the writings of Moses and others in the Old Testament we find that the ancient Jews (Israelites) did not believe in heaven or hell, or in reward or punishment after death. They also did not believe in the resurrection of the soul or the body. Job longed for death thinking that it would end his mental agony. In *Psalms* we read:

> "In death there is no remembrance of Thee; in the grave who shall give Thee thanks?" (vi, 5)
>
> "The dead praise not the Lord, neither any that go down into silence." (Cxv, 17)
>
> Solomon speaks:
>
> "All things come alike to all; there is one event to the righteous and to the wicked, to the good and to the clean and to the unclean . . . as is the good , so is the sinner." (Ecci. ix, 2)
>
> "All go into one place; all are of the dust and all turn to dust again."
>
> "Who knoweth the spirit of man that goeth upward and the beast that goeth downward to the earth? (Eccl. iii. 20-21)

There are many such passages, which show that before the Babylonian captivity, the Israelites had no belief in reward or punishment or in the resurrection of the soul. But when the ancient Jews were conquered by the Persians (536 BC), they came in contact with a nation that had a belief in one God, in heaven and hell, in the resurrection of the dead, and in the last day of judgment. Under the rule of Persia from 536–333 BC, the Jews were greatly influenced by the Persian religion. They gave up their idolatry and gradually developed social organization.

About this time, the Jews were divided into two classes, the Pharisees and Sadducees. Those who adopted the religious ideas of the Parsees were called Pharisees, and those who followed strictly the Jewish ideas, ceremonies, ritual and beliefs were called

Sadducees. Pharisees believed in angels and spirits, and in resurrection of the dead. The Sadducees were orthodox and did not believe in the resurrection of the dead. In Matt. XXII, 23, we read, "The same day came to him the Sadducees which say that there is no resurrection."

The Old Testament as a whole has no reference to the doctrine of resurrection. The only reference to resurrection is found in the *Book of Daniel* (*c.* 165 BC). There we read, "Many of those who sleep in the dust will awake, some to eternal life, others to eternal shame (12.2).

The clearest statements about resurrection appear in the documents from the end of the first century AD: the Syriac *Apocalypse of Baruch* (50:2); the Liber *Antiquitatum Biblicarum:* "God will revive the dead and raise up from the earth those who sleep." (3.10); after that, judgment will be held and everybody will receive according to his deed.

Gradually the Pharisees grew very powerful and after the death of Jesus, their doctrines of the resurrection of the dead, and of reward and punishment after death, and the belief in angels and spirits, became the cardinal principles of the new Christian sect. Thus we see that the idea of resurrection first arose in Persia and afterwards took a prominent place in the writings of the New Testament, and since then it has been largely accepted by the Christians of the Western countries.

Christianity

In earlier Christianity the resurrection of Christ was the fundamental fact. The New Testament (Bible) seems to have taken over the general idea of resurrection from contemporary Judaism. The Testament contains a few details about resurrection. Three days after Christ's crucifixion, his mother Mary, going to his tomb, found its stone rolled away and the tomb empty. Thereafter Jesus appeared to her and sporadically to a few other followers. That is all; the accounts are thus meager, but the faith in the Resurrection of Jesus remained unshakable.

The first Christians expected the second coming of Christ to happen in their lifetime. But it did not happen.

The mode of resurrection is dealt with by Paul in *Corinthians* (1:15): The spiritual body that rises is not the old body but a new one, just as a new plant comes out of a seed. But this important point is generally overlooked.

Under Greek influence the early Church developed the idea of an immortal soul that continues to exist after death and is reunited with the body at the resurrection.

Islam

Islam shares with Christianity the belief in a general resurrection of the dead, followed by a judgment.

However modern Science denies miracles. It teaches that this universe is guided, not by miracles, but by definite Universal Laws. There is no scientific explanation for resurrection. On the contrary the doctrine of Reincarnation is founded on the Universal Law of Cause and Effect, and on the psychical, moral and ethical laws.

Hinduism

In Hinduism, as we have already seen, there is deep belief in reincarnation. That is, after the death of a body, the soul enters into another earthly existence by taking up a new body according to the effects of its past actions. But there is no belief in resurrection. However Paramahansa Yogananda (1893–1952),[1] one of the great sages of India, in his inspiring Autobiography entitled *Autobiography of a Yogi* narrated the resurrection of his Master Sri Yukteswar.

Swami Yogananda was scheduled for several public addresses in Bombay. Sitting on his bed in a hotel at Bombay at three O'clock in the afternoon of June 19, 1936 – one week after the vision of Lord Krishna—he was roused from meditation by a beatific light. Waves of rapture engulfed him as he beheld the flesh and blood form of Sri Yukteswar.

"My son!" Master tenderly spoke.

"Is it you, Master, the same lion of God? Are you wearing a

body like the one I buried beneath the cruel sands of Puri?"

"Yes my child, I am the same. This is flesh and blood body. Though I see it as ethereal, to your sight it is physical. From cosmic atoms I created an entirely new body, exactly like the physical body you laid beneath the sands at Puri. I am in fact resurrected – not on earth but on an astral planet called *Hiranyaloka* (Illumined Astral Planet). There I am aiding advanced beings to rid themselves of astral karma and thus attain liberation from astral rebirths."

Sri Yukteswar explained the nature of *Hiranyaloka,* the life of the inhabitants, and what souls can enter it; he also described his role in the *Hiranyaloka.* Sri Yukteswar spent two hours with Swami Yogananda in the Bombay hotel room and answered his every question. Promising to come to him whenever Swami Yogananda enter into nirvikalpa samadhi and call on him, he vanished from Swami Yogananda's sight.

Swami Yogananda was not the only one privileged to behold the resurrected Master Yukteswar. One of the Master's devoted disciples was an aged woman, affectionately known as *Ma* (Mother). Her home was close to the Puri hermitage. The resurrected Master appeared before her door and talked to her for several minutes in the bright outdoors. (For further details, read "Chapter 43. The Resurrection of Sri Yukteswar," in *Autobiography of a Yogi*, Los Angels: Self-Realization Fellowship, 1990).

Reference

1. He came to United States of America in 1920 and founded Self-Realization Fellowship in Los Angels, California. He was one of the first Eastern sages to spread his teachings in the Western world.

33

Fatalism *Vs.* Free Will

Introduction

It is a great pity that the doctrine of karma is mistaken for fatalism. Fatalism means that all events are subject to fate and happen inevitably. Some are fatalists in their attitude towards the problems of life. They think everything in the future is already predetermined by God or by the Law of Karma, and so nothing can be done except to resign themselves to an inexorable fate. This thinking is bound to lead to the development of a negative or passive mentality and to undermine all efforts and initiative in life. But luckily such people do not practice what they profess. In fact they behave as if everything in the world depended upon their personal will. So fatalism, though a widely prevalent dogma among certain communities, is not a very active force in human life. Like all other aspects of religious faith, few people take this dogma seriously and their submission to fate does not mean much in actual life.

Fate

Fate is otherwise known as luck. It is the non-definable mysterious thing, which brings pleasure or pain, success or failure to a person. It raises a beggar to the level of a multimillionaire. It hurls down a mighty king to the level of a prisoner. However whimsically the fate may appear to operate, it works in harmony with the Law of Causation. Karmic effect is named as fate.

Fate is one's own creation. Man thinks and acts and thus creates his own fate. He creates a web, like the silkworm and entangles himself in its meshes through the knots of ignorance, desire and action.

Fatalism *Vs.* Karma

The doctrine of karma is diametrically opposed to the doctrine of fatalism. It provides a most rational and scientific explanation of fate. The differences between fatalism and the doctrine of karma are:

Fatalism	*Doctrine of Karma*
• Excuse for inertia and timidity	Incentive to better one's condition
• Weakens will and determination	Presupposes freewill
• Message of despair and not of hope	Infuses hope and prompts right effort
• Annihilates faith	Promotes faith in oneself and in God
• Infuses fear in the mind	Source of solace and comfort
• Destroys ethics	Upholds ethics and justice
• Checks growth and evolution	Gives chance to grow and evolve.

The doctrine of karma gives a positive assurance that although the present (the effect of one's own past actions) is unalterable and irrevocable, one may better his future by changing his thoughts, habits, tendencies and mode of action. It brings hope to the hopeless, help to the helpless, joy to the cheerless and new strength to the weak. It awakens and inspires the depressed and gloomy. It enlightens the ignorant. It teaches: "Do not blame others for your sufferings. Do not accuse God. You are reaping what you have sown in your past life. Your present sufferings are the effects of your past bad actions. You are the author of your present state. The present is unchangeable. Do not weep, do not cry over spilt milk. There is no use of crying over it. Instead of weeping, do virtuous actions now. Think rightly. You will have a brilliant future."

The doctrine of karma is based on ethics. It says: "If you hurt another person, you hurt yourself."

Every act of yours produces in you a double effect: one in the form of good or bad tendency in your inner nature, and the other in the form of reward or punishment. Your past action influences your present life in two ways: First, in the form of your tendency or character and second, as fate. Every action creates a subtle impression in your subconscious mind. The impression causes a tendency. Tendency develops into a habit by repetition of the action. The habit manifests as character. Character develops into destiny. (*See* Chapter 8. Karma and Character, *above*).

Free Will

The faculty of choosing is termed free will. Karma in its true sense includes both destiny and free will to choose and act or self-effort. Of these the latter is the most important factor in life. *Matsya Purana*, one of the Hindu scriptures, says, "Know that destiny is the result of one's own action performed in a previous bodily existence. Hence the wise man calls one's effort superior. So even adverse destiny is vanquished by the heroic efforts of people exerting themselves in auspicious actions."

Though you have no freedom to determine the effects of your actions, you have freedom to decide the course of actions or your self-effort. King Janaka and others attained to perfection by performing selfless actions. You can change your thoughts and desires, your character. Your will is ever free. Through selfishness your will has become impure. You can make it pure, strong and dynamic by getting rid of your base desires, and likes and dislikes. What you are now at present is the result of what you thought and did in the past. What you would be in the future will be the result of what you think and do now. You can create better conditions for the future. You can rise to the highest state of perfection.

A boatman without oars, rudder and sails is carried away helplessly by the winds and currents; but a clever boatman with oars, sails and rudder ably directs the boat in any direction he likes and reaches the other shore safely. Similarly, If you know the Laws of Nature --the Law of Thought, the Law of Karma, the

Law of Cause and Effect – you can sail fearlessly in the ocean of worldly life (*samsara*) and reach the other shore of fearlessness and immortality quite safely. You can utilize the helpful forces to your best advantage and neutralize the negative forces skillfully, with the knowledge of the Laws. Knowledge is the torch light. Exercise your discriminative faculty. Know the difference between selfish action and selfless action. Know that selfish action leads you to rebirth, but selfless work liberates you from the cycle of births and deaths. It will purify your heart and lead you to God-realization. So choose the path of selfless service and attain eternal freedom.

The Extent of Free Will

What is the extent of free will do you have? Both the scriptures and sages tell you that you have a high degree of free will. Humans are the only species that have free will. You have been endowed with intellect and power of discrimination. These extraordinary gifts bring with greater responsibility. Think carefully before you do anything, because as you know your future depends on your present actions.

Although you lack perfect freedom of choice, you can free yourself from the bondage of karma by making best use of the freedom you have. You can use your power of discrimination to distinguish right from wrong, and the real from the unreal. You have the ability to make conscious decisions, verify their validity in the light of reason and act on them. You also have the privilege of drawing on the vast knowledge and experiences of all those who have come before you. You have the opportunity to reach the supreme goal of life by performing actions without attachment and doing selfless service.

As you create your destiny through your actions, you must be vigilant about what you do. By listening to your inner voice and consulting scriptures and saints to confirm its validity. If you perform your present actions skillfully with devotion and non-attachment, you will attenuate old bad karmas and at the same time generate positive and elevating karmas. They purify your heart and you will eventually attain Self-realization.

34

Destiny and Self-Effort

Destiny

Your present condition, as explained before, is the result of your own past thoughts and action. That is what is known as your destiny. Thought is the real karma. Thought moulds your action. Thought materializes and becomes action. If you allow the mind to dwell on good and elevating thoughts, you will develop a noble character. Then you will naturally do noble and laudable actions. If you entertain evil thoughts, you will develop a base character. This is the immutable Law of Nature. Therefore shape your character by cultivating sublime thoughts. The *Brahadaranyaka Upanishad* says:

> "Verily one becomes good by good action, bad by bad action." (3.2.13)

You sow an action and reap a habit. You sow a habit and reap a character. You sow a character and reap your destiny. Hence destiny is of your own making. You yourself have built it, and you can undo it by entertaining noble thoughts and by doing virtuous actions. Destiny is determined by your conduct. The *Chandogya Upanishad* says:

> "Those whose conduct here has been good will quickly attain a good birth . . . But those whose conduct here been evil, the prospect is, will quickly attain an evil birth. . . ." (5.10.7)

Manu Smrti, one of the ancient Hindu scriptures, declares,

> "Actions, which spring from the mind, from speech and from the body, produce either good or evil results; by actions are caused the (various) conditions of men, the highest, the middle and the lowest." (12. 3)

However sore the straits may be in which you find yourself, you have put yourself there by your own previous indifference to the laws. Whatever laws you broke, you broke of your own free will, the free will given to you in the beginning by your Creator. You alone chose to be where you are at this moment. This, at least, allows you the dignity and self-respect of knowing that you made your own mistakes.

Freedom

Whatever may be your present condition you can shape your future through right thinking and right effort. You are the maker of your own destiny. Freedom is your birthright. It is hidden in the consciousness of your ever-free Self. Lord Krishna in *the Bhagavad Gita* speaks of the freedom of man in doing actions: "Let a man raise himself by himself, let him not lower himself, for he alone is the friend of himself, he alone is the enemy of himself." (6. 5)

> "The self is the friend of a person who has conquered himself by the Self; to the unconquered person, his own self stands in the place of an enemy like the (external) foe." (6. 6)

So conquer the lower mind with the help of the higher mind. The lower mind is filled with passion and darkness. The higher mind is pure and strong.

Binding Knots

Ignorance, desire and selfish action are the three knots that bind you to the wheel of *samsara* (worldly life). When desire for a sensual object arises in your mind, you begin to think where and how you can get it. Then action follows the thought. The desire, thought and the action always go together. Good desires give rise to good thoughts and good actions. Evil desires lead to evil thoughts and evil actions.

So do not allow the desires to control your thoughts. When a desire arises, think well. Reason out whether it will bring maximum happiness to you and others and no pain to others. If it is otherwise, reject it ruthlessly. A desire, when controlled, becomes transmuted into will. Always entertain holy and sublime desires and thoughts. Develop passion for Self-realization. This one strong and holy desire will annihilate all other worldly desires. Cut the three knots of ignorance, desire and selfish action and realize your own essential nature. Then you transcend the operation of Law of Karma.

You can Outgrow Environment

Do not feel helpless because of your adverse circumstances. Many, who have born in poverty and in adverse circumstances, have become great men. They rose above the environmental forces by their strong will and determination. Gigantic will is developed through good actions done in countless births. The potencies of these actions collect together, and in a birth bursts out—as in the case of Buddha, Jesus, Sankaracharya and Vivekananda.

Sri Sankaracharya, the exponent of Advaita philosophy, a spiritual giant and genius, was born in very poor and unfavorable circumstances. He out grew them by his strong will and tireless efforts and became on of the greatest saints of the world.

Sri T. Muthuswamy Aiyer, the first Indian High Court Judge in Madras during the British regime, was born in absolute poverty. He had to study at night under city street lanterns. He had no enough food. He was clad in rags. But he struggled hard and achieved greatness. He rose above environmental forces by his strong will and determination.

The life of James R. Mac Donald is another example. He rose from poverty to power, from a field-laborer to the status of the

Prime Minister of Britain. His first job was writing addresses in the envelopes for ten shillings per week. He was too poor to buy tea, so that he drank water. Gradually through right efforts he rose to the position of a Prime Minister. There are thousands of such instances all over the world in all ages.

Everyone is born with his own innate tendencies and potentialities. Good tendencies and potentialities caused by good thoughts and actions are valuable assets for you. They give you strength and determination to overcome unfavorable circumstances. The *Bhagavad Gita* says:

> " . . . he who fell from Yoga is born in the home of the pure and wealthy or he is born in a family of even the wise Yogis . . . .There he comes in touch with the knowledge acquired in his former body and strives more than before for perfection." (6. 41–43)

Therefore do not grumble of bad environment. You are not a creature of environment. You can control and modify it by your good actions and self-effort.

Self-effort

Destiny is only self-effort that has been done in previous births. The self-effort of today becomes the destiny of tomorrow. Self-effort and destiny are one and the same. Just as the present becomes the past and the future becomes the present, just as there is only the present, so also there is only self-effort. Note the words of *Yoga Vasistha* taught by ancient Sage Vasistha to prince Rama, "There is nothing like destiny other than the effect of our previous efforts." (*Yoga Vasistha, II*: 6. 4)

> "Our previous efforts are called our destiny." (II: 6-36)
> "Our achievements are determined by our efforts. Our effort is therefore our destiny." (II: 6-2)
> "Our previous and present efforts, in case they are in contrary directions, are the two rams fighting with each other. The more

> powerful of the two always overthrows the other." (II:6–10)
> "Whether they are the past or the present efforts, it is the stronger ones that determine our destiny. In either case, it is man's own effort that determines his destiny by virtue of its strength." (II:6–8)
> "Man determines his own destiny by his thought. He can make those things also happen that were not destined to happen." (V:24–28))
> "The soul of man is powerful enough. Only those things happen in this world which it creates by its own free efforts, not others." (V:24–35–36)
> "One should therefore overcome one's unfavorable destiny (the effect of one's past efforts) by greater effort in the present, gnashing his teeth." (II:5–11)
> "There is nothing in the world that cannot be achieved by man by the right sort of effort." (III:96–8)

Therefore you are not a helpless being. You have a free will of your own. You can change destiny in any way you like. You can become a saint by right desire, by right thinking and by right action. By right thinking and self-effort you can become a master of your destiny.

You are like a farmer who has a plot of land. The acreage, the nature of the soil and the conditions of weather are all predetermined, but the farmer is quite at liberty to till the land, manure it, sow the seeds, water the plants, and get good harvest or to allow the land to remain as a wasteland.

Have a new angle of vision. Arm yourself with discrimination, cheerfulness, and an undaunted spirit. A glorious future is in your hands. You can work miracles. You can do wonders. Do not give up hope. You can have command over the elements and nature. You can neutralize the effects of the evil influences and the antagonistic forces that may operate against you. The power is within you. Here is a story of Markandeya to illustrate the power of self-effort:

Markandeya was a great devotee of Lord Siva. His father

Mrikandu performed rigorous austerities to get a son. Lord Siva appeared before him and said, "O Rishi, Do you want a good son who will die in his sixteenth year or a bad and foolish son who will live for a long time?"

Mrikandu replied: O my venerable Lord, bless me with a good son." That son was Markandeya.

The boy Markandeya came to know about his fate and began to worship Lord Siva wholeheartedly with intense faith and devotion. On the morning of the last day decreed as the day of his death, the boy entered into deep meditation and samadhi in front of Siva Linga. The messengers of Yama (the king of death) were not able to approach him. Hence, Yama himself came to take away his life. The boy prayed to Lord Siva for protection and embraced the Linga. Yama threw his noose around the Linga and the boy. Lord Siva became angry and came out of the Linga immediately and destroyed Yama to protect the boy.

Then the Devas approached Lord Siva and pleaded for pardoning Yama for his mistake. Then Lord Siva brought Yama back to life at the request of the gods. He also conferred a boon to the boy Markandeya that he should live forever as a boy of sixteen years of age. He has become a *Chiranjivi* (ever living). In South India, even now elders bless a boy when he does prostration to them: "Live as a *Chiranjivi* like Markandeya."

Markandeya is thus an example for changing one's destiny through self-effort of austerity and intense devotion to the Lord.

Similarly Savitri changed the destiny of her husband Satyavan through the power of her strict chastity.

Patachara is another example for rising to the supreme state through self-effort. Her story is as follows:

Patacharya was born in an ancient town of Sravasti (North India) in the family of a businessman. When she attained maturity her parents selected a well-to-do young man of good looks and character for her husband; but Patachara did not want to marry him. She married a youth of her own choice. Her parents were displeased with her and she left her parental home and town with her husband to live in another land.

Many years passed by. After the birth of two sons Patachara had the desire to visit her parents. So, accompanied by her husband and children, she left for Sravasti. On the way through the forest, a poisonous snake bit her husband. No aid was near by and he died. With terrible grief over this loss, Patachara continued her journey; but misfortune pursued her still further. While her children were sleeping under the shade of a tree a wild bird came and carried away the younger child; later her elder boy was swept away by a strong current while crossing a stream. This filled her cup of sorrow to the brim. Thus, having lost all the members of her small family, Patachara with unbearable grief walked on in a daze. The chosen ones of God, however, must give up all worldly attachment and support and learn to take refuge on Him alone. Perhaps to learn this Patachara had yet another disappointment in store.

On arriving at Sravasti, she could not find the home of her parents. On making enquiry she learned that some time back the roof of her parental home had collapsed and both parents had been buried under the debris. She lost her balance. She roamed around the town weeping loudly and relating her tale to everyone that she happened to meet.

Lord Buddha was in Sravasti at that time. The grief stricken Patachara went to him, fell at his feet and told him of her irreparable loss. Buddha consoled her, saying that life in the world was transient, and his words calmed her mind. She took refuge in the *Sangha* and became a nun of Buddhist Order. Henceforth she spent her life in the service of humanity, in teaching the message of Buddha and urging the people to follow the eightfold path of Dharma.

Through her lifelong spiritual discipline she gained so much spiritual strength that she was able to bring peace to the hearts of thousands of men and women. While addressing a gathering of five hundred women, Patachara's words created such a deep impression on their minds that they all became initiated disciples of Buddha. To influence the hearts of such a large number of people through public speaking alone is rare in history and there is no doubt that it must have been her life and character that added force and conviction to her words. Patachara is a shining example of one who through self-effort was able to raise her own life from the level of ordinary worldly existence to spiritual joy, supreme peace and spiritual power. (Source: *Pitaka,* a Buddhist Scripture)

The great spiritual Master Swami Sivananda exhorts us: "Do not say, 'Karma, karma, my karma has brought me to this.' Exert, exert. Use self-effort. Do austerities, concentrate, purify and meditate. Do not become a fatalist and yield to inertia. Do not bleak like a lamb. Roar, 'OM, OM. Om' like a lion of Vedanta. Remember friends, you are the master of your destiny.

"You are gaining new experiences and new knowledge every day. Your mind is evolving every second. You can change your desires, thoughts and actions. Your old tendencies may resist and recur again and again. But through resolute efforts you can change your thoughts, desires and actions and can become a virtuous person and attain perfection and immortality."

35

Karma and Astrology

Introduction

In considering the relation of astrology to karma we should first clarify the meaning of the term 'karma.' Karma refers to the universal Law of Cause and Effect. It is identical with the biblical saying: "Whatsoever a man soweth, that shall he also reap." No one who plants orange can expect to harvest apples. The Law of Karma is similar to the Newton's Law of Mechanics that states: "For every action there is an equal and opposite reaction." Everyone has to reap the fruits of his past actions in this life or in the future births. Life is not limited to one incarnation in this world. It is a continuous experience over many incarnations. The Law of Karma is a way of maintaining universal justice.

The doctrine of karma is inseparable from the theory of reincarnation. Both provide you with opportunities for spiritual development. Though you cannot change your present destiny brought up by that part of your accumulated past karma that has now come into force, called *prarabdha karma* (active karma). Within that framework you are free to choose your present thoughts and deeds. By rightly exercising your free will or power of choice, you can refine your destiny and march towards of our ultimate goal of God-realization or Self-realization.

Astrology and its Relation to Karma

Now let us examine the relation of astrology to karma. Paramahansa Yogananda (1893–1952), one of the first Indian spiritual masters to spread his teachings widely in the West, was familiar with astrology, since his Guru Sri Yukteswar was a master of all the ancient arts and sciences. He quotes, in his inspiring autobiography entitled *Autobiography of a Yogi,* what his master Yukteswar said to him:

> "Astrology is too vast, both mathematically[1] and philosophically, to be rightly grasped by men of profound understanding.
> "Astrology is the study of man's response to planetary stimuli. The stars have no conscious benevolence or animosity; they merely send forth positive and negative radiations. Of themselves, these do not help or harm humanity, but offer a lawful channel for the outward operation of cause-effect equilibrium that each man has set into motion in the past.
> "A child is born on that day and at that hour when the celestial rays are in mathematical harmony with his individual karma. His horoscope is a challenging portrait, revealing his unalterable past and its probable future results. But only men of intuitive wisdom can rightly interpret the natal chart; these are few. . . .
> "What man has done, he can undo. None other than himself was the instigator of the causes of whatever effects are now prevalent in his life. He can overcome any limitation, because he created it by his own actions in the first place, and because he possesses spiritual resources that are not subject to planetary pressure. (p. 188)

All your thoughts, words, deeds and experiences are recorded in your subconscious mind as subtle impressions(*samskaras*). When your present physical body dies, your mind with all stored-up *samskaras* as a part of the subtle body transmigrates and enters new physical bodies in successive reincarnations. So the mind remains the same throughout. That is, your present primary life pattern – dispositions, attitudes, characteristics, talents and potentials – is the outcome of the past *samskaras.*

"The (astrological) natal birth-chart," says Stephen Arroyo, "reveals in symbolic form the individual's primary life pattern."[2] It obviously reveals a blueprint of your soul's present *prarabdha* karma, which is considered as your destiny or fate. The *sanchita* (reserve or dormant) karma is not indicated in the birth-chart, since it is not allotted to this lifetime.

Although the birth-chart shows the karma in force and hence the restrictions that bind you, the chart is also a tool that enables you to see clearly in what areas of life you need to work toward transforming your current mode of life. You become what your thoughts are. If, therefore, you can subtly alter your modes of thought and attitude, you can march towards liberation. It is your attitude toward events that is crucial. It will determine whether you suffer your karma or grow out of it.

The Chart thus shows what you are now because of what you have thought and done in the past. The habit pattern is powerful and real. A strong commitment to self-development and a firm determination and will to develop new habit patterns is necessary. Astrology, by providing you with a blueprint of your tendencies, offers you a way of not only realizing exactly what your karma is, but also a way of rising above it. This idea is confirmed in Edgar Cayce's psychic reading # 5124–L–1:

Not that man is good or bad according to the position of the stars; but the position of the stars indicates what the individual entity has done about God's plan in earthly activities.

You are responsible for your destiny and problems as shown in the natal chart. You could then even say that the birth-chart shows your karma. Indeed astrology could legitimately be called a science of karma. However, as quoted by Paramahansa Yogananda in the *Autobiography of a Yogi*, "Superstitious awe of astrology makes one an automaton, slavishly dependent on mechanical guidance. The wise man defeats his planets – that is, his past – by transferring his allegiance from the creation to the Creator. The more he realizes his unity with Spirit, the less matter can dominate him. The soul is ever free; it is deathless because birthless. It cannot be regimented by stars. When he properly places his sense of identity, he leaves behind all compulsive patterns. There is no greater power than that inward protection."

"Then, dear Master, why do you want me to wear an astrological bangle?" asked Swami Yogananda after a long silence. Sri Yukteswar replied:

"It is only when a traveler has reached his goal that he is justified in discarding his maps. During the journey, he takes advantage of any convenient shortcut. The ancient rishis discovered many ways to curtail the period of exile in delusion. There are some mechanical features in the Law of Karma that can be skillfully adjusted by the fingers of wisdom.

"All human ills arise from some transgression of universal law. The scriptures point out that man must satisfy the Laws of Nature, while not discrediting the Divine omnipotence. He should say: 'Lord, I trust in Thee, and know Thou can't help me, but I will do my best to undo any wrong I have done.' By a number of means – by prayer, by will power, by meditation, by consulting saints, by use of astrological bangles – the adverse effects of past wrongs can be minimized or nullified.

"Just as a house may be fitted with a copper rod to absorb the shock of lightening, so the bodily temple be protected in certain ways.

"Electrical and magnetic radiations are ceaselessly circulating in the universe; they affect man's body for good and ill. Ages ago our rishis pondered the problem of combating the adverse effects of subtle cosmic influences. The sages discovered that pure metals emit an astral light which is powerfully counteractive to negative pulls of the planets. Certain plant combinations were also found to be helpful. Most effective of all are faultless jewels of not less than two carats." (*Autobiography of a Yogi*, pp. 188–90).

References

1 The scientific knowledge of the ancient rishis (sages) was very great; in the *Kaushitaki Brahmana* of India we find precise astronomical passages indicating that over 5000 years ago the Hindus were far advanced in astronomy, which had a practical value in determining the auspicious time for astrological ceremonies. The

Jyotish (a body of *Vedic* astronomical expositions) contains the scientific lore that kept India at the forefront of all ancient nations. *Brahmagupta*, one of the *Jyotish* works, is an astronomical treatise dealing with the motion of planetary bodies in our solar system, the earth's revolution, the Law of gravitation and other scientific facts that did not dawn in the Western world until the time of Copernicus and Newton.

2 *Astrology, Karma and Transformation*, Sebastopol, CA.: CRCS Publications.

36

Social Dimensions of Karma

Collective Karma

Karma is not merely an individual affair. It is collective as well. "People often suffer from the effects of the actions done by others, effects which thus do not strictly belong to their own karma" says H. P. Blavatsky, in her book entitled *The Key to Theosophy* (Wheaton, Illinois: Quest Books, 1972, p. 101). At the highest level of our being we are not separate from others, and so we share the collective karma. It is not a question of personal karma but of shouldering responsibility together. Though we are surely conditioned by our past karma, we also have a responsibility to our particular time and situation and this is our duty or inner obligation. The choices we make have effects far beyond ourselves. We have a social responsibility as well as a responsibility to make our own personal life situation better.

Our Social Responsibility

Our social responsibility means—

- Our concern for suffering neighbors
- Our concern for the social impact of our own actions
- The part we play in the making of social policy on issues of family planning, social welfare, health care, environmental protection, etc.

In the *Bhagavad Gita*, Lord Krishna emphasizes action over

inaction, and selfless service to mankind. He exhorts us: "Do your bounded duty, for action is superior to inaction . . . (3.8); "the world is bound by actions other than those performed for the sake of sacrifice. Therefore perform actions for the sake of sacrifice alone, free from attachment." (3.9)

From a moral perspective, our duty is to all beings. It transcends inherited karmic patterns. The purpose of the moral life is to promote overall good, the welfare of all, the establishment of the Kingdom of God on earth.

A horse wearing blinders is prevented from being distracted in its forward motion. It does not possess the freedom to remove the restriction caused by the blinders. We, human beings, however, while wearing the "blinders" given by karmic destiny, have the possibility of throwing off the karmic limits by free choices. This is of course a great responsibility imposed on us by the free will given to us by God. (*See* Chapter 34. Destiny and Self-effort, above).

Social Problems

All the societal problems that we face today have risen from our acting contrary to the good of the greater whole, from the materialistic worldview. There is unprecedented degree of interdependence among nations and peoples. The major concerns of the society are interrelated and global in their implications. Thus, for example, human rights infringed in one place affect all of us; an act of terrorism in one place threatens world peace. Deforestation, air pollution, soil erosion and expansion of deserts have global implications, causing drastic changes in climatic patterns. Every commission and omission of ours affects all domains and regions. We can no longer deny responsibility for our acts and for each other. The underlying cause of all the societal problems of today is thoughtless materialism.

Inequitable Economic System

Mechanization, which is a form of materialism, has led to the exploitation of nature to the hilt. It fostered dichotomy between knowledge and values, between science and spirituality, between the rich and the poor, between industrialized countries and the developing nations and between the present and future generations.

In market-oriented countries, individual enterprises aim at maximization of profits. Industry has no concern for the social costs of its operations. It does not consider its impact on the environmental degradation, air and water pollution and health hazards to people. The gulf between the "haves" of the world and the "have-nots" is also ever widening.

The terms of trade between the industrialized world and the third world are inequitable. In the third world large landowners export cash crops including food, while the rural poor are landless and hungry.

According to karma, the chaos and anarchy we witness today express an underlying disorder. The major problems, notably, poverty, hunger, disease, population explosion in the poorest parts of the world, terrorism, threat of nuclear war, ethnic conflict, environmental degradation, depletion of natural resources, international debt, inflation – are apparently distinct, but really inter-connected. They arise in different circumstances and parts of the world, yet their impact is global. Mass poverty is related to affluent people's pursuit of power and wealth. Environmental degradation is connected with resources-and–energy intensive industrial production. The threat of nuclear war and the ethnic conflicts are closely tied to the turmoil caused by economic and social injustice and abject poverty. Also inter-linked are poverty, international debt and inflation. Self-aggrandizement, greed, corruption and exploitation of weaker are rampant. Consequently there is an upsurge among people against oppression and social injustice and inequality.

All these developments reflect the violation of the law of life, and by virtue of karma we have precipitated a global crisis. This crisis compels us to rethink, to introspect and to understand our mistakes and take corrective actions. The Law of Karma is a guiding light for us in our difficult journey toward world peace, harmony and justice.

37

Bondage of Karma

Meaning

The universal Law of Karma is a Law of Action and Reaction. Every thought, every word or every deed is an action. For every action that an individual performs, there is an equal and opposite reaction. Good action produces good reaction; evil action produces evil reaction. The doer of an action has to reap the fruit of his action sooner or later. That is, he is bound by the effects of his actions. This is one aspect of bondage of karma.

Prompted by thirst for satisfying desires for objects of senses, an individual performs millions and millions of actions during his lifetime. His present body may die before he enjoys the fruits of all his actions. So he is born again to experience the results of the accumulated actions. While experiencing them, he goes on performing fresh actions. Some of them may go into the accumulated karma to be experienced in the next life or lives. Thus the individual is subject to the wheel of births and deaths. This is another aspect of bondage of karma.

Causes of Bondage

What are the causes of our bondage and consequent sufferings or afflictions (*klesas*)? Patanjali, an ancient sage who codified the philosophy and practice of Yoga in *Yoga Sutras* has made a deep analysis of the fundamental causes of our misery and suffering (*Sutras*, 2.3–9). The causes of our misery and suffering are—

(1) Ignorance
(2) Egoism
(3) Attachment
(4) Aversion or hatred
(5) Clinging to life.

These are not really separate; one leads to the next.

1. *Ignorance.* Ignorance is the root cause of our suffering. It does not mean a mere lack of knowledge. It means unawareness of the Reality. It is taking the non-eternal as eternal, impurity as purity, evil as good, not-self as Self. We are neither the body, nor the mind and senses. We are eternal, pure and blissful Self (Atman). But out of ignorance, we identify ourselves with our bodies, minds and senses. This illusion is the root cause of our bondage and suffering. It is a veil that covers the Reality and shows the ego as the all-important entity in life.

2. *Egoism.* Ego is the sense of "I, me, mine." Out of ignorance we take the body-mind complex to be our Self and consider the activities of the body and mind as our own. Egoism takes several forms: ambition, pride, desire for name and fame, desire for sensual objects, craving for money, wealth, position and power. All these lead to restless activities, expectations, anxieties, disappointment, discontentment, stress and strain and the consequent diseases. We indulge in ceaseless selfish activities in order to satisfy our egoistic desires and bind ourselves to the worldly life and bondage of karma, and go through the wheel of births and deaths. Here is a story of "Self-fish."

In a place some fishermen were catching fish. A kite swooped down and snatched a fish. At the sight of the fish, about a hundred crows chased the kite and made a great noise with their crawling. Whichever way the kite flew with the fish, the crows followed it. The kite flew to the west and the crows followed it there. The kite flew to the east and still the crows followed it there. The kite flew to the south and north, but with the same result. As the kite began to fly here and there in confusion, the fish dropped from its mouth. The crows at once let the kite alone and flew after the fish. Thus relieved of its worries, the kite sat on the branch of a tree and thought, "That wretched fish was the root of all my troubles. I have now got rid of it and therefore I am at peace."

As long as you have the "self-fish"—worldly desires, you have to perform actions and consequently suffer from worry, anxiety and restlessness. No sooner do you renounce the worldly desires than your activities fall away and you enjoy peace.

3. *Attachment and Aversion.* Things or persons, that make us feel happy, good or pleasant and inflate our ego, attract us. We develop a sense of attachment toward them. (*Yoga Sutras,* 2.7). Such attraction and the consequent attachment are the outcome of taste (*vasana*) enjoyed earlier. The fear of losing or actual loss of things to which we are attached give rise to disappointment, anxiety and sorrow.

We may dislike persons, things and circumstances that make us unhappy or uncomfortable or threaten our security and happiness. (*Yoga Sutras,* 2.8). Aversion arises out of misery experienced earlier. A sustained attitude of repulsion casts into the subconscious a subtle stream of impressions of aversion. The likes and dislikes bind us to innumerable persons and things and condition our life to an unbelievable extent. They are the breeders of lower desires. They naturally keep us tied down to the worldly life.

4. *Clinging to Life.* All living beings want to continue to live. All of us are attached to life. (*Yoga Sutras*, 2.9).

Pleasure and Pain

As a result of the bondage of karma we experience pleasures and pains depending on the nature of actions that we have performed. Every thing that happens to us is the result of actions performed by us in the past, either in this life or in some previous incarnation.

Most of us, however, do not generally consider the underlying causes of many of the things that happen to us; instead we are contend to attribute them to circumstances, chance or fate, and also try to counteract. For instance, when we get a stomachache we seek to overcome by taking some patent medicines, instead of finding out what is wrong with our eating habits and correcting them. Similarly people and government spend millions of dollars for treating serious diseases like cancer and heart diseases, while at the same time producers of meat and manufacturers of cigarettes and alcoholic drinks spend millions of dollars for promotion of sale of these products and encourage people to become addicts to them though they are the cause of the deadly diseases.

Freedom from Bondage

How can freedom from karma be obtained? You have to perform actions without the sense of doership and without any desire for their fruits. Actions without attachment are no actions at all. Lord Krishna in the *Bhagavad Gita* exhorts us:

> "Perform action, being steadfast in Yoga, abandoning attachment and balanced in success and failure. Evenness of mind is Yoga." (2. 48)

(For details, *see* Chapter 39. Freedom from Karma and Rebirth. *below*). Selfless service purifies your heart and gives you the knowledge of Self. Self-knowledge liberates you from miseries and the cycle of births and deaths. (*See* also Chapter 21. Selfless *Service, above*).

38

Purpose of Suffering

Suffering

We often face adversity and misfortune and undergo sufferings and calamities. We move in a circle of ever-increasing anxieties and sorrows. We jump from one fire into another, from one pit into another, from one sorrow into another. We grope in darkness and stumble at every step. Pain is everywhere. Rest and peace nowhere. Why? Because we are holding on to the objects of senses. More we hold on anything for ourselves, the more we have the suffering. When we become sick and tired of holding on to what we have, we give up our hold. Temporary dispassion at least!

This reminds us of what monkeys do particularly in South India where tender coconuts are popular. We drink the tender coconut water just with a small opening, and then throw it away, because to cut that and take the kernel we need a big machete. So we just drink it and throw it. The monkeys wait for it. They love that jelly-like kernel inside. So they immediately run to that, any monkey which reaches it, puts the hand into the hole, collects all the jelly inside, nice handful of jelly. It wants to take the hand out; it has become a big handout! Now to take the hand out, it has to give up the grip. If it wants to hold on the grip it cannot take the hand out. That is what many of us do in our life.

You take a big grip and at the same time want to get the hand out and say, "I want freedom." But you are not a "freedom," but a "free dumb." Give up; the hand will come out. If you do not give up, the hand gets stuck. Just think of the monkeys. How many times you get into the same situation of those monkeys.

That is what you call *Maya*. Give up the jelly, hand is free. Hold the jelly, hand is bound. So if you are really interested in freedom, give up. Lord Krishna, in the *Bhagavad Gita*, says:

> "Fix the mind on Me, be devoted to Me, sacrifice to Me, bow down to Me, thou shall come even to Me; truly do I promise unto thee." (18.65)

Poor God has to come to promise us. Why should God promise? Because we are used to getting promises. Hence even God has to come and promise. Only then we begin to believe a little. Renounce everything. But it is not just simply giving up. Lord Krishna says further,

> "Abandoning all duties, take refuge in Me alone; I will liberate thee from all sins; grieve not." (18.66)

"Abandoning" means, "giving up the notion of doership." It also means, "surrendering the fruits of actions." God promises that He would liberate us. We read it, and forget it. We read it again and forget it. When the problem comes, we read it. When the problem is over, we forget that.

During the time of delivery pain, the lady cries, "God, enough. No more. I don't want any more child." For how long this dispassion! Until the baby comes out. When it is one year old, it is all-alone in the house. The mother feels that the child should have a company. Now all the dispassion disappears. Maya overcomes your feeble dispassion.

What does cause suffering and misery? Our selfishness, our past evil thoughts and deeds are the causes of our suffering. We undergo suffering because of our involvement in the passing phase and affairs of life, forgetting our real nature. We neglect to turn our thoughts to the eternal source of our existence.

Purpose of Suffering

If we understand the purpose of suffering we will welcome it. By undergoing suffering we purge out our karma. Suffering means experiencing of the effects of a past karma. Tibetans say that suffering is a "brim that sweeps away all our negative karma."

The purpose of suffering is purification. The ancient Tamil saint Tiruvalluvar in his *Thirukkural* says:

As fire refines gold and makes it glow
So pain illuminates the penance-doer. (267)

So if you are interested in becoming purified, look for suffering. But do not inflict suffering on you. When it comes welcome it. There was a saint; he was somehow festered with a lot of wounds and they started even creating worms inside. The worms were literally eating. He said, "Okay, Lord, probably this is the way you are taking karma away." One day he saw a little worm just slipped and dropped down. He said, "Oh, no, no, no, I still have a lot to be cleaned up. Please don't go away." He slowly took it up and put it on the wound: "Come on finish your job. Don't go out so soon." Why? Because he knows the truth, the purpose of suffering.

After all what is pain? It is not something that terrifies you. If you understand the pain as a means of purification, purging past bad karmas, you would never be afraid of it. When it comes, you will accept it, saying, "Yes, my friend come. You are coming to help me." The moment you are afraid of it, then it would pain you more. When you face it, smile at it, may be even the pain might hesitate a little to come to you. I always see this truth when one dog chasing another dog. All of a sudden a dog will be chasing another one. The running dog will hide its tail behind the hind legs and run, screaming. He will be fast behind his heel. When it reaches its home, it will immediately stop, turn around, stop there. The moment it stops running and turns around, the chasing dog will stop there. It will think, "All this time it was running. Now he has stopped and looking at me. There must be something. Oh, I should be careful." Similarly, the more you run from the pain, the more the pain will run after you. Stop running; look at it, "Hey, who are you?" And the pain, "Oh, I think there is something. He seems to be getting some backing there. I better be careful." Your fear creates more pain than the pain itself. How many people, when they go to the dentist, become nervous even before opening the mouth; they become shaking and perspiring. Probably the dentist may be just putting a cotton swab, but they may think that he is putting a crowbar into the mouth. So do not be afraid of pain. How will that fearlessness come? By knowing that there is a great power behind. You are fully supported by that, fully protected by that. So you need not be afraid of anything. A great saint says, "I am not afraid of anything or anybody in this life, not even the death, not even the hell. Why? Because there is somebody who is taking care of me. I have that faith. I have taken refuge at His feet. Who can do anything to me? Who will even dare to do that?" Another saint, looking at the death that is coming to him, says, "Hey, death, please don't come. Not because I am afraid of you. Probably you didn't get the message. Perhaps you didn't know that the Lord has accepted me and taken me under His protection. Get out. Arumugavan is my Lord. If by chance He sees you , without any hesitation He will destroy you immediately. To save your life, get out." To whom he is addressing? To the one who is coming to take his life away. And that is what you call faith. That is what you call real devotion, real Bhakti. Often your faith is tested. You have to face all the tests. That is what suffering means. No pain, No gain.

Suffering also helps us to turn toward God. Normally we do not think of God. Only when some problem or some suffering comes and squeezes us, forces us, we think of God and we pray to Him to remove our suffering. Hence the saying: "Adversities are blessings in disguise."

Beyond Suffering

Eight Hasidic scholars were translating an ancient Hebraic text. When they came across the line, "Suffering is grace," they stopped short, sharing with each other in great candor. Although they had heard this text many times, they really did not comprehend it. "How can suffering really be grace?" each asked the other.

Then, one of the rabbis suggested, "just outside of the town lives crippled Jonathan. Jonathan has known great travail and many illnesses in his life. His son was killed by the great floods that ruined his land and covered his home with mud. But as he was burying his son and cleaning up the soil that ruined his house, he began to sing to God. Some years later, his wife became quite ill because he could hardly grow enough food to support the family. But that did not stop his song. Later, he broke his leg and could not afford a physician, so it never healed quite properly and left him with a rather painful limp; Jonathan seemed still unruffled. Jonathan, even in those sparse fields, even during the drought, constantly spoke and sang to God. If anyone knows how suffering may be grace, Jonathan would be the person to ask. He is so poor and has had such misfortune, yet he seems to be at peace."

So the eight rabbis set out to the impoverished farm of Jonathan and his wife. Meeting Jonathan at the porch, they were invited to share in the meager supper. Of course, the rabbis demurred, noting that he had so little and was so generous to share, which brought them to the reason for their visit. They told Jonathan of their difficulty in honestly translating, "Suffering is grace." They felt that he, of all the people they knew, might be able to elucidate its meaning, because somehow all his misfortunes seemed not to have diminished his heart-felt devotion.

"How, Jonathan, with the loss of your child and farm, and you and your wife's poor health, can you still sing to God? How have you found that suffering may be grace?

To which Jonathan sheepishly replied, "I am very sorry you made this long trip and that I cannot help you. You have come to the wrong man to ask this question. I am not suffering."

So suffering is grace and it strengthens one's intense devotion to God.

Spiritual Evolution

Surely, if there were no suffering in the world, there would not have been any evolution of human beings toward the highest state of perfection or realization of the Divinity within us. It is through suffering alone we understand the real foundation and purpose of existence. It is through misery that we attain progress toward the subtle and spiritual realm of existence. We realize the fullest grandeur and beauty of life, only when we pass through the fire of tribulation and sorrow.

Every new birth presupposes a period of agony. Every seed breaks up with pain and manifests the charm of its hidden foliage and fruit. The glowing stream of gold runs out of the dull ore when heated in the fiery furnace. The aroma of certain leaves and barks spreads out only when crushed and bruised. So also the human life which is attended with the most painful experiences exhibits its highest glory.

39

Freedom from Karma and Rebirth

Introduction

We have studied in the Chapters 9. Universal Laws, 10. The Doctrine of Karma and 37. Bondage of Karma that we are subjected to the reactions of our actions, and that as a result of the operation of the Law of Karma we are bound by the wheel of births and deaths. This moral Law of Cause and Effect is often viewed as a form of cosmic accountancy of fixed debits and credits, and is thus feared as a punitive retributive law. But it is not a fearful law. As suggested by Huston Smith in his *The Religion of Man*, it is more appropriate to think of karma organically in terms of cosmic harmony that, when disturbed, must be restored.

The Law of Karma—A Teacher

The Law of Karma gives us a logical explanation for the existence of suffering and evil. The effects produced by our actions teach us how to bring harmony into our lives. We learn lessons from experiences. We would realize the folly of selfish desires and evil thoughts, and thus be prompted to cultivate unselfishness and perform selfless service for the welfare of all.

God has given us the great power of free will, the power of choosing for ourselves. This rare opportunity can be utilized to choose the Path of Divine Love and to attain eternal peace as its culmination. A balanced life of universal love, selfless service and the inner knowledge of the identity of the Self with God will lead us to the state of *jivanmukti,* liberation while alive. Then our soul will stand acquitted of all the accumulated karmas.

This is similar to the learning of a violinist from his dissonant, spine-chilling sounds, what movements of bow and fingers to avoid, and finally discovering how to play beautiful, soulful music. How long this will take depends on his effort and talent. The same is true in mastering the human instrument through the experience of karma.

Objectors to rebirth nevertheless often ask, "If all of us have lived thousands of lives why are we not much further advanced?" Such questioners equate reincarnation with progress, whereas it only provides the *opportunity* for progress. Consider the daily "reincarnation" cycle. If mere multiplication of days made one automatically wise, then all octogenarians would be sages! Buddha well appreciated that the vast majority advance quite slowly. He likened man's pilgrimage to climbing a mountain. "By steep or gentle slopes the climber comes where breaks that other world. Strong limbs may dare the rugged road . . . . . .The weaker must wind from slower ledge to ledge with many places of rest . . . . .The firm soul hastes; the feeble tarries. All will reach the sunlit snows."

Bondage

Do the nets of karma and rebirth eternally bind our soul? Is there any possible escape from them at any time? "Yes. There is," reply the scriptures of ancient India. As stated in Chapter 37. Bondage of Karma, above, ignorance of our real nature is the root cause of our bondage and suffering. We, out of ignorance, identify ourselves with the body-mind complex and thus develop a false notion that we are the agents *(karta)* of the actions performed by the body-mind complex. It is the physical body with the mind and senses that performs various actions, but the soul within the body does not act. It is mere actionless silent witness or observer. Because of the false sense of doership we invite the nemesis of reactions of actions. Thus this nemesis binds the soul (*jiva*) to worldly life.

From ignorance arises ego or sense of "I, me mine," and ego, in turn, causes desires, attachments and aversion and clinging to life. The desire for the objects of senses drives us to take efforts to obtain them. We become attached to the things, which give us pleasure or happiness and hate those things that hurt us. Therefore the desire to possess and develop relations with external things is the vital spring of all actions.

With the false notion of doership if we perform actions with the expectation of their fruits, their effects bound us and also we have to take rebirth again and again to enjoy the fruits of our actions.

Removal of Causes

All the causes of bondage and afflictions exist in the mind. The mind is full of impurities arising out of ignorance, evil thoughts, egoistic selfish desires, attachments, aversion, impressions of past experiences and so on. The first thing is to purify the mind. In fact all the major religions have prescribed certain "don'ts" and "dos" – restraints and observances for purification. In the Yoga tradition they are known as the *Yamas* and *Niyamas*. *Yamas* (restraints) consist of five self-restraints: non-hurting, non-lying, non-stealing, celibacy and non-possessiveness (*Yoga Sutras*, 2.30). *Niyamas* consist of five observances: purity, contentment, austerity, self-study and surrender to God (*Yoga Sutras*, 2.32). These are similar to the Ten Commandments of the Christian and Jewish faiths and the ten virtues of Buddhism. The *Yamas* and *Niyamas* seek to remove all evil tendencies and mental and emotional disturbances and thus purify the mind. The purification makes the mind fit for the practice of Yoga, and also attenuates the afflictions (*klesas*). The *Bhagavad Gita* advocates renunciation of the fruits of actions. Along with the practice of restraints and observances prescribed by the scriptures, performance of actions without sense of doership and without attachment and doing selfless service to needy people purifies our mind. The cause of karmic bondage is performance of actions with the expectation of reward and the attachment to their fruits. But the performance of actions without attachment and selfless service to others without any expectation, not even a word of thanks from the recipients do not bind us. So such dispassionate service do not create fresh karmic effects; they, instead, promote positive emotions of love, compassion and sacrifice. These positive emotions contribute to the attenuation of the *klesas*.

The mere attenuation of the *klesas* alone is not enough. So long as they remain in "seed" form, the practitioner is not free from the danger, because when favorable conditions arise, the klesas can become active again. Therefore the seeds have to be scorched and the potentiality of the *klesas* has to be destroyed.

The *klesas* are reduced to an unproductive state, the state of roasted seeds, through the practice of meditation (*Yoga Sutras*, 2. 11). The *klesas* are burnt up by the fire of discriminative knowledge attained through meditation or supreme devotion.

Finally, the scorched *klesas* are totally destroyed by resolving the mind back into its source, *Prakriti* (Nature) (*Yoga Sutras,* 2.10). That is, we have to go beyond the mind. We will be able to go beyond the limitations of the mind, when we attain the highest state of super-consciousness known as samadhi. This state is achieved through the practice of meditation and/or supreme devotion, and it brings liberation.

The practice of meditation is part of Raja Yoga. For details refer texts on Raja Yoga or Meditation. This Yoga consists of eight limbs or stages: *Yama, Niyama, Asanas (*postures), *Pranayama* (breathing exercises), *Pratyahara* (withdrawal of the senses), *Dharana* (concentration), *Dhyana* (meditation) and *Samadhi* (super-consciousness). *Yoga Sutras*, 2.29). The first five stages prepare our mind and body for the higher stages. They constitute the means for overcoming the obstacles to meditation.

As mentioned earlier the practice of *Yamas* and *Niyamas* purifies our mind.

Asanas are physical postures. They are practiced to perfect the body, making it supple and free from disease (For details, refer manuals on Hatha Yoga).

Pranayama means control of *prana* (life-breath). The process of breathing is regulated through breathing exercises. *Pranayama* regulates the mind and purifies and strengthens the nervous system.

Pratyahara means withdrawal and control of the senses. The mind comes into contact with the objects of the world through the five senses of sight, hearing, touch, taste and smell. These sensual experiences set the mind to wandering and restless. We should therefore acquire the ability to voluntarily draw the senses inward and thus insulate ourselves from the distractions of the world outside.

Dharana means concentration or one-pointedness. In concentration the dissipated powers of the mind are gathered together and focused on the object of concentration (i.e., mantra or the name of God) through continued voluntary attention. Through concentration the diffused mind is focussed and hence made more powerful and penetrative.

Dhyana means state of meditation. Prolonged and unbroken concentration leads to meditation. Concentration makes the mind one-pointed and steady. Meditation expands the focused mind to the super-conscious state by piercing through its conscious and subconscious levels. Through deep meditation we can reach the state of super-consciousness and thus attain perfection. Persistence and intensive practice of meditation is needed.

Samadhi or Super-conscious State is the final stage of Raja Yoga. Prolonged and deep meditation leads to this state. In this state the meditator becomes one with the Divine Self (*Paramatman*) and transcends all imperfections and limitations, and attains Enlightenment.

Enlightenment and supreme Divine Love are interrelated. The attainment of *samadhi* becomes easier when the Yogi delights in the Love of God. (*Yoga Sutras*, 1.23). Lord Krishna says in the *Bhagavad Gita*:

> "Among all the Yogis, I consider him to be the best, who worships Me with intense faith and whose mind is immersed in Me." (6.47)

Jesus Christ shows his disciples how one can escape from the wheel of rebirth:

> "Verily verily, I say unto you, if a man keeps my saying, he shall never see death."

What Christ says is that if you are faithful to his teaching, you will never see death, i.e., you will become free from transmigration or rebirth. He also says:

> "If ye continue in my word, then are ye my disciples indeed; And ye shall know the truth (Holy Spirit) and the truth shall make you free."

Devotion to God helps meditation and meditation in itself is a form of Divine Love. If one has never truly loved a human being, the visible manifestation of God, one can never love God, the invisible Lord. The Biblical Commandment to "love thy neighbor as thyself" has no significance without understanding the terms "*love*" and "*Self.*" Self is the living God within us, and the true love is unconditional love, love for love's sake, without any prejudice or expectation. It is a love with total surrender to God; it is a love with the heart, soul and mind.

Love has not been universally grasped by the followers of religions. Crusades, tortures and persecutions have taken place in the name of God in various parts of the world. This is nothing but barbarianism. In the Sermon on the Mount Jesus emphatically states,

> "Love your enemies. . . . . and pray for them which . . . . persecute you; that ye may be the children of your Father, which is in heaven." (Matt. 5: 43 – 45)

This concept of love implies seeing our own Self in all beings. Love is God and God is love. With love there is no enmity, no hatred, no jealousy. Universal love is both the result and the cause of God-consciousness. It is attainable through the practice of both meditation and intense devotion to God in daily life. God-realization or liberation is the goal of life and the karmic effects and rebirths serve as stepping stones for our soul for reaching the summit of perfection.

Beyond Liberation or Self-realization

The attainment of freedom from karma does not necessarily involve inaction; it only requires transcendence of egoism and selfishness. The sages liberated while alive are *Jivanmuktas.* They continue to work in order to set an example to ordinary people and also to promote human welfare. As they have neither egoism nor desire for fruits, they are not bound by actions. The *Bhagavad Gita* declares:

> "Having abandoned attachment to the fruits of actions, ever content, depending on nothing, the sage does not do anything though engaged in activity." (4.20)
> "Content with what comes to him without effort, from envy and the pairs of opposites, even-minded in success and failure, though acting, he is not bound." (4.22)
> "To one who is devoid of attachment, who is liberated, whose mind is established in knowledge, who works for the sake of sacrifice, the whole action is dissolved." (4.23)

The sages work for the well being of the world without any attachment to the fruits. They find inaction in action. They have no sense of doership. They know they do nothing at all; Nature does everything. They have a balanced state of mind. They are not attached even to things that are necessary for the maintenance of their bodies. They ever rest in their essential nature of *Satchidananda* (Truth-knowledge-bliss). Their mind is rooted in wisdom. Their actions and their results melt away. They are in fact no actions at all.

Though the modern world is deeply immersed in materialism, and terrorism and ethnic and economic conflicts continue to pose threats to peace, yet righteousness continues to prevail. This is entirely due to the eternal teachings of great Avatars (God-Incarnates) like Krishna, Buddha, Jesus and Sri Ramakrishna, and the ceaseless and tireless spiritual services rendered by great saints like Mahavir, Sankaracharya, St. Francis, Guru Nanak, Swami Vivekananda, mystic saints of various religions and the living saints of today. Their actions of purity and insight stand to create a world of spirituality in the midst of materialism, a world of peace and bliss in the midst of chaos and suffering.

40

Liberation

Meaning

Liberation is the goal of life. It means the realization of the ultimate Reality. It is the realization of the Self or God within us. It is the knowledge of Brahman, the pure Absolute. According to Sankaracharya liberation is the realization of the Atman, which is identical with Brahman. Its nature cannot be expressed in words or symbols. Atman is beyond all descriptions. It is difficult to comprehend the ultimate Reality. It can only be known when it is actually experienced.

Liberation is not becoming something that previously did not exist. It is just the regaining of the lost identity of the individual Self with the universal Self, the discovery of an already existing real fact.

Types of Liberation

In all the religious traditions of India, a distinction is made between liberation attained while still alive (*jivanmukti*) and liberation attained after leaving the body (*videhamukti*).

A person who attains liberation while still living on earth with his physical body is called *jivanmukta.* He is free from egoism, beyond the three gunas of nature, and free from desires and selfishness. He is established in the Self. He sees his Self in all beings and all beings in his Self. He is not bound by actions, for he has no sense of doership and any personal motive. He just performs actions as an instrument of God. He is beyond pleasure and pain and other dualities. He renders service for the welfare and spiritual development of people, and his service is God's service.

Upanishads

The *Upanishads* have outlined not only the ultimate goal of liberation, but also expounded pathways to realize it.

One, who has a vision of Brahman, becomes liberated. All the knots if his heart are cut off, and all his deeds cease. He realizes the Light of lights. The *Mundaka Upanishad* describes this state as:

> "The sun shines not there, nor the moon and stars; there lightning shines not, where then could the fire be? Everything shines only after that shining Light. This Light illumines all the whole world." (2.2.11)
>
> ". . . One's deeds and the Self, consisting of intellect, all become one in the Supreme immutable Being." (3.2.7)
>
> "Just as the flowing rivers disappear in the ocean, casting off name and form, so, the knower, freed from name and form, attains to the Divine person, higher than the high." (3.2.8)
>
> "He, verily, who knows the Supreme Brahman becomes *Brahman* himself. . . . ." (3.2.9)

The knower of Brahman is not touched by what he has done and what he has left undone. His past actions are burnt away like the straw on fire. Future actions are inaction. He has become one with the Cosmic Self. He becomes free from sorrow and sins. He is freed from all the angularities of the heart and attains immortality.

Similar declarations are found in the *Brahadaranyaka Upanishad:*

> ". . . The man who does not desire, he who is without desire, who is freed from desire, whose desire is satisfied, whose desire is the Self, his breaths do not depart. Being Brahman he goes to Brahman." 4.4.6)
>
> "When all the desires that dwell in the heart are cast away,

then does the mortal becomes immortal, then he attains Brahman here (in this very body)." (4.4.7)

A similar statement is found in the *Katha Upanishad* also:

"When all desires that dwell within the human heart are cast away, then a mortal becomes immortal and (even) here (while alive) he attains to Brahman." (2.3.14)

Desire is the root of empirical existence. One who is free from desires realizes Brahman while alive, i.e., while he lives in the physical body. To fail to realize Him is to live in ignorance, to be subject to the wheel of births and deaths. The knower of Brahman is immortal. Others continue to undergo suffering.

The *Kena Upanishad* also gives the same view:

"If here (on earth) (a person) knows It (Brahman), then there is truth, and if here he knows It not, there is great loss. Hence seeing (the Real) in all beings, wise men become immortal. . . ." (2.5)

If we do not know the Brahman while living on earth, our loss is great, for we, then, are lost in the life of mind and body and do not rise above it to our superamental existence. The wise sees the same Brahman in all beings.

The *Katha Upanishad* declares:

"If one is able to perceive (Him) before the body falls away, (one would be free from misery); (if not) he becomes fit for embodiment in the created world." (2.3.4)

Sankaracharya interprets this verse thus: "If here, in this life, a man is able to know the Brahman before the falling of the body, he is freed from the bond of *samsara*; if he is not able to do so, he takes embodiment on earth."

The *Isa Upanishad* emphasizes the vision of oneness:

> "One, who sees all beings in his own Self and his own Self in all beings, does not feel any revulsion by reason of such a view. When, to one who knows, all beings have become one with his own Self, then what delusion and what sorrow can be to him who has seen the oneness?" (6,7)

When the unity is realized by an individual, he becomes liberated from sorrow, which is the product of dualities. When he perceives his Self in all beings, there can be no source of disturbance or care. The vision of the oneness of all beings is the foundation of freedom and joy.

Along with the supreme knowledge, the observance of moral rules, the practice of meditation and devotion to God are recommended by the *Upanishads* as pathways to liberation.

The *Mundaka Upanishad* classifies knowledge into lower and higher. The knowledge of *Vedas* and sciences is lower. "And the higher is that by which the Imperishable (Brahman) is known." (1. 1. 5). The knowledge of Brahman or Self alone is higher, and the knowledge of everything else, including the knowledge of scriptures, is lower.

Bhagavad Gita

The *Bhagavad Gita* synthesizes the pathways of Meditation, Karma (Action), Jnana (Knowledge) and Bhakti (Devotion):

> "Fix thy mind on Me, be devoted to Me, sacrifice to Me, bow down to Me. Thou shall come even to Me. . . . (18.65)

The words "fix thy mind on Me" refer to meditation, in which the mind is set on the Self. The words "be devoted to Me" and "bow down to Me" denote devotion to God. The words "sacrifice to Me" refer to Karma Yoga, in which all actions and selfless service are dedicated to God. And the words "thou shall come even to Me" refer to Jnana Yoga, by which the oneness of one's Self with the Brahman is realized.

The *Gita* teaches renunciation of attachment rather than of action, and dedication of all actions to God:

> "Not by non-performance of actions does man reach actionlessness, nor by mere renunciation does he attain to perfection." (3.4)
>
> "Verily none can ever remain for even a moment without performing action; for, everyone is made to act helplessly indeed by the *gunas* born of nature." (3.5)
>
> "He who performs actions, offering them to Brahman and abandoning attachment, is not tainted by sin as a lotus leaf by water." (5.10)
>
> "Therefore, without attachment do thou always perform actions that should be done; for, by performing actions without attachment man reaches the Supreme." (3.19)

One cannot attain to the state of perfection by simply sitting quiet abandoning action. In fact no one can remain even for a moment without performing action, for everyone is forced to act by the *gunas* of nature. But actions performed and dedicated to God without a sense of doership and without attachment to their fruits, do not bind the doer. Therefore, if we perform actions without attachment, for the sake of the Lord and without any motive, we will attain purity of heart and finally Self-realization or liberation.

Vedanta

According to the Vedanta philosophy, liberation means the realization of one's real nature, namely, the eternal Atman (Self). Cultivation of moral virtues, devotion to God and the pursuit of knowledge lead to the attainment of Self-realization. Sankaracharya, an exponent of Non-dualistic Vedanta, in his *Vivekachudamani* states:

> "The first step to liberation is the extreme aversion to all perishable things, then follow calmness, self-control, forbearance, and complete relinquishment of all selfish work enjoined in the scriptures." (69)

> "Then come hearing (of the truth from the Guru), reflection on that, and long, constant and unbroken meditation on the truth. After that the learned seeker attains the supreme *nirvikalpa* state and realizes the bliss of *nirvana* (liberation)." (70)

According to Dualistic Vedanta (*Visistadvaita*) propounded by Ramanujacharya (eleventh century), the bondage of the Self is real, and it can be overcome not by the knowledge alone but with pure devotion and grace of God. The liberated soul only becomes similar to Brahman, but not identical with Brahman as held by Sankaracharya. The liberated soul does not lose its individuality, but retains it. It is only egoism that is annihilated in the state of liberation. Karma Yoga, Bhakti Yoga and self-surrender to God are the chief means to attain liberation. According to Ramanujacharya there is no *jivanmukti* so long as soul is embodied.

Jainism

According to the doctrine of Jainism, liberation means ultimate release from suffering and *samsara* (the cycle of births and deaths). It also denotes the ultimate state of supreme peace and bliss. It is attained when all karmas are destroyed. The Self that attains perfect liberation (*siddhi*) possesses the great attributes of perfect knowledge, perfect perception, perfect right vision, infinite power, perfect peace and extreme fineness.

Karma is the root of *samsara.* It envelops the real nature of the Self. Karma clings to the self due to the forces of attachment and aversion.

In order to attain liberation the self must cut off all connection with karmic matter. Jainism prescribes the practice of right belief, right knowledge, and right conduct as the pathway to liberation. Right faith means firm conviction in the fundamental principles of Jainism taught the teachers of this faith.

Right knowledge means the knowledge that reveals the nature of things as they are.

Right conduct means doing whatever is right, good and proper. It consists in observance of five vows – vows of non-injury, non-stealing, chastity and detachment from worldly concerns with watchfulness in walking, speaking, eating, in taking up and setting down, and in excreting, and with control of mind, body and speech. That is, acting in accordance with the right faith and knowledge without any attachment or aversion is right conduct. These three jewels are to be realized in one's self. Thus is attained liberation.

Buddhism

The main aim of Buddhism is to seek liberation from sufferings. It is known as *nirvana,* whose literal meaning is "blowing out." It means complete extinction of all cravings, passions, attachments, ignorance and other defilements. *Nirvana* is the cessation of all sufferings. It is a state of highest happiness, tranquility and bliss. It is attainable only by morality, perfect knowledge and meditation. The pathway to nirvana consists of eight limbs:

1. Right view
2. Right aspiration
3. Right speech
4. Right action
5. Right livelihood
6. Right effort
7. Right mindfulness
8. Right absorption (samadhi)

Right view means a knowledge of the basic tenets of Buddhism. Right aspiration consists in the strong desire to attain liberation, and sustained zeal for removing all fetters on the path of liberation. Right speech means truthful and meaningful speech. Right action means morally good actions of body, speech and mind. Right livelihood means earning one's livelihood by just means. It prohibits unlawful and immoral means of livelihood such as killing animals, cheating and stealing. Right effort is to work continuously for the purification of one's own heart by cultivation of virtues. Mindfulness implies awareness, vigilance, recollection and remembrance; it promotes tranquility of mind. Samadhi is absorption in tranquility and equanimity through deep meditation.

The Bodhisattva's Way. In the Mahayana form of Buddhism the way to *nirvana* has been universalized. A truly religious being must seek his liberation in and through the liberation of all beings. Such a being is called a *Bodhisattva*; his will is fixed on Enlightenment. But he works for the safety and happiness of all other beings. He takes upon himself the task and happiness of all other beings. He takes upon himself the task of universal liberation. In order to fulfil this task he practices the following ten virtues to their perfection:

1. Liberality
2. Morality
3. Patience
4. Vitality
5. Meditation
6. Wisdom
7. Skillfulness in means
8. Aspiration or resolution
9. Strength or power
10. Knowledge

The *bodhisattva*'s way stresses the doctrine of self-reliance. It also stresses the unity of life and the unity of Buddhahood.

Sikhism

The Sikh way to liberation is devotion to God. The heart of this devotion is the practice of constant remembrance of God's name. It does not mean mere repetition of God's name. It needs total commitment to God by feeling and realizing His presence everywhere at every moment. It also includes worship of and wholehearted devotion to God.

The seeker of God must cultivate such virtues as mercy, humility, forbearance, truthfulness, contentment, love, faith, tolerance, austerity and such others. He must perform pure actions imbued with loving devotion to God.

The goal of devotion is the realization of God. Liberation is conceived in terms of the union of the individual soul with the Supreme Soul. The liberated person experiences peace, bliss, satiety and ecstasy.

The Effects of Liberation

The first effect of attaining liberation is freedom from sufferings and karmas. (*Yoga Sutras*, 4.30). The ignorance, which is the root cause of karmic effects and sufferings, is destroyed. The liberated person then becomes a *jivanmukta*. He does not fall again into ignorance and start generating karmas that bind. All actions in the state of liberation are necessarily done in complete identification with the Divine Consciousness without even the slightest identification with the individual ego, for, ego and other causes of sufferings have been destroyed by the intuitional knowledge. That is why no karmic effects accrue to the *jivanmukta*.

The second effect of attaining liberation is the sudden expansion of consciousness in the realm of Infinite knowledge. When the last veil of illusion is removed, the enlightenment that blossoms is of an entirely new kind. In the realm of Infinity, there is no realm of magnitudes. So the *jivanmukta* transcends knowledge and passes into the realm of pure consciousness.

41

Some Karma Yogis

There were great Karma Yogis in different countries since ages. In this Chapter the life and services of some Karma Yogis are presented.

BUDDHA (560 BC–486 BC)

Buddha was the founder of Buddhism. His original name was Siddharta. His father was Suddhodana, king of the Sakhyas; his mother's name was Maya. He was born in a grove near the city of Kapilavastu in the Himalayas within Nepal. The astrologers predicted that he would become either a universal monarch or a Buddha, a perfectly enlightened soul for the salvation of mankind.

The king took all precautions to prevent him from becoming a monk. He surrounded Siddharta with all kinds of luxury and indulgence in order to retain his attachment for sensual pleasures. He got him married and put him in a walled palace with gardens, etc. Siddharta's wife gave birth to a son named Rahula.

One day Siddharta managed to get out of the walled enclosure of the palace and roamed about in the town along with his servant Channa. The sight of a de-crept old man, a sick man, a corpse and a monk finally induced Siddharta to renounce the world. He retired into the forest of Uruvila, the modern Buddha Gaya, Northern India. He practiced severe *tapas* (penance) and self-mortification. He became exceedingly weak.

At that moment some dancing girls were passing that way singing joyfully. The song was:

> Fair goes the dancing when the Sitar is tuned. Tune us the Sitar neither low nor high And we will dance away the hearts of men . The string over-stretched breaks, the music dies, The string over-slack is dumb and the music dies, Tune us the Sitar neither low nor high.

Siddharta realized then that he should not go to extremes in torturing the body by starvation but should adopt the middle path. Then he began to eat food in moderation and took to the middle path.

One day sitting underneath a large bo-tree (pipal tree) Siddharta meditated from morning till night with firm determination. He entered into deep samadhi and attained *nirvana*. Siddharta became Buddha, the enlightened. After seven days he came to the normal consciousness. His heart was filled with profound mercy and compassion. He discovered the cause of suffering and the way to escape from it – the noble Eight-fold Path. He wanted to share his doctrine with humanity.

Buddha traveled all over India and preached his doctrine and gospel to all without exception. He preached his doctrine for over forty-five years traveling from place to place.

"He is the one who has carried it (Karma Yoga) into perfect practice, says Swami Vivekananda, " . . .He was, in the conduct of his life, absolutely without personal motives; and what man worked more than he? . . . The whole human race has produced but one such character, such high philosophy, such wide sympathy. This great philosopher preached the highest philosophy, and yet had the deepest sympathy for the lowest of animals and put forth any claims for himself. He is the ideal Karma Yogi, acting entirely without motive."[1]

His disciples and followers have spread his teachings in the East and the West in many countries.

SUPRIYA (FIFTH CENTURY BC)

Supriya was a Buddhist nun. She was the daughter of Anatha Pindada, a rich man of Sravasti. Her fond parents brought her up in the lap of luxury. It is said that she had an exceptionally brilliant mind; she even remembered her former birth. Mahaprajapati Gautami, the foster mother of and aunt of Buddha initiated her into Buddhism at the age of seven. Along with her prayers and meditation she found time to serve the sick and the poor and the destitute.

At one time when Lord Buddha was living in the monastery of Jeta-vana, the prosperous town of Sravasti, was in the grip of a devastating famine. A large number of people were dying. Sravasti did possess sufficient means to buy food for the starving people and tide over the crisis, but the selfishness and avarice had hardened the hearts of the rich people.

One day a starving child was found lying at the entrance of the monastery. Ananda, the chief disciple of Buddha deeply moved to see the child's miserable condition, went to the Master and said, "The people round about are dying of hunger. What is our duty under this situation?" Many rich people of the town had come to listen the teaching of the Master. Buddha addressing them said, "All of you are wealthy people. If you desire you can easily save the lives of people who are dying in such large numbers." Hearing the words of the Master, some said, 'Our granaries are empty." Others said, "Sravasti is a big town and the population is large. It will be impossible to feed them all." Anatha Pindada was absent at that time. The Master looked around and said again, "Is there no one here who can save his brothers and sisters from the grip of this terrible famine?"

No one answered, but after a moment of silence, a young girl got up and speaking confidently said, "My Lord, thy handmaiden is ready to obey thy command. To be able to serve people is a good blessing even at sacrifice of one's life." Needless to say the girl was none other than Supriya. The audience was amazed, but they thought that she spoke heedlessly without responsibility. The

Master smiling at her, said, "My child, how will you feed this vast multitude?" Supriya answered, "By thy grace, O Master, my begging bowl will never remain empty. It will feed the hungry, bring the dying back to life and the famine will come to an end."

Ananda's heart was filled with joy to hear the sweet words of Supriya and blessed her. The Master also blessed her.

The news that Supriya had taken a vow to remove the famine of Sravasti spread like wild fire. A wave of enthusiasm arose in the hearts of people. From house to house she went begging for food. Her love for humanity had already found an echo in every heart, and everyone in the town was ready to give her a helping hand. The famine of Sravasti thus came to an end. This selfless service of Supriya made herself immortal in the annals of Buddhist literature.

ST. BRIGIT (453 AD – 525)

St. Brigit was a patron saint of Ireland and the foremost woman of her day. She was a rare gifted woman who dedicated her life to God.

With the advent of Christianity in the fifth century, Ireland passed from the Iron Age to the golden age. About seventy years after the spread of Christianity, Brigit was born in a kingdom of Leinster. Her father Dubthach was a minor pagan prince and her mother was a Christian bondwoman.

Brigit was born into slavery, for the mother was sold to another master before the birth of her child. As she grew up, Brigit performed the usual tasks of bondwoman: tending the flock, grinding the corn and washing the feet of the guests. When she reached an age to be of service, her father claimed her and she returned as a menial to his household.

Brigit had a noble and intellectual mind; she regarded the humblest slave girl as a sister, and was equally at ease with her father's guests. This quality of deep compassion later enabled her in life to touch the hearts of those with whom she was dealing, be they bishop, king or slave.

As a young girl she was always generous in giving away her father's possessions to the poor and distressed. This became an embarrassment to her father. He found her generosity so expensive that he finally decided to sell her to the Christian King of Leinster. He put her into his chariot and reached the fortress. He went to the king to bargain a price for the new slave; while Brigit was left waiting in the chariot a leper approached her for help. But she possessed nothing she could give, and turning pitifully away from the leper's eyes, Brigit suddenly noticed in the chariot her father's bejeweled sword. Without hesitation she presented it to the leper who gladly took it and hastened away. Dubthach explained to the king the reason for selling Brigit, and returned to his chariot to take her. Immediately he noticed his sword, the most valuable possession was gone. He was infuriated.

When the king heard her action, he championed the cause of the slave girl who could find the leper's need was greater than that of her father. He asked her father to free her bondage, saying, "Leave her alone, for her merit before God is greater than ours." After Brigit had received her freedom from slavery, her father had her well educated and ultimately arranged to marry a poet. But Brigit insisted on dedicating herself to monasticism and finally took her vows as a nun.

In an age when woman took no part in society, she became the pioneer, drawing her country-women of all classes from the sheltered life of the family into a life of service to the community.

Brigit founded convent settlements throughout the country, traveling by chariot from one place to another supervising their building works and exhorting people to dedicate their lives to God and to serve their fellow beings. These settlements were centers of religious and secular learning giving instruction in craftsmanship and practical experience in farming, harvesting, milling, dyeing , weaving and health-care. They were abodes of brotherly love, asylums for the poor and the afflicted.

Brigit dedicated her life to the Divine and desired nothing of the comforts of the world. The greatest in the land and the humblest went to her for counsel and guidance. She was unostentatious.

When visited by the famous she was often found tending her sheep. She was admired for her courage, steadfastness in truth, balance of mind and common sense. She was prophet honored in her own country in her own time.

The most famous of Brigit's foundations was in Leinster where she built for herself a cell of wattle and clay. Around her cell grew up one of the most famous centers of learning in Ireland. It is now known as Kildare. In Kildare Brigit spent most of the seventy years of her life. (See John O' Hanlon, *Lives of the Irish Saints*, 1875).

SANKARACHARYA (788–820)

Sankaracharya was the most influential of all Hindu religious thinkers. He was the foremost among the master-minds, which India has produced. He was great metaphysician, a practical philosopher, an infallible logician, a gifted poet and a stupendous spiritual force. He was a fully developed Yogi, Jnani and Bhakta. He was a proponent of Advaita (Non-dualistic) Vedanta. He was born at a time when darkness prevailed over India and bigotry reigned supreme. Sankaracharya overpowered all negative forces and restored *Sanathana dharma* and Advaita Vedanta in the land.

He was born in a brahmin family of the village Kaladi in Kerala, southern India, Sankara's father died when he was seven year old. Her mother took special care to educate her son in all the scriptures.

At the age of eight years, Sankara renounced the world and became a monk, promising her mother that he would serve her at death bed. He proceeded to find out a Guru to get himself formally initiated into the sacred order of sannyasa. Sankara met Swami Govindapada in Badrinath in the Himalayas. Govindapada initiated him and taught him the philosophy of Advaita and asked Sankara to go to Benaras. At Benaras at the age of sixteen Sankara wrote all his famous commentaries on the *Brahma Sutras, the Upanishads* and *Bhagavad Gita*. He then began to propagate his philosophy.

Sankara toured all over India. He met the leaders of different schools of thought. He convinced them by arguments and established the supremacy of Advaita Vedanta.

When her mother was seriously ill, Sankara came to Kaladi and in his presence she gave up her physical body. His relatives did not help him in performing the funeral rites. He had to perform them all alone.

Then Sankara continued his tour, vanquished all the religious opponents and preached his Advaitra Philosophy wherever he went. He established Mutts (monasteries) at Sringeri (South West), Puri (East), Dwaraka (West) and Joshi (North) and placed his eminent disciples in charge of them. Sankara also organized ten Orders of Sannyasins

In Benaras a student was cramming the Sutras of Sanskrit grammar. Sankara heard it. He immediately sang a small song, the famous *Bhaja Govindam* song in order to teach the uselessness of such studies in attaining the liberation of the soul.

In addition to the Commentaries mentioned earlier, Sankara also wrote several original works such as *Viveka Chudamani,, Atma Bodha, Aparaoksha Anubhuti, Ananda Lahari*, etc. His philosophy can be summed up in the following words:

> Brahman alone is real, the world is unreal; the Atman is identical with Brahman.

Within a very short span of about fifteen years the work he turned out was so vast that it could ordinarily take several life-times. He was indeed a great Karma Yogi.

SAINT FRANCIS XAVIER (1506–1552)

St. Francis Xavier was an erudite philosopher, theologian, Karma Yogi and the cofounder of Roman Catholic Society of Jesus. He was born in Spain. He studied in the University of Paris, and took his Master of Arts Degree in 1530 and became Professor in the same University. Xavier was a linguist. He knew five languages:

Spain, French, Portuguese and Basque. Xavier's fellow student Ignatius Loyola used to say very often, "Master Francis! What shall it profit a man if he gains the whole world and loses his own soul?"

Xavier seriously contemplated on the profound import of the words of Ignatius. He abandoned all ambition, worldly position and income. He embraced poverty and chastity and resolved to live for Christ alone.

Xavier spent much of his time in prayer and meditation. He distributed all that he had to the poor. He set on foot to Venice. He underwent a lot of hardship on the way. He passed through the Alphine snow. A co-traveler fell down and swallowed up in a huge mass of snow. Xavier, risking his own life, went to the spot and pulled him up from the snow.

Xavier arrived in Venice in 1537. He started his selfless service in Venice. He tended the sick in hospital and served them. He nursed the sick and prayed with them. He went to the prison, served the prisoners and prayed with them.

Xavier proceeded to Rome on foot. He visited villages and preached the gospel of Christ. He declined to accept presents when they were offered by the people. He fell ill and underwent a lot of difficulties during the period of his sickness.

In 1541 Xavier set sail from Lisbon for India with three or four old garments and two books. He did the humblest services to the passengers. He washed the clothes of the poor and the sick passengers. He washed the bodies of sick persons and fed them with his own hands.

In 1542 Xavier landed in India and reached Goa. He lived in a hospital and served the sick. He moved from village to village and begged for the lepers, the starving people and the prisoners. He visited prison and schools and taught the prayers and the Commandments.

Xavier caused forty-five churches to be built along the coast. He traveled on foot continuously. He took only one meal a day.

After visiting Malacca, Ceylon and Japan, he came back to India and passed away at the age of forty-five years.

His life was an illustrious example of dedicated selfless service and humility.

BROTHER LAWRENCE (1611 – 1691)

Brother Lawrence was born of poor parents. At the age of eighteen he underwent a conversion when he saw a tree stripped of the leaves in winter. He began to think about the deep mystery and power of life that would make the tree produce fresh leaves and flowers after some time. This thought weaned him away from worldly life and made him seek the divine, the source of all life and consciousness.

When he grew up he was for a time in the army and in the service of a nobleman, and finally became a cook in a monastery in Paris. He did that humble service for thirty years with his soul enwrapped in God. In the midst of busy work in the kitchen he still preserved God-mindedness He soon became well known for his holiness. Even noble men and high dignitaries sought his advice. His little book the *Practice of the Presence of God* contains his conversations and letters. He always felt the presence of God. His work itself was his prayer.

"The time of business," said Brother Lawrence, "does not differ with me from the time of prayer. In the noise and clatter of my kitchen, while several people are at the same time calling for different things, I experience God in as great tranquility as if I were upon my knees at the Blessed Sacrament."

He described his method as under:

> At the beginning of my duties I would say to the Lord with confidence, 'My God, since You are with me, and since, by Your will, I must occupy myself with external things, please grant me the grace to remain with You, in Your presence. Work with me, so that my work might be the very best. Receive as an offering of love both my work and all my affections.'
>
> During my work, I would always continue to speak to the Lord

as though He were right with me, offering Him my services and thanking Him for His assistance. And at the end of my work, I used to examine it carefully. If I found good in it, I thanked God. If I noticed faults, I asked His forgiveness without being discouraged, and then went on my work, still dwelling in Him.

Thus continuing in this practice of conversing with God throughout each day and quickly seeking His forgiveness when I fell or strayed, His presence has become as easy and natural to me now as it once was difficult to attain.[2]

Brother Lawrence was thus an illustrious example for making work as worship and Karma Yoga.

SRI SARADAMANI DEVI (1853–1920)

Sarada Devi was the consort and first disciple of Sri Ramakrishna. She was a pure Divine soul. She dedicated her life for selfless service. She was born in a small village of Jayarambati in Bengal. Her parents, Ramachandra Mukhopadhyaya and Syamasundari were deeply religious, though poor. They had a vision foretelling the birth of a divine being as their daughter.

Sarada lived the simple life of an Indian village girl. She used to worship the clay models of Kali and Lakshmi. She meditated on Divine Mother with deep concentration. Even in her early age she had experiences and mystic visions. She received training in domestic duties and began to help her mother in household work. She acquired a knowledge of Indian culture, religion and philosophy from temple festivals, domestic worship, village dramas and family functions.

In accordance with the then prevailing customs, little Sarada was betrothed at the age of six to Sri Ramakrishna who was then practicing severe austerities. Sarada spent some days in his parental home. On his return to Dakshineswar she returned to her parental home.

When Sarada was fourteen years old, Sri Ramakrishna visited his native village of Kamarpukur. Then she spent three months with him at his home. He taught her many things from cookery, household to meditation and spiritual life. Sarada found in him a man of exalted devotion to God and absolute purity.

Four years passed. Sarada came of age and desired to be with her husband but did not express it, and was helping her mother in doing household work.

She came to know of the rumor that Sri Ramakrishna had become insane. She felt a strong urge to see him. In the absence of railway or any other modern transport facility, she was taken by walk by her father. On the way she fell ill and she and her party rested in a rest house. She obtained relief as a result of a vision of Kali at night.

On arrival at Dakshineswar Sarada went to her husband's room and could see how kind he was. She found that the rumor about him was false. She stayed at Dakshineswar till 1885. She could see that Sri Ramakrishna used to often pass into deep Samadhi even during nights.

Sri Ramakrishna had by now finished practicing all the disciplines of Hinduism and attained a variety of experiences. He also realized the truths of other religions and the underlying unity of all faiths.

After the marriage when Sarada was growing into womanhood he had fervently prayed to the Divine Mother to remove all traces of carnality from her mind so that she might remain pure. During the early days of her stay at Dakshineswar he once asked her whether she had come there to drag him to worldly life, but she replied, "I have come only to help you in the path of religious life."

It was during these early days of her stay there that he performed a form of worship. Invoking the Divine Mother in Sarada, he worshipped her. When the worship was over, she went into deep samadhi. Both realized their identity of being as the one Brahman. Sarada Devi retained the sense of her identity with the Divine throughout her life.. Both of them never had any physical relationship and lived as pure celibates throughout their lives. Sarada Devi's body and mind became the instruments of the Divine Mother who played through the body and mind of Ramakrishna. They saw in each other only the Divine Mother. He was the "Divine man," and she was the "Divine woman."

Sarada Devi was a mother to his disciples, to their disciples in turn and to her own disciples. She was more than a mother, for through her, the Divine Mother whom Ramakrishna worshipped and realized, manifested. It is no wonder that she is known as the Holy Mother.

She rendered selfless service to Ramakrishna and his disciples as a form of Divine worship. His teaching had a profound effect on her receptive mind. She practiced the highest spirituality. She was used to be totally absorbed in meditation. She rendered service to Sri Ramakrishna until his passing away like a mother taking care of her child.

Sri Ramakrishna taught her the great mantras, instructed her how to initiate people in them and be a guide to those who sought spiritual refuge.

When Sri Ramakrishna was suffering from cancer of the throat, the Holy Mother busied herself in nursing the Master, cooking suitable food for him and attending to his needs.

Sri Ramakrishna left his body on August 16, 1886. Sarada's heart was filled with despair and grief. Sri Ramakrishna appeared in a vision and told her, "Where have I gone, after all? I have only passed from one room to another."

Two weeks after the Master's passing away, the Holy Mother went on pilgrimage through North India along with some woman disciples and three monastic disciples of the Master. The party returned to Calcutta before August 1887.

In 1888 disciples made arrangements for her stay in Calcutta. In 1893 she performed a severe form of austerity with a view to removing psychic disturbances. She used to have very rare spiritual experiences. An increasing number of people began to flock her for guidance, instructions and spiritual initiation.

The Holy Mother's youngest brother died in 1899 leaving behind his widow Surabala under her care. Stricken with grief over her husband's premature death, Surabala became insane. She gave birth to a posthumous daughter called Radhu. Radhu was not properly cared by her insane mother. The Holy Mother played the part of a mother. Radhu and her insane mother were a constant source of trouble and anxiety to the Holy Mother.

The Holy Mother gave herself away in the service of all. Her mind dwelt on God in spite of all the distractions caused by Radhu and other relatives.

Her motherly love and compassion for all never allowed her personal suffering to stand in the way of giving spiritual refuge to those who sought it. She was giving refuge to all accepting their sins and digesting the same. On Tuesdays and Saturdays, when she was staying at her Calcutta residence, several hundreds of disciples and devotees would bow down before her and touch her feet. She, then, used to feel a severe burning sensation all over her body on account of her vicarious sufferings.

The hospitality of the Holy Mother was unique. Those who had the privilege of visiting her would not be sent back without being treated as guests as long as they stayed. Many local devotees used to visit her at odd hours. They all, however, received the same warm and cordial hospitality. She had the power of weaning people from evil ways. Some devotees had mystical experiences after their contact with the Holy Mother.

In 1919 her health seriously declined. After a final ecstasy on July 20, 1920 she left her body.

Sarada Devi was neither wife nor mother. Yet she was a mother in a higher sense. The Holy Mother and God are inseparable. Her teachings are the revelations of a Savior.[3]

SWAMI VIVEKANANDA (1863–1902)

Swami Vivekananda was a versatile genius and the greatest disciple of Bhagavan Sri Ramakrisha. He was born in Calcutta, India. His original name was Narendra Nath Datta. Narendra as a boy had a peculiar experience when he would go to sleep. As soon as he closed his eyes a wonderful spot of light of changing colors would appear between his eyebrows. It would expand and bathe his whole body with a flood of radiance. He was very naughty and hard to manage. His memory was prodigious.

While he was studying in college Narendra was attracted to

the Brahmo Samaj Movement. In his longing to know the Reality, he went to Maharishi Devendra Nath Tagore and other religious leaders and asked them, "Sir, have you seen God?" Everyone was startled by this question, and no one could satisfy him.

Narendra heard about Sri Ramakrishna from the principal of his college. He decided to go to Dakshineswar, four miles north of Calcutta in order to know if Sri Ramakrishna had the direct experience of God. Narendra soon found in Sri Ramakrishna a genuine man of God.

When Narendra visited him again after a few weeks, Sri Ramakrishna received him affectionately and called him to sit on the bed by his side. Then Sri Ramakrisha, in an ecstatic mood, touched Narendra, the latter became unconscious of the external world. The rationalistic mind of Narendra received a rebuff. He could not account for that strange experience. He was extremely drawn to the Master.

When Narendra was dreaming of the fulfillment of his spiritual longing, in 1884 his father, who was the only support of the family, suddenly died of heart disease. He had spent more than he had earned, and at his death the family sank into dire poverty. The burden of support of six or seven people fell upon Narendra. He had passed his B. A. examination and was admitted to Law studies. The son of a rich father now became the poorest of the poor in the college. Many times he went to his classes without food.

With the increasing intensity of desire for self-illumination, the studies for the examination in Law became a torment to Narendra. Very often he was visiting the Master. Sri Ramakrishna, with infinite love and patience, began to train him.

As the end of the Master came nearer, Narendra's passionate desire for the God-realization increased and intensified. The Master would often send Narendra and other disciples to meditate. Narendra became blessed with many rare experiences including a state of Nirvikalpa Samadhi.

Three or four days before his passing away, Sri Ramakrishna called Narendra near and commissioned him for future work. On August 16, 1886, Sri Ramakrishna attained mahasamadhi.

Narendra began to organize the Master's young disciples into a monastic brotherhood. The first monastery of the Ramakrishna Order was started.

In 1888 Narendra—now Swami—left Calcutta and embraced a wandering life. He went to Varanasi, Ayodhya and other spiritual centers in North India and returned to the monastry after gathering manifold experiences in life.

In 1891 the Swami wandered allover India, met with all sorts of people – from beggars to princes, giving illuminating discourses. He reached Kanyakumari, the southernmost extremity of India.

Hie long wandering brought him face to face with the abject poverty of India. He wanted to go to America to ask the West for the means to ameliorate the material condition of India and to take to it the gospel of Vedanta for its spiritual uplift. Swami was thinking of attending the Parliament of Religions to be held at Chicago in 1893.

At America. During the months of March and April, 1893 the Swami's disciples started raising funds for his visit to America. Before leaving for America, on invitation he visited the Maharaja of Khetri. At his request he assumed the name of Vivekananda. He sailed from Bombay on May 31, 1893. On the way he visited China and Japan. He was very much impressed by the religious influence of ancient India over the empires of the Far East.

Swami reached Chicago at the end of July. He came to learn from the Information Bureau that the Parliament would commence after the first week of September, and that no one would be admitted as a delegate without proper references. This was a great unexpected blow. Then, too, his purse was being emptied. He cabled to his friends in Madras for help and applied to an official religious Society to appoint him one of its delegates, but the head of the Society declined. Swami proceeded to Boston which was less expensive than Chicago. On the way in the train, a rich lady from Massachusetts became his friend. She was struck by his noble personality and illuminating conversation, and gladly asked him to stay in her home and introduced him to Prof. J. H. Wright of Harvard University. Swami discussed all kinds of subjects with the learned Professor for four hours. The Professor became so deeply impressed with his rare ability that he insisted that he should represent Hinduism in the Parliament. He explained his difficulties. Prof. Wright said, "To ask you, Swami, for credentials is like asking the sun to state its right to shine!" The Professor wrote at once to his friend , Dr. Barrows, the Chairman of the Committee of selection of delegates, stating, "Here is a man who is more learned than all our learned professors put together." He presented him with a ticket to Chicago and also gave him letters of introduction to the Committee.

But on his arrival at Chicago he found that he had lost the address of the Committee. He was lost and did not know where to go. Nobody could guide a colored man. Tired and helpless, he spent the chilly night in a big empty box found in a corner of the station. In the morning he wandered from door to door for food only to meet with insults. At last exhausted he sat down quietly upon the roadside. At this juncture the door of a fashionable residence opposite to him opened and the lady of the house came down and gently asked him whether he was a delegate to the Parliament of Religions. Swami told her his difficulties. The kind-hearted lady invited him into her house. After breakfast she took him to the office of the Parliament. Swami was grateful to Mrs. Hale beyond words. She and her husband and children became his warmest friends.

Swami was accepted as a delegate. On September 11, 1893 the first session of the Parliament was opened. The delegates were asked to introduce themselves in brief speeches. Swami let his turn go hour after hour until the end of the day. At last when the Chairman insisted Swami rose. His face glowed like fire. When he pronounced the simple opening words, "Sisters and Brothers of America," the audience rose up with shouts of applause, and cheered wildly for two whole minutes. It was only a short speech, but its spirit of universality, its earnestness and catholicity completely captivated the whole assembly. In the course of his addresses in subsequent sessions Swami placed before the audience the cardinal truths of Vedanta and the concept of universal religion. He also delivered talks to a wider public. By the time the Parliament had come to an end, he had become, beyond comparison, its most popular speaker. He was in demand everywhere. He had to face the crudest publicity, the most brutal curiosity and lavish hospitality. The news papers proclaimed him a Prophet and a Saint.

The news of this extraordinary success spread throughout India. The unknown monk became a world-figure. But in the midst of this immense popularity Swami was mindful of his duties to the sunken masses of India.

In order to serve the cause of his motherland Swami accepted the offer of a lecture tour of the United States. At the beginning of the winter of 1894, Swami returned to New York after a whirlwind tour through various centers of learning and culture in America. He gave his whole time to teaching and everyday instructed a band of chosen followers in Raja Yoga and Jnana Yoga. Many prominent persons became his ardent followers.

By June 1895 Swami had placed his real constructive work on a solid foundation. He also finished his famous treatise on *Raja Yoga*, which soon attracted the attention of American psychologists like William James. Whatever financial returns he received went toward the consolidation of his work. All through the year Swami's work was hectic, lecturing both privately and publicly. He began to feel himself wearing out. But he was satisfied that the ideals of the Sanatana Dharma, the Eternal Religion, were spreading and percolating through the thought world of America.

Having almost exhausted himself by this restless work of class and public lecturing, Swami eagerly sought a place of retreat where he could give some rest to his scattered nerves and continue his task of training young minds for future action. One of the students, Miss Dutcher offered the use of her cottage at Thousand Island Park, the largest island in the St. Lawrence River. In this enchanting environment a group of twelve devoted students spent seven blessed weeks with their beloved teacher, listening to his inspiring words. His wisdom was pouring itself as a grand revelation of the many-sidedness of the Eternal Truth. Some glimpses of his ecstatic teaching of this period can be had in his *Inspired Talks*.

Having fulfilled his great mission of training and initiating disciples at Thousand Island Park, Swami returned to New York. In the later part of 1895 he visited England to carry to the English people the message of Vedanta. Returning to America he established the Vedanta Society of New York in February 1896 with the aim of preaching and practicing Vedanta. Some of the great works like *Raja Yoga, Bhakti Yoga* and *Karma Yoga* had already been published.

In England and Europe. Swami again visited England from April to the end of July 1896 and from October to December 1896. On the way he visited Paris. In London he held classes and gave interviews. Many became his sincere friends and supporters. Among them was Miss Margaret Noble (afterwards Sister Nivedita). Swami's illuminating lectures on Jnana Yoga made a direct appeal to the intelligentsia of England. He met with Prof. Max Muller of Oxford. Max Muller wanted to write a book on Sri Ramakrishna's life and teaching. All available facts were soon provided to him. His book was soon published under the title *Ramakrishna: His Life and Sayings.* This book aided in giving Swami and his mission a firmer hold on the English-speaking world. Talented souls became Swami's disciples.

In 1896 he made a tour of the Continent on invitation. He met Prof. Paul Deussen, the celebrated Indologist of Germany. After the European tour Swami again came to London and spent another two months and delivered a fresh course of lectures on Vedanta and Advaita. This heavy strain told seriously on his health. But the voice of India was calling him back. He sent Swami Saradananda to New York and brought from India Swami Abhedananda for the work in London.

Returned to India. On December 16, 1896 Swami with his disciples left for India. On January 15, 1897 he arrived at Colombo. He received a grand welcome. He stayed in Ceylon for about ten days and addressed several meetings. When he arrived at Madras a grand welcome was waiting for him. Swami gave a series of lectures conveying his message to India in various provinces.

When Swami reached Calcutta in February 1897 Bengal gave

a grand reception to her distinguished son. Hundreds of people used to visit him daily. A brilliant group of young men joined the Ramakrishna Order. Swami organized the monks for a life of renunciation and service. He established the Ramakrishna Mission Association. Gradually various monastic centers, Homes and relief centers came into existence.

From May 1897 to January 1898 Swami toured the historic cities of Northern India, sowing the seed of his message to India.

After he returned to Calcutta, the Math was shifted to Belur at the western bank of the Ganges. For some time Swami devoted himself to the training of his own disciples both Eastern and Western so as to enable them to implement his plan for the regeneration of his mother land.

Swami then set out on a journey through historic India with a select group of his disciples. His health was so much undermined that he had to be brought back to Bengal.

Swami, in spite of his failing health, resumed his work and performed the consecrating ceremony of the new Belur Math, which became the permanent Headquarters of the monks of the Ramakrishna Order. His dream of starting a monastery in a cool, secluded region of Himalayas was also realized. The Advaita Ashrama was founded in March 1897 in the interior of the Himalayas at Mayavati. Other institutions also came into existence under Swami's direction in different parts of India.

Second Visit to the West. In June 1899 he left for the West on his second visit. After breaking his journey in London he went to the United States and stayed for almost a year. He visited California and founded new Vedanta centers at San Francisco, Oakland and Alameda. He received the gift of a property of one hundred and sixty acres of forest land, where an Ashram was established to train students in the monastic life.

In July 1900 Swami left for Paris, where he was invited to the Congress of the History of religion. He stayed in Paris for about three months and left for Egypt and came back to India in December 1900. He visited Advaita Ashrama, and made a last pilgrimage with his mother to the holy places of Eastern Bengal and Assam. His health became much worse. Yet he gave frequent interviews to the devotees from all parts of India till the end. He left the body on July 4, 1902.

Swami was indeed a very great Karma Yogi. Within about ten years he rendered restless service, even at the cost of his health, for the benefit of humanity both in the West and in India. In that short period he did so much work that would ordinarily take several lifetimes. What a great dedicated genius and Sage he was! His greatness and service knows no comparison. No doubt he left his body, but he lives in his eternal messages and he will continue to inspire people everywhere until the world realizes its oneness with God.

References

1. *Karma Yoga and Bhakti Yoga*, New York: Ramakrishna-Vivekananda Center, 1955, pp. 110–11.
2. Br. Lawrence, *the Practice of the Presence of God,* PA: Whittaker House, 1982, pp. 82– 83.
3. For full details, refer Swami Nikhilananda, *Holy Mother*, New York: Ramakrishna-Vivekananda Center; *Sri Sarada Devi, the Holy Mother*, Madras: The Ramakrishna Math.